THE
BIGGEST PUB
JOKE
BOOK
Ever!
2

Text and design copyright © 2003 Carlton Books Limited

First published by Carlton Books Limited 2003

ISBN 1 84222 939 7

Printed and bound in Great Britain

THE
BIGGEST PUB
JOKE
BOOK
Ever!
2

Compiled by
David Southwell, Sam Wigand and John Mullet

CARLTON

CONTENTS

Introduction

Imagine you're down the pub with your mates. You've caught up with the gossip and sorted out whether your home team will win the league/avoid the drop this season and agreed that your local rival's new striker really is a complete donkey. Now what? After the third pint the jokes start. Let's face it, a drink and a laugh is the main point of going down the boozer in the first place and, like most people, without the beer you probably can't remember jokes at all.

The point is, are your jokes any good? Will they reduce the lads to helpless hilarity and raise your standing (fnar, fnar) with the ladies? Or will they fall as flat as an anorexic's chest? Are you the local Jack the Lad, or just another spotty contender? If you feel deficient in the quip department, this is the book for you. If you already know lots of jokes, well, you can never have too much of a good thing, can you?

Booze may not actually make you more attractive to the opposite sex but it has been scientifically proven that a GSOH does. OK, not exactly proven, but it's probably true. Certainly if you make people laugh they'll like you and buy you drinks, which can't be a bad start. What is completely undisputed is that the boozer is the true home of the dirty joke. Stuff that wouldn't raise a titter at the office will go down like a randy nun's knickers once you're down the pub. Alcohol is the magic ingredient that causes any joke to reduce crowds of grown men (and even, sometimes, women) to helpless, side-hugging laughter.

All you need for a really memorable night out is a good pub, a bar full of your mates, numerous pints, and a close reading of this book. In here you'll find everything you need to keep a pub full of happily inebriated punters entertained all evening. There are one-liners, funny stories, humorous book titles, religious jokes, animal jokes and sex jokes. None of it is even remotely politically correct and much of it is in appalling taste. So success is guaranteed. Just sit comfortably and browse through the book. You might not think you can remember much of it afterwards but, once you have an appreciative audience and a pint in your hand, you'll be surprised what comes back to you. Of course, whether you remember next day just how popular you were (or, for that matter, where you were) is another matter.

This book won't give you bigger balls or instant sex appeal (well, it might but we're not promising), but it will improve your social life and get you a name for being a good laugh. There is enough material between these covers to keep your sense of humour fully fuelled for life. Just amuse yourself for a few hours now and again, as it were, and you will never be short of a good story or a quick quip to bring the house down.

Dogs & Ducks

Jokes About the Animal Kingdom

You're nobody until you've been ignored by a cat!

****

How can you tell if you're in an elevator with an elephant? You can smell the peanuts on his breath.

****

It's always blackest just before you step on the cat.

****

If you're colour-blind, how do you tell a grape from an elephant? Stamp on it a while. If you don't get any wine, it's an elephant.

****

What do you know when you see three elephants walking down the street wearing pink sweatshirts? They're all on the same team.

****

How do you know if you pass an elephant? You can't get the toilet seat down.

How do you catch a yellow elephant? First find a yellow elephant. Then look at it through the wrong end of a telescope, pick it up with a pair of tweezers and put it in a matchbox.

****

Make your mark in the world, or at least spray in each corner.

****

Why do elephants have trunks? Where else would they pack their luggage?

****

From an Associated Press bulletin: When a San Francisco insecticide manufacturer ran a contest in August, 1994, looking for the most cockroach-infested house in the country to demonstrate its pest control prowess, Rosemary Mitchell of Tulsa, Oklahoma, really wanted to win, and she did. The prize: a house call from a roach expert, entomologist Austin Frishman, aka television's 'Dr Cockroach', who began work on the home after estimating that her one-story house harboured between 60,000 and 100,000 roaches. Mitchell said, "I keep a pretty clean house," but admitted that she had to check the bed thoroughly every night and shake the shower curtains off every morning. Frishman said that he had seen a lot worse and rated Mitchell's house only a three on a scale of one to five.

****

Why is it that elephants never forget? Well, what do they have to remember?

****

In ancient Rome, the cat was considered a symbol of liberty. Anyone who watches a cat can see that he always does exactly as he pleases.

****

Have you heard of the wallet made of elephant foreskin? When you rub it, it turns into a briefcase.

****

The other day, I was walking my dog around my building...on the ledge. Some people are afraid of heights. Not me; I'm afraid of widths.

****

A man and his dog walk into a bar. The man says: "I'll bet you a round of drinks that my dog can talk." Bartender: "Yeah! Sure...go ahead." Man asks the dog: "What covers a house?" Dog says: "Roof!" Man asks the dog: "How does sandpaper feel?" Dog says: "Rough!" Man asks the dog: "Who was the greatest baseball player of all time?" Dog says: "Ruth!" Man says to the bartender: "Pay up. I told you he could talk." Bartender throws both of them out the door. Sitting on the sidewalk, the dog looks at the man and says: "Should I have said Gehrig, then?"

****

What do elephants use for vibrators? Epileptic pygmies.

****

Cats are intended to teach us that not everything in nature has a function.

****

A snail got mugged by two tortoises. When he went to the police, they questioned him as to what happened. He said: "I don't know; it all happened so quickly!"

****

What do elephants use for tampons? Sheep.

****

How do porcupines make love? Veerry carefully!

****

Why do elephants have long trunks? Because sheep don't have strings.

****

What has two tails, two trunks and five feet? An elephant with spare parts.

****

What did the peanut say to the elephant? Nothing, peanuts can't talk.

****

What did the vet say to the dog who kept licking his balls? "Thanks, darling."

****

Three agricultural scientists were determined to discover how much a pig could eat before it just had to take a shit. To this end they procured a Yorkshire sow and pushed a large cork into her arse. After six weeks of force-feeding, the sow was the size of the Goodyear airship and threatening to burst. Being humane types, the scientists agreed that the cork must now be removed. No one wished to volunteer for the job, however, so in true scientific tradition, they decided to train a monkey for the task and swiftly put a small gibbon through a crash course in cork-pulling. The day came and the pig was airlifted out to the desert for safety's sake. Special equipment was set up to monitor the event. Picture the scene: in the middle of the desert, the pig. Behind the pig, the monkey. One mile behind him, the first scientist with a video camera. One mile behind that scientist are the other two scientists with a seismometer. Finally, the monkey reaches up and pulls out the cork. SPLAT! When the massive geyser has subsided, the two scientists find themselves knee-deep in pigshit. Grabbing shovels, they wade forward and dig out the first man who has been buried up to his neck. When they free him they find that he is laughing hysterically. "What's so funny?" they ask. "You should have seen the monkey trying to get the cork back in!"

✳✳✳✳

The more people I meet, the more I like my dog.

✳✳✳✳

Why do elephants prefer peanuts to caviar? Peanuts are easier to get at the pub.

****

Why do hummingbirds hum? Because they don't know the words.

****

How do you know if there's an elephant in bed with you? She has a big 'E' on her pyjama jacket pocket.

****

How do you know if there is an elephant under the bed? Your nose is touching the ceiling.

****

How can you tell if an elephant has been in your refrigerator? Footprints in the butter.

****

How do you know if there are two elephants in your fridge? Two sets of footprints in the butter.

How do you know if there are three elephants in your fridge? Can't get the fridge door closed.

✱✱✱✱

How do you know if there are four elephants in your fridge? There's a Mini parked outside it.

✱✱✱✱

Why are there so many elephants running around free in the jungle? The fridge isn't large enough to hold them all.

✱✱✱✱

How do you put an elephant into a fridge? Open the Mini door, take the elephant out, open the fridge, put the elephant inside, close the fridge.

✱✱✱✱

The Lion, King of Beasts, gathered all the animals for a meeting. All of them showed up except the elephants. Why? They were stuck in the Mini.

✱✱✱✱

Why did the turtle cross the road? To get to the Shell garage.

****

Why did the pervert cross the road? His dick was stuck in the chicken.

****

I went to the cinema the other day and in the front row was an old man and with him was his dog. It was a sad, funny kind of film; you know the type. In the sad part, the dog cried his eyes out, and in the funny part, the dog laughed its head off. This happened all the way through the film. After the film had ended, I decided to go and speak to the man. "That's the most amazing thing I've seen," I said. "That dog really seemed to enjoy the film. It's remarkable!" "Yeah, it is," said the man. "He hated the book."

****

An elephant is walking through the jungle when she gets a thorn in her foot. She is in absolute agony when she sees an ant strolling by. The elephant asks the ant for help but the ant refuses, unless the elephants is prepared to let the ant have his wicked way with her. "Anything! Anything!" replies the elephant. So out comes the thorn and up gets the ant and proceeds to enjoy himself. Meanwhile, in a tree directly above them, a monkey, who witnessed the whole episode, was in fits of laughter. He laughed so much he fell out of the tree on top of the elephant. "Ouch!" says the elephant. "Yeah," says the ant, "take some more, bitch!"

****

Why do elephants wear pink tennis shoes? White ones get dirty too fast.

****

When you go out into the world, always remember, being placed on a pedestal is a right, not a privilege.

****

The cat agenda: variety is the spice of life. One day, ignore people; the next day, annoy them. Only play with them when they're busy.

****

Three rats are sitting at the bar talking. The first says: "I'm so hard, once I ate a whole bag full of rat poison!" The second says, "Well I'm well hard; once I was caught in a rat trap and I gnawed it apart!" Then the third rat gets up and says, "'Bye, chaps, I'm off home to screw the cat..."

The life sentence of Taro the dog was commuted in February 1994, permitting his release from the Bergen County Jail and his deportation from New Jersey. Taro had been sentenced to die under the state's 'vicious dog' law, but appeals had continued until Taro had spent more than 1,000 days behind bars in his climate-controlled kennel and had cost American taxpayers more than $100,000 in expenses.

****

So this mouse walks in the jungle with his elephant friend, looks back and says: "Wow, look how much dust we leave behind!"

****

Why do seagulls live near the sea? Because if they lived near the bay, they would be called bagels.

****

A butcher is leaning on the counter towards the close of day when a wee dog with a basket in its jaws comes pushing through the door. "An' wot's this then?" he asks. The dog knocks the basket sharply into the butcher's shins. "You little bugger." As he reaches down to smack the dog, he notices a note and a tenner in the basket. The scribble on the note asks for three pounds of his best mince. The butcher reckons this is too easy. He goes to the window and reaches for the dried up stuff that's been sitting out all day. The dog growls at him. The butcher turns around and, glaring at the mutt, gets the best mince from the fridge. Weighing out about 2 ½ pounds, he drops it on the scale with his thumb. "Hmmmmm, a bit shy. Who'll know?" Again, the dog growls menacingly. "Alright, alright," as he throws on a generous half pound. He wraps it up, drops it in the basket, and drops in change from a fiver. The dog threatens to chew him off at the ankles. Another fiver goes in the basket. The butcher is quite impressed and decides to follow the little dog home. The dog quickly enters a high-rise building, pushes the lift button, enters the lift, and then pushes the button for the twelfth floor. The dog walks down the corridor and smartly bangs the basket on the door. The door opens, the dog's owner screams abuse at the dog and then tries to kick the dog inside. "Hey, what are you doing?" says the buthcher. "That's a really smart dog you've got there." "Stoopid dog – that's the third time this week he's forgotten his key".

****

A dog went into a telegram office, took out a blank form and wrote, "Woof. woof. woof. woof. woof. woof. woof. woof. woof." The clerk examined the paper and told the dog: "There are only nine words here," he said. "You could send another 'woof' for the same price." "But," the dog replied, "that would be silly."

****

"If you pick up a starving dog and make him prosperous, he will not bite you. This is the principal difference between a dog and a man."
Mark Twain

****

I turned on my lawn sprinkler as my dog was crossing the yard. He thought it was the lamp-post getting even with him.

****

Why do elephants paint the soles of their feet yellow? So that they can hide upside-down in custard.

****

Why do elephants wear sandals? So that they don't sink in the sand.

****

Why do sheep-shaggers wear green wellies? So they can stick the sheep's back legs down them.

****

How do you keep a skunk from smelling? Hold his nose.

Why do ostriches stick their heads in the ground? To look for the elephants who forgot to wear their sandals.

✳✳✳✳

Psychiatrist: "What's wrong with your brother?" Sister: "He thinks he's a chicken." Psychiatrist: "I see. And how long has be been acting like a chicken?" Sister: "Three years. We would have come in sooner, but we needed the eggs."

✳✳✳✳

The Washington Post reported in September 1993 that at the Third Annual Slugfest in Fairfax County, Va. , 'Slippery' beat 49 other slugs in the Tour de Slug race. Also featured at the festival: slug face-painting, the slime toss, and the official drink – green 'slimeade'. A 12-year-old boy demonstrated his skill at flicking his tongue in and out of his mouth with his slug, Mickey, attached. He said that despite washing Mickey several times with soap beforehand, "the slime still sticks between your teeth. I've still got some slime from yesterday."

✳✳✳✳

What did the one crocodile say to the other crocodile? "What's with the long face?"

Do you know why elephants paints their toenails red? So that no one will see them hiding in the cherry trees. If you have never seen an elephant in a cherry tree, then you already know how effective it is.

****

Why don't they play poker on the African savannah? There are too many cheetahs.

****

Why do elephants wear springs on their feet? So they can jump up in trees and rape monkeys.

****

A parrot has a habit of shagging chickens, so the farmer tells him that if he does it again he will pull out every feather on its head. The parrot jumps on the hens again, and his head feathers are duly pulled out. Meanwhile, the farmer's wife, who has pretensions to culture, is having a formal dinner. She appoints the parrot to be butler and to tell the guests where to put their hats and coats. The party proceeds without mishap, with the parrot announcing, "Ladies to the right! Gentlemen to the left!" Suddenly, two bald-headed men enter, and the parrot says: "You two chicken-fuckers come out to the hen house with me."

In a two-day period in New York City recently, a homeless man, a train maintenance worker, and a dog were killed on the subway tracks. Ninety people telephoned the Transit Authority to express concern about the dog, but only three called about the worker, and no-one phoned in about the homeless man.

✱✱✱✱

Which pine has the longest needles? A porcupine.

✱✱✱✱

I put contact lenses in my dog's eyes. They had little pictures of cats on them. Then I took one out and he ran around in circles.

✱✱✱✱

Why don't elephants drink martinis? Have you ever tried getting an olive out of YOUR nose?

✱✱✱✱

Two boy silkworms pursued a luscious girl silkworm. They ended up in a tie.

✱✱✱✱

When do giraffes have eight legs? When there are two of them.

****

How do you train King Kong? Hit him with a rolled-up newspaper building.

****

Why do elephants have wrinkled knees? From playing marbles.

****

The Chicago Tribune reported in June 1994 on a local sex therapist, Robert Herd, who works exclusively helping animals to mate. He says a surprising number of dogs and horses exhibit sexual dysfunction.

****

A burglar has just made it into the house he's intending to ransack, and he's looking around for stuff to steal. All of a sudden, a little voice pipes up, "I can see you, and so can Jesus!" Startled, the burglar looks around the room. No one there at all, so he goes back to his business. "I can see you, and so can Jesus!" The burglar jumps again, and takes a longer look around the room. Over in the corner by the window, almost obscured by curtains, is a cage in which sits a budgie, who pipes up again: "I can see you, and so can Jesus!" "So what?" says the burglar, "you're only a budgie!" To which the budgie replies: "Maybe, but 'Jesus' is the rottweiler!"

****

What is the loudest noise in the jungle? A giraffe eating cherries.

****

A panda spent the night in bed with a prostitute. The following morning as he is about ready to leave, the prostitute yells after him: "Hey, aren't you going to pay me?" The panda appears confused so she throws a dictionary at him and tells him to look up 'prostitute'. The definition reads: "A woman who engages in promiscuous sexual activity for pay." The panda throws the dictionary back at the prostitute and tells her to look up 'panda'. The definition reads: "An animal that eats bamboo, shoots, and leaves."

****

Two vampire bats wake up in the middle of the night, thirsty for blood. One says: "Let's fly out of the cave and get some blood." "We're new here," says the second one. "It's dark out, and we don't know where to look. We'd better wait until the other bats go with us." The first bat replies: "Who needs them? I can find some blood somewhere." He flies out of the cave. When he returns, he is covered with blood. The second bat says excitedly: "Where did you get the blood?" The first bat takes his friend to the mouth of the cave. Pointing into the night, he asks: "See that black building over there?" "Yes," the other bat answers. "Well," says the first bat, "I didn't."

****

Psychiatrist: "What's your problem?" Patient: "I think I'm a chicken." Psychiatrist: "And how long has this been going on?" Patient: "Ever since I was an egg."

****

Why do hens lay eggs? If they dropped them, they'd break.

****

A hunter goes hunting and he tracks an elephant. He almost shoots it, then he looks into the elephant's eyes and decides that he is not up to it. Ten years later, he goes to the circus. There is a group of elephants performing. One of the elephants walks up to him and kicks him! Why?

****

Diner: "Do you serve chicken here?" Waiter: "We serve anyone, sir."

✳✳✳✳

What did Tarzan say when he saw 1,000 elephants coming over the hill? "Look, there's 1,000 elephants coming over the hill."

✳✳✳✳

What did Tarzan say when he saw 1,000 elephants with sunglasses on, coming over the hill? Nothing, he didn't recognise them.

✳✳✳✳

What's six feet long and hangs from trees in Africa? Elephant snot.

✳✳✳✳

A farmer down the road has a fairly large herd of cows and three bulls. Each bull keeps a strict eye on his portion of the cows. A rumour comes around that the farmer is going to get another bull and the three bulls are standing in the field discussing this. The first bull says, "Well, there's no way he's going to get any of my cows." The second bull agrees, "Yeah, I'm not giving up any. He can wait till next year and get some of the new ones." The third bull, who was a bit smaller, says, "I don't have as many as you guys, so I'm not giving any up." Finally, the new bull arrives. The first three gather at the edge of the field to watch him being unloaded from the trailer. To their consternation, the biggest, meanest Aberdeen Angus bull they have ever seen, with hooves like flint anvils, comes strolling down the ramp and glares at them. He's at least three times bigger than any of them. The first bull looks around nervously and says, "Well, now, I suppose it would be a neighbourly thing to give this guy some cows. I think I'll give him twenty of mine." The second bull says, "Yeah, I guess so; I'll give him thirty of mine." They look over at the small bull. He's busy pawing the grass, snorting, and shaking his head. They go over and ask him what he's doing, and suggest that he should give up some cows too. "Yes, I know," he says, "I'm just making sure he knows I'm a bull!"

✳✳✳✳

A blind man with a guide dog at his side walks into a department store. The man walks to the middle of the shop, picks up the dog by the tail and starts swinging it around in circles over his head. The manager, who has seen all this, thinks it a little odd, so he approaches the blind man and says: "Pardon me. May I help you with something?" The blind man says: "No thanks, I'm just looking around."

✳✳✳✳

Why do elephants wear tiny green hats? To sneak across a pool table without being seen.

****

One afternoon, there was a good witch who was flying along when all of a sudden she heard this soft crying from down below. When she landed, she saw a yellow frog. Touched by his sadness, the witch asked why he was crying. "Sniff. None of the other frogs will let me join in all their frog games. Boo hoo." "Don't cry, little one," replied the witch, and with a wave of her magic wand, the frog turned green. All happy now, the frog was checking himself over when he noticed that his penis was still yellow. He asked an embarrassed witch about this, and she told him that there were some things that she just couldn't do, but that the wizard could fix things up for him. So happily, the little green frog hippity-hopped along his merry way. Feeling quite happy about herself, the witch once more took to the skies, and once again, she heard some crying, but this time of a thunderous sort. So down to the ground she flew, only to discover a pink elephant. The witch asked him why he was crying. "Sniff. None of the other elephants will let me join in all their elephant games. Boo hoo." Now, if you have ever seen an elephant cry, you know it to be a pathetic sight, but a pink elephant crying is just downright heart-breaking, and that is just how the witch felt. So once again, she waved her magic wand, and – poof – the elephant was all grey. All happy now, the elephant was checking himself all over when he noticed that his penis was still pink. He asked an embarrassed witch about this, and she told him that there were some things that she just couldn't do, but that the wizard would fix things up for him. At this point, the elephant started wailing again: "I don't know where the wizard is," he sobbed. "Oh, that's easy," said the witch, "Just follow the yellow-pricked toad."

****

What's the last thing that goes through a bee's mind when it hits a car windscreen at 70mph? Its arse.

****

What's worse than a giraffe with a sore throat? A centipede with athlete's foot.

****

Why didn't they invite the giraffe to the party? He was a pain in the neck to talk to.

****

A baby rabbit was orphaned. Fortunately, though, a family of squirrels took it in and raised it as if it were one of their own. This adoption led to some peculiar behaviours on the part of the rabbit, including a tendency for it to eschew jumping but rather to embrace running around like its step-siblings. As the rabbit passed through puberty, however, it soon faced an identity crisis. It went to its foster-parents to discuss the problem. It explained how it felt different from its brothers and sisters, was unsure of its place in the universe and was generally forlorn. The father squirrel just sat back and cracked another nut, ,saying: "Don't scurry, be hoppy."

****

What's grey and puts out forest fires? Smoky the Elephant.

****

Why do ducks have flat feet? To stamp out forest fires.

****

Private Atkins joins the French Foreign Legion and is stationed at a remote outpost in the North African desert. After several weeks in barracks he feels a moist yearning for female companionship. He approaches the evil-looking, scar-faced sergeant, and asks him what the men do for sexual relief around here. "Zere eez only ze camel, oui?" the sergeant tells him with a leer. "I'm not desperate enough to brave that!" replies Atkins, and takes a brisk walk and another cold bath. A week later he's more desperate and asks the sergeant again. "Ze camel, I told you. Use ze camel!" comes the reply. Atkins actually has a look at the camel this time. It's like a flea-ridden carpet full of coat-hangers with camel shit matted in the hair round its rump. Atkins doesn't fancy it. Much. A week later, delirious with unvented lust, he goes to the sergeant again, only to be told: "Merde! Ze camel, I tell you, ze camel!" That night Atkins creeps out to the camel. "At least its got a pulse," he tells himself as he climbs onto a hay-rack and proceeds to roger the camel to his satisfaction. As he dismounts he sees the sergeant staring open-mouthed in horror and admiration. "How inventive and practical you Engleesh are. Ze other men, zey usually ride ze camel to ze brothel in town!"

✳✳✳✳

Some veterinarians are prescribing Prozac for dogs. Animal rights activists are thrilled. Things have finally come full circle. Finally, a drug for animals that has been tested on humans first.

✳✳✳✳

How does the male elephant find the female elephant when she's lying down in tall grass? Very attractive.

✳✳✳✳

Why do elephants have four feet? Because lady elephants have big vaginas.

****

An old woman saved a fairy's life. To repay this, the fairy promised to grant the old woman three wishes. For the first wish, the old lady asked to become young and beautiful. Poof! She became young and beautiful. For the second wish, the old lady asked to be the richest woman in the world. Poof! She was the richest woman in the world. For the last wish, she pointed at the cat she had kept for years. She asked that he be turned into the most handsome man on earth. After all, he had been her best friend for so many years. Poof! The fairy turned the cat into the most handsome man on earth. The old lady and the fairy said their goodbyes. After the fairy left, the handsome man strolled over to her and asked: "Now aren't you sorry you had me neutered?"

****

What is that stuff between elephants' toes? Careless elephant drivers.

****

Why do elephants have Big Ears? Because Noddy won't pay the ransom.

****

A polar bear was out driving one day when he suddenly started having engine trouble. He pulled into the next service station and asked the walrus there to take a look at it. The walrus drove the car into the workshop and put it up on the hoist. After looking at it for a bit he returned and said to the polar bear, "You've blown a seal," to which the bear replied, "No, honestly! That's just mayonnaise from lunch."

****

A talent scout is walking down the street and comes across a man and his dog. The little dog is singing. He has a lovely voice and the talent scout says, "Come to my office. I want to sign you and this marvellous dog to a contract. This dog can make us both rich." The man brings his little dog to the talent scout's office. The little dog is just about to finish singing 'La Donna E' Mobile', when a large dog runs into the room and grabs him by the scruff of the neck. She (it's a bitch) runs away with him in her mouth. The talent scout yells, "Stop her! She's taking away our fortune!" The man replies, sadly, "It's no use. That's his mother. She doesn't want him to be on stage. She wants him to be a doctor."

A man goes to a dog-breeder to buy a guard dog, only to be presented with a scruffy terrier mongrel. "What use is that?" he asks. "Ah, but he's a trained killer, this one," promises the breeder. "Watch: Guard Dog? That chair!" In a blur of little snappy teeth and yapping, the chair is reduced to splinters. "Amazing!" says the man. "Can I have a go? Guard Dog? That box!" In seconds the box is shredded to mere fluff. Delighted, he buys the mutt and rushes home to show his lady wife. "Look at our new guard dog," he says. "He's a trained killer!" "What, that thing?" she replies. "Guard dog, my arse!"

****

Wife: "We've got such a clever dog. He brings in the daily newspapers every morning." Husband: "Well, lots of dogs can do that." " Wife: "But we've never subscribed to any papers."

****

How do you make a dog go 'meow'? Freeze it in liquid nitrogen, then take a chainsaw to it.

****

A man went to a doctor to have his penis enlarged. Well, this particular procedure involved grafting a baby elephant's trunk onto the man's penis. Overjoyed, the man went out with his best girl to a very fancy restaurant. After cocktails, the man's penis crept out of his pants, felt around the table, grabbed a bread roll and quickly disappeared under the tablecloth. The girl was startled and exclaimed: "What was that?" Suddenly the penis came back, took another bread roll and just as quickly disappeared. The girl was silent for a moment, then finally said: "I don't believe I saw what I think I just saw...can you do that again?" With a strained smile the man replied: "Darling, I'd like to, but I don't think my arse can take another bread roll!"

✱✱✱✱

How do you make a dead elephant float? Well, you take ten dead elephants, ten tons of chocolate ice-cream, five tons of bananas...

✱✱✱✱

"No!" said the lady millipede, crossing her legs, "no, a thousand times no!"

✱✱✱✱

There was a herd of cattle all standing on a hill when an earthquake struck. All of the cows fell down, but the bull remained standing. The farmer, noticing this, went out and asked the bull, "Why didn't you fall down like the rest of the herd?" The bull replied: "We bulls wobble, but we don't fall over."

Why did the Iraqi chicken cross the road? To take over the other side.

****

Why did the chicken cross the road again? Because it was a double-crosser.

****

Why do pygmies wear giant condoms on their heads? Because if an elephant steps on them, they're fucked!

****

A farmer with lots of chickens posted the following sign: "Free Chickens. Our Coop Runneth Over."

****

Men and women have been calling to fish, pleading with them and swearing at them without response since the beginning of time. Scientists have set out to translate fish language. They are not far along yet, but have made some headway. Various clicks and whistles have been recorded that indicate that one fish has a way to communicate what is on his mind to another fish. If the research continues as planned, it should be only a matter of time until man will be able to reproduce fish noises and communicate what is on his mind to bass, perch and catfish. All right-minded fishermen agree that fish-talk research projects should be cancelled and the scientists on them forced to seek other employment. The reasoning behind this point of view is simple and sound. If the research continues to its logical conclusion, fishing will cease to be the pleasant and relaxing sport that it now is. Fishing will become a business of bellowing speeches in fish language designed to convince fish that they would be better off on the bank or in the boat than they are in the water. In such circumstances, any fool knows who the men who'll catch all the fish will be...they'll be politicians.

✶✶✶✶

"What is it, Lassie? A boy fell down a mine shaft and broke his ankle and is diabetic and needs insulin? Is THAT what you're trying to tell me?"

✶✶✶✶

A Norwich University professor has been studying cow flatulence for 20 years, and has determined that the average cow emits 200 to 400 litres of methane gas PER DAY, resulting in a total annual world cow methane output of 50 million metric TONS! This is why you should never allow a cow inside your sleeping bag!!

Why couldn't the pony talk? Because he was a little hoarse.

****

A man went to visit a friend and was amazed to find him playing chess with his dog. "I can hardly believe my eyes!" he exclaimed. "That's the smartest dog I've ever seen." "Oh, he's not so clever," the friend replied, "I've beaten him three games out of five."

****

Once upon a time, there was a non-conforming sparrow who decided not to fly south for the winter. However, soon after the weather turned cold, the sparrow changed his mind and reluctantly started to fly south. After a short time, ice began to form his on his wings and he fell to earth in a barnyard almost frozen. A cow passed by and crapped on this little bird and the sparrow thought it was the end, but the manure warmed him and defrosted his wings. Warm and happy, the little sparrow began to sing. Just then, a large tom cat came by and hearing the chirping investigated the sounds. As Old Tom cleared away the manure, he found the chirping bird and promptly ate him. There are three morals to this story: 1) Everyone who shits on you is not necessarily your enemy. 2) Everyone who gets you out of shit is not necessarily your friend. 3) If you are warm and happy in a pile of shit, keep your silly beak shut.

The After-Work Crowd

2

Jokes About Jobs, Bosses and Lawyers

Mr Matthews sat in his attorney's office. "Do you want the bad news first or the terrible news?" the lawyer said. "Give me the bad news first." "Your wife found a picture worth a half-million dollars." "That's the bad news?" asked Matthews incredulously. "I can't wait to hear the terrible news." "The terrible news is that it's of you and your secretary."

✱✱✱✱

Work hard and save your money and when you are old you will be able to buy the things only the young can enjoy.

✱✱✱✱

When Willie retired from the railway after 50 years' service, the company presented him with an old coach to keep in his garden as a memento. One wet day, his friends found him sitting on the step of the coach, smoking his pipe with an old sack over his shoulders to keep out the rain. "Hullo, Willie," said his pals, "why are ye no' inside on a day like this?" "Can ye no' see?" replied Willie, with a nod toward the coach. "They sent me a non-smoker."

✱✱✱✱

How can you tell if your barrister is worthless? Ask him if he's a member of the Bar.

I worry all the time: I worry about worrying too much. I worry when I'm not worried that there's something I should be worried about. I worry when I'm worried whether I should worry about what I am currently worried about or whether I should worry about something else that worries me, even if I'm not worried about it, but should be worried about it, or at least worry about the fact that I'm worrying about not possibly having to worry at all, about worrying.

****

A lawyer was trying to console a weeping widow. Her husband had passed away without a will. "Did the deceased have any last words?" asked the lawyer. "You mean right before he died?" sobbed the widow. "Yes," replied the lawyer, "they might be helpful, if it's not too painful for you to recall." "Well," she began, "he said, 'Don't try to scare me. You couldn't hit the broad side of a barn with that gun.'"

****

If you see a lawyer on a bicycle, why don't you swerve to hit him? It might be your bicycle.

****

A president of a democracy is a man who is always ready, willing and able to lay down your life for his country.

A nun is undressing for a bath and while she's standing naked, there's a knock at the door. The nun calls, "Who is it?" A voice answers, "A blind salesman." The nun decides to get a thrill by having the blind man in the room while she's naked, so she lets him in. The man walks in, looks straight at the nun and says: "Uhhhh, well, hello there. Where would you be wanting the blinds fitted...?"

✶✶✶✶

If you perceive that there are four possible ways in which a procedure can go wrong and circumvent these, then a fifth way, unprepared-for, will promptly develop.

✶✶✶✶

The merchandizing manager of a large food chain was on holiday. While driving through rural Norfolk he developed a headache and decided to stop in the next town and buy some aspirin. Stopping at a small grocery store, he went in and got his aspirin. While in the store, more out of habit than anything, he walked around to see how it was merchandized. To his amazement, only about two of the ten aisles in the store were devoted to the basic staples and the other eight aisles were filled with salt. He had never seen anything like this in his life and wondered what caused this huge demand for salt in a small rural town in Norfolk. Seeing the proprietor in the rear of the store, he said, "My God, you sell a lot of salt." At which the owner said: "Who, me?

Wurr, boy. I don't 'ardly sell any salt at all, but that fellow that sells me salt, does he know how to sell salt."

****

Why should lawyers wear lots of sunscreen when holidaying at a beach resort? Because they're used to doing all of their lying indoors.

****

He who beats his sword into a ploughshare usually ends up ploughing for those who kept their swords.

****

Diplomacy is the art of saying "Nice doggy" until you find a large enough rock.

****

A very large department store chain in the UK is very low on sales. The head of personnel, Mr Jones, informs the head of each department store that they are to send all employees over the age of 60 out on early pension. The early pension plan is implemented. After three months Mr Jones, in going over store reports, notices that the Croydon store has an employee over the age of 60. Mr Jones calls

Mr Smith at the Croydon branch to find out why Mr Green is still with the firm. Mr Smith explains to Mr Jones that Mr Green is the best salesman that the store has ever had. He brings hundreds of thousands of pounds into the shop a year – to let him go would be a real loss. The following week, Mr Jones goes to the shop and down to the sales floor to secretly watch Mr Green in action. Mr Green says to a customer: "You know, with that new fishing rod that you bought, you should really have some new fishing clothes." The customer is convinced and Mr Green outfits him in hundreds of pounds'-worth of new fishing clothes. Mr Green continues: "You know, you are going to look so spiffy in that new outfit with your new fishing rod that it would be a pity not to be seen. Instead of just standing on the bank of the river, you should be seen in a new fishing boat." The customer is convinced and Mr Green sells him a new fishing boat. Mr Green is so convincing that he also sells the customer a new boat trailer and a new car to go along with the new boat, new outfit, and new fishing rod. By the time the sale is rung up, Mr Green has sold thousands and thousands of pounds'-worth of merchandise. Mr Jones is absolutely astounded. He tells Mr Smith to give Mr Green a raise. He says to Mr Smith, "I have never seen such an outstanding selling job in my life. It is unbelievable that the customer came in for a simple fishing rod and Mr Green sold him thousands of pounds'-worth of merchandize." Mr Smith says: "That's not even the beautiful part. That customer didn't even come in for a fishing rod. He came in to buy his wife a box of tampons. Mr Green convinced him that since his weekend was already shot, he might as well go fishing..."

The scene is a dark jungle in Africa. Two tigers are stalking through the brush when the one to the rear reaches out with his tongue and licks the arse of the tiger in front. The startled tiger turns around and says: "Hey, leave it out, alright?" The rear tiger says, "Sorry", and they continue. After about another five minutes, the rear tiger again reaches out with his tongue and licks the arse of the tiger in front. The front tiger turns around and cuffs the rear tiger and says: "I said stop it!" The rear tiger says, "Sorry", and they continue. After about another five minutes, the rear tiger once more licks the arse of the tiger in front. The front tiger turns around and asks the rear tiger: "What is it with you, anyway?" The rear tiger replies: "Well, I just ate a lawyer and I'm trying to get the taste out of my mouth."

✻✻✻✻

We need either less corruption or more chance to participate in it.

✻✻✻✻

Between the pigeons and the politicians, it's hard to keep the courthouse clean.

✻✻✻✻

A travelling salesman stops at a petrol station to take a crap. The toilet has two stalls and there's a man already there using one of them. The two men acknowledge each other and go about their business. The salesman finishes first and, as he pulls his trousers up, some coins drop into the toilet bowl. He looks at it, thinks for a moment and throws a £20 note into the bowl. The other man, astonished, asks: "Why the hell did you do that?" The salesman says: "You don't expect me to put my hand in there for 35 pence do you?."

****

A conclusion is the place where you got tired of thinking.

****

By the time you can make ends meet, they've moved the ends.

****

Lawyers are the only profession where the more there are, the more are needed.

****

A man goes to an office and sees a crying secretary. "Excuse me, but what is the matter with you?" "My boss told me that I'm not pretty enough to make so many typing errors..."

Where can you find a good lawyer? In the cemetery.

****

A man walks into a department store, finds the manager and says, "I really need a job; how about giving me a chance?" The manager says, "Certainly, but you have to sell these 500 toothbrushes in a week to get the job." Our hero takes the toothbrushes and leaves. Next week, he comes back with the toothbrushes and finds the manager. "I didn't get any of these sold, but please, please, give me another chance." The manager says, "OK, but you have to take another 500 toothbrushes." Our man takes the toothbrushes and tries his luck again. Again our man comes back with the 1000 toothbrushes, talks to the manager, gets another 500 toothbrushes and tries his luck. So he comes back in a week, not with 1500 toothbrushes but with a bag of money. The manager gives him the job and wants to know his trick. Our hero says: "Well, the idea came to me a couple of days ago. I set up a table on a busy street corner with a bowl of chips, a bowl of shit, and a sign saying 'Free Chip and Dip'. Someone would come along, dip the chip, and say, 'Yuck! That tastes like shit.' and, of course, I would reply, 'Yeah. So, want to buy a toothbrush?'"

****

The easiest way to find something lost around the office is to buy a replacement.

There were two grocers, Smith and Jones, in the same street. Smith had a sign in his window, "Avocados, 20 pence a pound". A woman goes in and asks for some. "Sorry, love", said Smith, "I haven't got any in just now. Come back on Wednesday." So she goes on up the street to Jones' shop. His avocados are £2.50 a pound, but at least he has them in stock. "That's a bit steep, isn't it? Smith's are only 20 pence a pound." "Yeah," says Jones, "so are mine when I'm out of stock."

****

I broke a mirror in my house. I'm supposed to get seven years of bad luck, but my lawyer thinks he can get me five.

****

The unemployment rate is so bad in Birmingham that when a post office posted a notice reading,"WANTED for Armed Robbery", 25 people responded.

****

Did you hear about the new sushi bar that caters exclusively to lawyers? It's called Sosumi.

****

When the Lord made man, all the parts of the body argued over who would be boss. The brain explained that since he controlled all the parts of the body, he should be boss. The legs argued that since they took the man wherever he wanted to go, they should be boss. The stomach suggested that since he digested all the food, he should be boss. The eyes said that without them man would be helpless, so they should be boss. And so it went on. The hands, heart, ears and lungs each demanded that they be made boss. Then the arsehole applied for the job, but the other parts just laughed, so the arsehole became mad and closed up. After a few days, the brain went foggy, the legs got wobbly, the stomach got ill and the eyes got crossed and unable to see. They all conceded and made the arsehole boss. This proves that you don't have to be a brain to be a boss, just an arsehole.

****

A fool and his money are soon elected.

****

When a lawyer tells his clients he has a sliding fee schedule, what he means is that after he bills you it's financially hard to get back on your feet.

****

An airliner was having engine trouble and the pilot instructed the cabin crew to have the passengers take their seats and prepare for an emergency landing. A few minutes later, the pilot asked the flight attendants if everyone was buckled in and ready. "All set back here, Captain," came the reply, "except one lawyer who is still passing out business cards."

****

There is a cartoon showing two people fighting over a cow. One is pulling the cow by the tail; the other is pulling on the horns. Underneath is a lawyer milking the cow.

****

A doctor, an engineer and a lawyer go out hunting in the woods one day. Each of them brings along his hunting dog, and they spend most of the morning arguing about which of the dogs is the smartest. Early in the afternoon, they discover a clearing in the forest. In the middle of the clearing is a large pile of animal bones. Seeing the bones, the doctor turns to the others and says: "I'm going to prove to you two that my dog is the smartest. Watch this." He then calls his dog over and says: "Bones. See the bones? Go get 'em." The dog rushes over to the pile, rummages around for a bit and then proceeds to build a replica of the human skeleton, perfect down to the last detail. The doctor grins smugly; after all, his dog has just built a human skeleton from animal bones. The engineer, however, is totally unimpressed. "That's nothing," he says. "Watch this." He calls his dog over, and points out the pile. "Bones. Get the bones." The dog rushes over, tears down the skeleton and in its place builds a perfect replica of the Eiffel Tower. It even has a little French flag waving at the top. The doctor is forced to agree that the engineer's dog is, in fact, smarter than his own. The lawyer, however, is still not impressed. "My dog is smarter," he says. "Watch." He then calls his dog over, points to the pile, and says simply "Bones." The dog rushes over to the pile, tears down the tower, eats half the bones, buries the other half, screws the other two dogs and takes the rest of the afternoon off.

****

Between grand theft and a legal fee, there only stands a law degree.

****

What is brown and black and looks good on a lawyer? A Dobermann.

****

A couple of months in the lab can often save a couple of hours in the library.

****

As productivity has not increased since the implementation of the seven-day working week, the stoppage of all company health and retirement plans, the 20 per cent pay cut, the ten-year pay freeze, the installation of video cameras in company restrooms, the hiring of the corporate truant officers to check up on all employees calling in sick, and the random drug and dirty underwear screenings, management has decided that the beatings and mandatory self-flagellations will continue until morale improves.

****

What do you call an honest lawyer? Hypothetical.

****

Creativity is great, but plagiarism is faster.

****

Artificial intelligence usually beats real stupidity.

****

Never volunteer for anything.

Have you heard about the lawyers' word processor? No matter what font or typesize you select, everything comes out in fine print.

****

Experience is what causes a person to make new mistakes instead of old ones.

****

A car company is planning to build a new model made from all its previous engineering errors. The new model will be called Total Recall.

****

A fellow had just been hired as the new managing director of a large high-tech corporation. The managing director who was stepping down, met him privately and presented him with three numbered envelopes. "Open these if you run up against a problem you don't think you can solve," he said. Well, things went along pretty smoothly, but six months later sales took a downturn and the new MD was really catching a lot of heat. About at his wits' end, he remembered the envelopes. He went to his drawer and took out the first envelope. The message read, "Blame your predecessor." The new MD called a press conference and tactfully laid the blame at the feet of the previous MD. Satisfied with his comments, the press - and the City responded positively, sales began to pick up and the problem was soon behind him. About a year later, the company was again experiencing a slight dip in sales, combined with serious product problems. Having learned from his previous experience, the MD quickly opened the second envelope. The message read, "Reorganize." This he did, and the company quickly rebounded. After several consecutive profitable quarters, the company once again fell on difficult times. The MD went to his office, closed the door and opened the third envelope. The message said: "Prepare three envelopes."

✳✳✳✳

What did the harassed lawyer say? "Get off my case."

✳✳✳✳

The boss returned from lunch in a good mood and called the whole staff in to listen to a couple of jokes he had picked up. Everybody but one girl laughed uproariously. "What's the matter?" grumbled the boss. "Haven't you got a sense of humour?" "I don't have to laugh," she said, "I'm leaving on Friday."

✳✳✳✳

When angry, count to ten before you speak. If VERY angry, count to 100, and then go and shout at someone junior.

****

What do you call a lawyer with an IQ of 50? Your Honour.

****

Secretary: "I would like to inform you that I have found a new position." Boss: "Fine. What are we waiting fo?, Let's try it."

****

Q: In front of you stand four men: Adolf Hitler, Idi Amin, Saddam Hussein and a lawyer. You are holding a gun which contains only three bullets. Who do you shoot? A: Use all three bullets on the lawyer. Its the only way to be sure.

****

"You're a cheat," shouted the attorney to his opponent. "And you're a liar," bellowed the opposition. Banging his gavel sharply, his Honour interrupted: "All right; now that both barristers have been identified, let's get on with this case."

A door-to-door vacuum cleaner salesman manages to bullshit his way into a woman's home in outback Australia. "This machine is the best ever," he claims, while pouring a bag of dirt over the lounge floor. The woman says she's really worried it may not all come off, so the salesman says: "If this machine doesn't remove all the dust completely, I'll lick it off myself." The woman says, "Do you want ketchup. We're not connected to the electricity yet."

✱✱✱✱

A businessman was having a tough time lugging his lumpy, oversized suitcase on to the plane. Helped by a stewardess, he finally managed to stuff it in the overhead locker. "Do you always carry such heavy luggage?" she sighed. "Never again," the man replied. "Next time, I'm riding in the bag, and my partner can buy the ticket."

✱✱✱✱

Take heart; the only person who always got his work done by Friday was Robinson Crusoe.

✱✱✱✱

A circuit judge in a small-town court was hearing a drunk-driving case and the defendant, who had both a record and a reputation for driving under the influence, demanded a jury trial. It was nearly 4pm.

And getting a jury would take time, so the judge called a recess and went out in the hall looking to empanel anyone available for jury duty. He found a dozen lawyers in the main lobby and told them that they were a jury. The lawyers thought this would be a novel experience and so followed the judge back to the courtroom. The trial was over in about ten minutes and it was very clear that the defendant was guilty. The jury went into the jury room, the judge started getting ready to go home and everyone waited. After nearly three hours, the judge was totally out of patience and sent the usher into the jury room to see what was holding up the verdict. When the usher returned, the judge said: "Well, have they got a verdict yet?" The usher shook his head and said: "Verdict? No, M'lud, they're still doing nominating speeches for the foreman's position."

****

A speaker was getting tired of being interrupted. He grabbed the microphone and said loudly, "We seem to have a great many fools here tonight. Would it be advisable to hear one at a time?" Someone in the back of the room said, "Yes. Get on with the speech."

****

Diplomacy is the art of letting someone else have your way.

****

It has been reported in a magazine that a certain cosmetics company has more than 36,000 sales representatives in the Amazonia region of Brazil, with sales growing at 50 per cent a year. The company representatives in Amazonia sell the complete range of products, from lipstick, moisturizer and mascara to men's bikini briefs, and accept for payment almost any barterable items, such as fish.

****

A man on trial at the Old Bailey had previously pleaded not guilty. However, once the jury, – eight women and four men – had been seated and the trial was under way, the defendant switched his plea. "Why the change?" asked the judge. "Were you persuaded to plead guilty?" "No Sir," the man replied, "when I pleaded not guilty, I didn't know women would be on the jury. I can't fool one woman, so I know I can't fool eight of them."

****

What do you get when you cross the Godfather with a lawyer? An offer you can't understand.

****

A lawyer named Strange was shopping for a gravestone. After he had made his selection, the stonemason asked him what inscription he would like on it. "Here lies an honest man and a lawyer," responded the lawyer. "Sorry, but I can't do that. In this country, it's against the law to bury two people in the same grave. However, I could put 'Here lies an honest lawyer'" "But that won't let people know who it is," protested the lawyer. "Certainly will," retorted the stonecutter. "People will read it and exclaim, 'That's strange.'"

✸✸✸✸

How do you know when your divorce is getting ugly? When your lawyer doesn't seem like the bloodsucking leech anymore.

✸✸✸✸

Why did the lawyer cross the road? To get to the car accident on the other side.

✸✸✸✸

A lawyer died and appeared before the pearly gates. When he arrived, a chorus of angels began to sing in his honour and St Peter himself came out to shake his hand. "Mr Morris," said St Peter, "it is a great honour to have you here at last. You are the first being to break Methuselah's record for longevity. You have lived 1028 years." "What are you talking about?" said Morris. "I'm 56." "56? But aren't you John Morris?" "Yes." "A lawyer?" "Yes." "From Knightsbridge?"

"Yes." "Let me check the records," said St Peter. He slapped his hand against his forehead. "Now I see the mistake; we added up your billing hours."

****

A new employee was habitually late. Finally, the foreman called him in. "Don't you know what time we go to work here?" he shouted. "No, sir," was the reply, "I haven't been able to work it out yet, because the rest of you are always here".

****

Sam Cohen, father of three and faithful husband for over 40 years, unexpectedly drops dead one day. His lawyer informs his widow that Stu Schwartz, Sam's best friend since childhood, is to be executor of the will. The day comes to divide Sam's earthly possessions – over a million pounds' worth. In front of Sam's family, Stu reads the will: "Stu, if you're reading this, then I must be dead. You were such a good friend for so long, how can I ignore you in this will? On the other hand, there are my beloved Sophie and my children to be looked after. Stu, I know you can make sure my family is taken care of properly. So, Stu, give what you want to her and take the rest for yourself." Stu then looks at the survivors and tells them that, in accordance with Sam's instructions, he will give fifty thousand pounds to Sam's widow. The rest he is retaining for himself. The family is beside itself. "This is impossible. Forty years of marriage and then this? It can't be." So the family sues. Their day in court arrives, and after testimony from both sides, the judge gives his verdict: "To Stuart Schwartz, I award fifty thousand pounds of the contested money. The remainder shall go to Sophie Cohen, widow of the deceased." Needless to say, the family is elated, but Stu is dumbfound. "Your Honour, how can you do this? The will made Sam's wishes quite clear: 'Give what you want to her and take the rest for yourself.' I wanted the lion's share. What gives?" The judge answered back, "Mr Schwartz, Sam Cohen knew you his whole life. He wanted to give you something in gratitude. He also wanted to see his family taken care of. So he drew up his will accordingly. But you misread his instructions. You see, Sam knew just what kind of a person you are, so with his family's interest in mind, he didn't say, 'Give what you want to her and keep the rest for yourself.' No. What Sam said was, 'Give what YOU want to HER; and keep the rest for yourself'."

****

This executive was interviewing a nervous young women for a position in his company. He wanted to find out something about her personality so he asked, "If you could have a conversation with someone, living or dead, who would it be?" The girl quickly responded, "The living one."

I'll share with you my own secret method for moving up the corporate ladder. It's called the Hind-lick Manoeuvre.

✱✱✱✱

In order to get a loan, you must first prove you don't need it.

✱✱✱✱

When I first started working, I used to dream of the day when I might be earning the salary I'm starving on now.

✱✱✱✱

Lawyers are people who can write a 10,000-word document and call it a brief.

✱✱✱✱

At the funeral of a lady were her doctor, a friend and her lawyer. Each had promised her that at her funeral they would toss £1000 into her grave. The doctor and friend each tossed in their £1000 cash, after which the lawyer removed the cash and placed a cheque for £3000.

✱✱✱✱

The president of a large corporation opened his directors' meeting by announcing: "All those who are opposed to the plan I am about to propose will reply by saying, 'I resign.'"

****

Prosecutor: "Did you kill the victim?" Defendant: "No, I did not." Prosecutor: "Do you know what the penalties are for perjury?" Defendant: "Yes, I do. And they're a hell of a lot better than the penalty for murder."

****

A man was walking down the street one day and he saw a "Salesman Wanted" sign in a window. He went in the store and the owner asked, "Can I help you?" "I'I'IIII w'w'waannnttt j'j'jjoooobbbb," said the man. "I don't know if this job would suit you because of your speaking problem," said the owner. "I'I'III h'h'avvee a'a'a wif'f'fe annd si' si' six k'k'ids a'a'ndd I'I n'neeeed th'th'e j'joobb," said the man. "Okay, here are three Bibles. Go out and sell them," said the owner. So the man went out and came back an hour later. "H'here'sss your mm'money," said the man. The owner was impressed, so he gave the man a dozen more Bibles and sent him out. The man came back in two hours and said, "H'here'sss your mm'money." The owner said, "This is fantastic. You sold more Bibles in three hours than anyone has sold in a week. Tell me, what do you say to the people when they come to the door?" "W'welll," said the man, "III r'r'ing the d'd'oor b'b'ell a'a'nd s's'say 'M'M'aaddammm, d'd'o y'y'ou w'w'ant t'to b'buy t'this B'Bible o'o'rrr d'd'o y'you w'w'w'ant m'me t't'o read it to you?'"

✳✳✳✳

Why do lawyers carry their certification on their dashboard? So they can park in the handicapped parking; it's proof of a moral disability.

✳✳✳✳

A man walked into a bar with his crocodile and asked the bartender: "Do you serve lawyers here?" "Certainly," replied the bartender. "Good," said the man. "Give me a beer, and I'll have a lawyer for my croc."

✳✳✳✳

The son of a Spanish lawyer graduated from college and was considering the future. He went to his father, who had a very large office, and asked if he might be given a desk in the corner where he could observe his father's activities. He could be introduced to his father's clients as a clerk. That way, he could decide on whether or not to become a lawyer. His father thought this a splendid idea and this arrangement was set up immediately. On his son's first day at work, the first client in the morning was a rough-hewn man with calloused hands, in workman's attire, who began the conversation by saying: "Mr Lawyer, I work for some people named Gonzales who have a ranch on the east side of town. For many years I have tended their crops and animals, including some cows. I have raised the cows, tended them, fed them, and it has always been my understanding and belief that I was the owner of the cows. Mr Gonzales died and his son has inherited the farm, and he believes that since the cows were raised on his ranch and fed on his hay, the cows are his. In short, we have a dispute as to the ownership of the cows." The lawyer said: "I have heard enough. I will take your case. DON'T WORRY ABOUT THE COWS." After the tenant farmer left, the next client came in, a young, well-dressed man, clearly a member of the landed class. "My name is Gonzales. I own a farm on the east side of the town," he said. "For many years, a tenant farmer has worked for my family tending the crops and animals, including some cows. The cows have been raised on my land and fed on my hay, and I believe that they belong to me, but the tenant farmer believes that since he raised them and cared for them, they are his. In short, we have a dispute over ownership of the cows." The lawyer said, "I have heard enough. I will take your case. DON'T WORRY ABOUT THE COWS." After the client left, the son came over to his father with a look of concern. "My father, I know nothing of the law, but it seems to me that we have a serious problem regarding these cows." "DON'T WORRY ABOUT THE COWS." said the lawyer. "The cows will be ours."

A little old lady walked into the head branch of a respected bank holding a large paper bag in her hand. She told the young man at the window that she wished to take the £3 million she had in the bag and open an account with the bank. As it was such a large sum she asked to meet the manager of the bank first. The teller seemed to think that was a reasonable request and after opening the paper bag and seeing the bundles of £50 notes, which amounted to around £3 million, he telephoned the manager's secretary to arrange this. The lady was escorted upstairs and ushered into the manager's office. Introductions were made and the lady stated that she would like to get to know the people she did business with on a more personal level. The bank manager then asked her where she came into such a large amount of money. "Was it an inheritance?" he asked. "No," she answered. "Was it from playing the stock market?" "No," she replied. He was quiet for a minute, trying to think of where this little old lady could possibly come into £3 million. "I bet on things," she stated. "You bet?" repeated the bank manager, "as in horses?" "No," she replied, "I bet people." Seeing his confusion, she explained that she just bet different things with people. All of a sudden she said, "I'll bet you £25,000 that by ten o'clock tomorrow morning, your balls will be square." The bank manager figured she must be off her rocker and decided to take her up on the bet. He didn't see how he could lose. For the rest of the day, the bank manager was very careful. He decided to stay home that evening and take no chances; there was £25,000 at stake. When he got up in the morning and took his shower, he checked to make sure everything was okay. There was no difference; he looked the same as he always had. He went to work and waited for the little old lady to come in at ten o'clock, humming as he went. He knew this would be a good day; how often do you get handed £25,000 for doing nothing? At ten o'clock sharp, the little old lady was shown into his office. With her was a younger man. When he inquired as to the man's purpose for being there, she informed him that he was her lawyer and she always took him along when there was this much money involved. "Well?" she asked, "what about our bet?" "I don't know how to tell you this," he replied, "but I am the same as I've always been only £25,000 richer." The lady seemed to accept this, but requested that she be able to see for herself. The bank manager thought this was reasonable and dropped his trousers. She instructed him to bend over and then grabbed a hold of him. Sure enough, everything was fine. The bank manager then looked up and saw her lawyer standing across the room banging his head against the wall. "What's wrong with him?" he inquired. "Oh, him?" she replied," I bet him £100,000 that by ten o'clock this morning that I'd have the bank manager by the bollocks."

✳✳✳✳

If a lawyer and a tax inspector were both drowning, and you could only save one of them, would you go to lunch or read the paper?

✳✳✳✳

Once overheard at the office water cooler: "The boss said that I would get a rise when I earned it. He's crazy if he thinks I'm gonna wait that long."

****

A man, who barely made it through the Black Monday stockmarket crash, called his stockbrokers the next day and asked, "May I speak to Mr Spencer, please?" The operator replied, "I'm sorry. Mr Spencer is deceased. Can anyone else help you?" The man said "No" and hung up. Ten minutes later, he called again and asked for Mr Spencer, his broker. The operator said, "You just called a few minutes ago, didn't you? Mr Spencer has died. I'm not making this up." The man again hung up. Fifteen minutes later he called a third time and asked for Mr Spencer. The operator was irked by this time. "I've told you twice already, Mr Spencer is dead. He is not here. Why do you keep asking for him when I say he's dead?" The man replied: "I just like hearing it."

****

You know it is going to be a bad day at work when...the gypsy fortune-teller offers to refund your money.

****

What is the ideal weight of a lawyer? About three pounds, including the urn.

****

Experts are people who know a great deal about very little and who go along learning more and more about less and less until they know practically everything about nothing. Lawyers, on the other hand, are people who know very little about many things and keep learning less and less about more and more until they know practically nothing about everything. Judges are people who start out knowing everything about everything but end up knowing nothing about anything because of their constant association with experts and lawyers.

****

A devout, good couple were about to get married, but a tragic car accident ended their lives. When they got to heaven, they asked St Peter if he could arrange for them to be married, saying that it was what they had hoped for in life, and they still desired wedded union. He thought about it and agreed, but said they would have to wait. It was almost one hundred years later when St Peter sent for them. They were married in a simple ceremony. So things went on, for thirty years or so, but they determined, in this time, that eternity was best not spent together. They went back to St Peter, and said, "We thought we would be happy for ever, but now we believe that we have irreconcilable differences. Is there any way we can get divorced?" "Are you kidding?" said St Peter. "It took me a hundred years to get a priest up here to marry you. I'll never get a lawyer."

****

Why didn't the mime artist feel so bad about his career? At least he wasn't a lawyer.

****

All work and no play will make you a manager.

****

How do you get a lawyer out of a tree? Cut the rope.

****

How many lawyers does it take to stop a moving bus? Never enough.

****

What's the difference between a lawyer and a skunk? Nobody wants to hit a skunk.

In a terrible accident at a railroad crossing, a train smashed into a car and pushed it nearly 400 yards down the track. Though no one was killed, the driver took the train company to court. At the trial, the engineer insisted that he had given the driver ample warning by waving his lantern back and forth for nearly a minute. He even stood and convincingly demonstrated how he'd done it. The court believed his story and the suit was dismissed. "Congratulations," the lawyer said to the engineer when it was over, "you did superbly under cross-examination." "Thanks," he said, "but he sure had me worried." "How's that?" the lawyer asked. "I was afraid he was going to ask if the lantern was lit."

✱✱✱✱

Q: How many lawyers does it take to change a light bulb? A: Such number as may be deemed necessary to perform the stated task in a timely and efficient manner within the strictures of the following agreement: Whereas the party of the first part, also known as "Lawyer", and the party of the second part, also known as "Light Bulb", do hereby and forthwith agree to a transaction wherein the party of the second part (Light Bulb) shall be removed from the current position as a result of failure to perform previously agreed upon duties, ie: the lighting, elucidation, and otherwise illumination of the area ranging from the front (north) door, through the entryway, terminating at an area just inside the primary living area, demarcated by the beginning of the carpet, any spillover illumination being at the option of the party of the second part (Light Bulb) and not required by the aforementioned agreement between the parties. The aforementioned removal transaction shall include, but not be limited to, the following steps: 1) The party of the first part (Lawyer) shall, with or without elevation at his option, by means of a chair, stepstool, ladder or any other means of elevation, grasp the party of the second part (Light Bulb) and rotate the party of the second part (Light Bulb) in a counter-clockwise direction, this point being non-negotiable. 2) Upon reaching a point where the party of the second part (Light Bulb) becomes separated from the party of the third part (Receptacle), the party of the first part (Lawyer) shall have the option of disposing of the party of the second part (Light Bulb) in a manner consistent with all applicable European, local and Government statutes. 3) Once separation and disposal have been achieved, the party of the first part (Lawyer) shall have the option of beginning installation of the party of the fourth part (New Light Bulb). This installation shall occur in a manner consistent with the reverse of the procedures described in step one of this self-same document, being careful to note that the rotation should occur in a clockwise direction, this point also being non-negotiable. Note: The above described steps may be performed, at the option of the party of the first part (Lawyer), by any or all persons authorized by him, the objective being to produce the most possible revenue for the party of the fifth part, also known as "Partnership". Charge: £2185.

****

A man went into the Town Hall of a small town, obviously desperate. He asked the man at the counter, "Is there a criminal lawyer in town?" The man replied: "Yes, but we can't prove it yet."

✳✳✳✳

What do you call a person who assists a criminal in breaking the law before the criminal gets arrested? An accomplice. What do you call a person who assists a criminal in breaking the law after the criminal gets arrested? A lawyer.

✳✳✳✳

How do you kill four thousand lawyers? You build a new Titanic and declare it cannot sink.

✳✳✳✳

What's the difference between a lawyer and a herd of buffalo? The lawyer charges more.

✳✳✳✳

If only one price can be obtained for a quotation, the price will be unreasonable.

Doctor's Orders

3

Jokes About Doctors
and Their Kind

Two country doctors out in the Yorkshire Dales were discussing the population explosion in the world. One physician said: "Why, at t'current rate o' population growth, there'll soon be no'but standing room on t'whole planet." After a thoughtful pause, the other doctor replied, "Aye, but that'll slow t'buggers down a bit."

****

Patient: "Well, doctor, what does the X-ray of my head show?"
Doctor: "Absolutely nothing."

****

A guy goes to the doctor with a mysterious pain and tells the doctor, "Doc, Doc, my penis has been burning lately." And the doctor says reassuringly, "Don't worry, son, that just means someone is talking about it."

****

A woman goes to a doctor with a problem. She's sitting on the chair next to the doctor, and she's very hesitant about describing her problem. Eventually, the doctor manages to discover that she thinks she may be sexually perverted. "What sort of perversion are you talking about?" asks the doctor. "Well," says the woman, "I like to be...Ohh...Ah...Ummm...I'm sorry, doctor, but I'm too ashamed to talk about it." "Come, come, my dear. I'm a doctor, you know; I've been trained to understand these problems. So what's the matter...?" So the woman again tries to explain, but gets so embarrassed that she just turns bright red and looks as though she might faint. Then the doctor has a bright idea. "Look," he says, "I'm a bit of a pervert myself. So if you show me what your perversion is, I'll show you what mine is. Okay? Is it a deal?" The woman considers the offer and after a short while agrees that it's a fair request. So after a slight pause, she says: "Well, my perversion is...my perversion...Oh...I like to be kissed on the bottom." "Shit, is that ALL," says the doctor. "Look, go behind that screen, take all your clothes off, and I'll come round and show you what MY perversion is." So the woman does as she is told and undresses behind the screen. She gets down on all fours thinking to herself, "Hmmmm, perhaps he might kiss me on the bottom." Anyway, 15 minutes pass and nothing has happened. So the woman peers around the side of the screen to see the doctor sitting behind his desk, his feet up on the table, reading a newspaper and whistling to himself. "Hey!" shouts the woman, "I thought you said you were a pervert?" "Oh, I am," says the doctor, "I've just crapped in your handbag."

✳✳✳✳

Be a better psychiatrist and the world will beat a psychopath to your door.

What do you call a man who ignores doctors' advice? The Health Secretary.

****

A woman goes to her doctor, who verifies that she is pregnant. This is her first pregnancy. The doctor asks her if she has any questions. She replies, "Well, I'm a little worried about the pain. How much will childbirth hurt?" The doctor answers, "Well, that varies from woman to woman and pregnancy to pregnancy; and besides, it's difficult to describe pain." "I know, but can't you give me some idea?" she asks. "Grab your upper lip and pull it out a little..." "Like this?" "A little more..." "Like this?" "No. A little more..." "Like this?" "Yes. Does that hurt?" "A little bit." "Now stretch it over your head."

****

Did you hear about the doctor who had his licence taken away because he was having affairs with his patients? Yes, it's a shame because he was one of the top veterinarians in the country.

****

A young woman, two months pregnant, went to see her obstetrician. He was in a hurry to leave on an emergency call, so he asked her to quickly bare her stomach, then reached into his desk and took out a rubber stamp, which he pressed beside her navel. He then rushed off. At home, she and her husband tried to read the tiny words printed on her belly, but they were too small. They then found a magnifying glass and tried to read the words. The stamp read: "When your husband can read this without his glasses, it's time to get yourself to the hospital."

****

A Manchester couple discovered the wife was pregnant, but the family simply couldn't afford any more children. They looked around and found an excellent Hispanic family to adopt the child. Then...they found out she was going to have twins. Fortunately, a family of Arab immigrants agreed to adopt the other child. Twin healthy boys were born and passed on to the families, who named them Juan and Amal. The biological parents kept in close touch with the adoptive parents in a very amicable relationship. One day, Juan's family sent a picture of the youth in his cricket uniform. The biological mother was so proud of her son. She said to her husband: "He is so handsome. I wish we had a picture like this of our other son, too." He replied, "Dear, they are twins. When you've seen Juan, you've seen Amal."

****

There is a businessman who is not feeling well, so he goes to see the doctor about it. The doctor says to him: "Well, it must be your diet;

what sort of greens do you eat?" The man replies: "Well, actually, I only eat peas; I hate all other green foods." The doctor is quite shocked at this and says: "Well man, that's your problem, all those peas will be clogging up your system, you'll have to give them up." The guy says, "But how long for? I mean, I really like peas." The doctor replies, "For ever, I'm afraid." The man is quite shocked by this, but he gives it a go and sure enough, his condition improves, so he realizes that he will never eat a pea again. Anyway, one night, years later, he's at a convention for his employer and getting quite sloshed. One of the reps says: "Well, ashully, I'd love a cigarette, coz I avn't ad a smoke in four years, I gave it up." Quite a shocker really, and the barman goes. "Really? I haven't had a game of golf in three years, because it cost me my first marriage, so I gave it up." The businessman says, "Thas nuvving, I haven't ad a pea in six years." The barman jumps up screaming, "Okay, everyone who can't swim, grab a table..."

****

There was a country doctor who was the only doctor for miles around. He wanted to go on a fishing trip , so he called the vet and asked him to look after things while he was gone. The vet asked: "Is anything happening?" The doctor replied, "Mrs Jones is about due, but I don't think the baby will come before I get back. Anyway, if it does, just deliver it. This is her third and the first two went really easily." The vet said "Okay", and the doctor went on the fishing trip. When he returned, he called the vet. "How did things go while I was gone?" "Pretty good." "Did Mrs Jones have her baby?" "Yes, it was an eight-pound boy. Everyone's doing fine." "Did you have any trouble?" "Well, there was just one little problem." "What was that?" "I had a terrible time getting her to eat the afterbirth."

****

A man and a woman were waiting at the hospital donation centre. Man: "What are you doing here today?" Woman: "Oh, I'm here to donate some blood. They're going to give me £5 for it." Man: "Hmm, that's interesting. I'm here to donate sperm, myself. But they pay me £25." The woman looked thoughtful for a moment and they chatted some more before going their separate ways. Several months later, the same man and woman met again in the donation centre. Man: "Oh, hi there. Here to donate blood again?" Woman: [shaking her head with mouth closed] "Unh unh."

****

Max Brown, a young father-to-be, was waiting anxiously outside the maternity ward where his wife was giving birth to their first baby. As he paced the floor, a nurse popped her head around the door. "It's a boy, Mr Brown," she said, "but we think you'd better go and have a cup of coffee, because there might be another." Max turned a little pale and left. Some time later, he rang the hospital and was told he was the father of twins. "But," the nurse went on, "we're sure there's another on the way. Ring back again in a little while." At that, Max decided that coffee was not nearly strong enough. He ordered a few beers and rang the hospital again, only to be told a third baby had arrived and a fourth was imminent. White-faced, he stumbled to the bar and ordered a double Scotch. Twenty minutes later, he tried the phone again, but he was in such a state that he dialled the wrong number and got the recorded cricket score. When they picked him up off the floor of the phone box, the recording was still going strong, "The score is 96 all out, and the last one was a duck."

✳✳✳✳

A therapist told a woman to use some imagination while making love with her husband to spice things up. She replied, "You mean imagine that it's good?"

✳✳✳✳

Patient: "Doc, Doc, if I give up wine, women, and song, will I live longer?" Doctor: "Not really. It will just seem that way."

✳✳✳✳

A group of psychiatrists go to tour an insane asylum that is known for its progressive rehabilitation methods. They begin by visiting some of the patients. The first patient they visit is a young woman. She is practising ballet. One of the psychiatrists asks: "What are you doing?" She replies, "I'm studying ballet so when I get out of here I can possibly join a troupe and be a productive member of society." "Wow, that's wonderful." The next person is a man reading a book with a pile of books next to him. The same question is asked of him, "What are you doing?" "I'm studying biology, chemistry, and physics, so I can enter medical school when I get out." Room after room, they witness the incredible success and attitudes of the patients, until they finally reach a room the asylum's director is reluctant to open. Finally, he is persuaded to open it. Inside is a man balancing a peanut on his penis. The psychiatrist exclaims, "My God what are you doing?" The man replied: "I'm fucking nuts and I'm never getting out of here."

✳✳✳✳

Doctor: "What seems to be the trouble? " Patient: "Doctor, I keep getting the feeling that nobody can hear what I say." Doctor: "What seems to be the trouble?"

✳✳✳✳

Patient: "My tongue tingles when I touch it to a cracked walnut wrapped in used toaster-oven aluminium foil, what's wrong with me?" Doctor: "You have far too much free time."

Patient: "How much to have this tooth pulled?" Dentist: "£90." Patient: "£90 for just a few minutes' work?" Dentist: "I can extract it very slowly if you like."

✳✳✳✳

There was once a guy whose tongue was so long that when he stuck it out for the doctor, the nurse went, "Aaaaaahhh!"

✳✳✳✳

Mrs Smith: "Help me, doctor! Little Tommy's swallowed the can-opener." Doctor: "Don't panic. He'll be alright." Mrs Smith: "But how do I open the frigging beans? The toast's getting cold."

✳✳✳✳

A woman goes to the dentist. As he leans over to begin working on her, she grabs his balls. The dentist says: "Madam, I believe you've got hold of my privates." The woman replies, "Yes. We're going to be careful not to hurt each other, aren't we?"

✳✳✳✳

A man, 92 years old, is told by his doctor that he has tested positive for HIV. Distraught and befuddled, he retires as usual to spend the afternoon at the park bench with other senior citizens. He tells his friend: "Can you believe it? I have HIV...at 92." His friend replies, "You think you have troubles? I have IBM at 80."

****

A woman goes to the hospital to visit a girlfriend who is about to have a heart transplant. She's worried about the friend so she speaks to the doctor. Girlfriend: "I'm worried about my friend, doctor. What if her body rejects the organ?" Doctor: "Well, she's 36 years old and healthy. How long has she been in business?" Girlfriend: "She's been working since she was 19 years old but what does that have to do with anything?" Doctor: "Well, she's been working 17 years and hasn't rejected an organ yet."

****

This guy took his nymphomaniac wife to the sex therapist for treatment. "This is one hot potato of a lady, doctor," he said, "maybe you can do something for her. She goes for any man, any age, any time, any where...and it is just driving me crazy with jealousy." "We'll see," the therapist said. He directed the wife into his examining room, closed the door behind her, and told her to get undressed. Then he told her to get up on to the examining table on her stomach. The moment he touched her buttocks, she began to squirm and moan. It was too much for him to resist, so he climbed up on top of her and began screwing her. The husband heard the moans and groans coming from the examination room and, very suspicious, burst into the room. He was confronted by the sight of the doctor astride his wife and banging away. "Doctor, what are you doing?" he asked. Flustered, the therapist replied, "Oh, it's you. I'm only taking your wife's temperature." The husband pulled out a large pocket knife and began to hone it deliberately on his boot. "Well, doctor," he said, "when you take that thing out, it had better have numbers on it."

✳✳✳✳

An old man of 87 went to the hospital to get a radical new surgical procedure done where they stretch the skin and pull all the wrinkles up on to the top of the scalp, making you appear years younger. On his way out of the hospital, he met an old friend who didn't recognize him at first. "Rob, is that really you?" said the friend. "You look years younger. I didn't know you had a dimple in your chin." "It's not a dimple, it's my belly button" said the old man and his friend laughed. "If you think that's funny, take a look at what I'm wearing for a tie."

✳✳✳✳

Patient: "I am having a hard time hearing. I can't even hear myself cough." Doctor: "Here is a prescription, take the medicine for seven days, then return for a check-up." Seven days later – Patient: "Thanks a million, doctor. At least, I can hear myself cough now. So what did you do to make me hear better?" Doctor: "Not much, I gave you an expectorant to increase your cough."

****

A woman walks into her sex therapist's office. She tells the therapist that her husband is not a very good lover, and they never have sex any more, and she asks what to do about it. The therapist tells her that there is an experimental drug that might do the trick. She tells the woman to give her husband one pill that night and come back in the morning and tell her what happens. The next day, the woman comes in, ecstatic, telling the therapist that the pill worked and that she and her husband had the best sex ever. She asks her therapist what would happen if she gave her husband two pills and the therapist says she doesn't know, but to go ahead and try it. The next day, the same thing happens, the woman comes in telling the therapist that the sex was even better than the night before and what would happen if she gave him five pills? The therapist says she doesn't know, but to go ahead and try it. The next day, the woman comes in limp but happy, and tells the therapist that the sex just keeps getting better and what would happen if she gave her husband the rest of the bottle? The therapist says she doesn't know; it's an experimental drug and she doesn't know what a full bottle could do to a person. Anyway, the woman leaves the therapist's office and puts the rest of the bottle of pills in her husband's morning coffee. A week later, a boy walks into the therapist's office and says: "Are you the dick-head who gave my mother a bottle of experimental pills?" "Why, yes, young man, I did. Why?" "Well, Mum's dead, my sister's pregnant, my arse hurts, and Dad's sitting in the corner going 'Here, kitty, kitty, kitty'..."

****

Patient: "Will it hurt, doctor?" Doctor: "Only when you get my bill."

****

After making love, the woman said to the man: "So, you're a doctor?" "That's right," replied the doctor smugly. "Bet you don't know what kind of doctor." "Ummm...I'd say that you're an anaesthetist." "Yes, that's right. Good guess. How did you know?" asked the man. "Because throughout the entire procedure, I didn't feel a thing."

****

A friend of mine went to the dentist recently. He commented that it must be tough spending all day with your hands in someone's mouth. He said, "I just think of it as having my hands in their wallet."

****

One day, a man walked into the dentist's office for some dental work. The dentist said: "Sir, you have a tooth I must pull, what type of painkiller would you like?" The man looked at the dentist and said, "None, thanks, I have experienced the second greatest pain in my life." The dentist said, "Sir, pulling this tooth will be painful, I suggest a painkiller." The man looked back at the dentist and said, "I have experienced the second greatest pain in my life. Nothing else will ever compare." The dentist said, "Sir, I'm telling you, use a painkiller." The man again said to the dentist, "I have experienced the second greatest pain in my life, I do not need painkillers, now pull the tooth." The dentist then said, "Okay, you asked for it, but first, tell me what was the second greatest pain in your life?" The man said, "Yes, I remember it well. I was hunting in some woods north of here one snowy day. Walking through the woods, the urge came upon me and I headed over to a tree. Well, I started to do my thing, and when the first part dropped, it set off a large bear trap that was hidden in the snow that closed on my balls. That was the second greatest pain in my life." The dentist then said, "Ouch! But then what was the first greatest pain in your life?" The man replied, "When I reached the end of the chain."

✳✳✳✳

Three nurses died and went to the Pearly Gates. St Peter asked the first one: "What did you do on Earth that you deserve to get in here? The first nurse replied, "I was an intensive care nurse and I saved hundreds of lives." "Welcome," said St Peter, "come right in. And what did you do?" he asked the second one. The second nurse replied,

"I was an emergency room nurse and I saved hundreds of lives." "Welcome," said St Peter, "come right in. And what did you do?" he asked the third one. The third nurse replied, "I was a managed care nurse and I saved the taxpayer hundreds of thousands of pounds." "Welcome," said St Peter, "come right in... but only for three days."

****

A patient goes to a psychiatrist. The psychiatrist gives him a Rorschach test; he shows a patient a circle with a dot inside it and asks, "What do you see?" The patient replies, "Two people are having sex in the middle of the circular room." The psychiatrist shows the patient another picture of a square with a dot inside it and asks, "What do you see?" Patient answers, "Two people are having sex in the square room." The psychiatrist shows the patient one more picture of a triangle with a dot outside it and asks: "What do you see now?" Patient replies, "What are you, some kind of pervert?"

****

"Oh, doctor," moaned the woman to the psychiatrist. "Everyone calls me a nymphomaniac." "I understand," said the doctor, "but I'll be able to take better notes if you'll let go of my penis."

****

Patient: "Doc, Doc, I keep thinking that I'm a deck of cards."
Psychiatrist: "Sit over there and I'll deal with you later."

****

Doctor: "Did you take the patient's temperature?" Nurse: "No. Is it missing?"

****

It is said that the limbic system of the brain controls the four Fs: Feeding, Fighting, Fleeing and Reproduction.

****

Patient: "Doc, Doc, I think I swallowed a pillow." Doctor: "How do you feel?" Patient: "A little down in the mouth."

****

Patient: "Doc, Doc, I can't stop stealing things." Psychiatrist: "Take these pills. They should help you." Patient: "But what if they don't?" Psychiatrist: "Then get me a video."

****

A city doctor started a practice in the countryside. He once had to go to a farm to attend to a sick farmer who lived there. After a few housecalls he stopped coming to the farm. The puzzled farmer finally phoned him to ask what the matter was. The doctor said, "It's your ducks at the entrance. Every time I enter the farm, they insult me."

✳✳✳✳

Gynaecologists have a power that makes some men envious. They can go into a room where a woman is waiting for them and say, "Get undressed. I'll be with you in a minute."

✳✳✳✳

After her operation, the famous lady soap-opera star was propped up in bed in her private room, as the doctor did his rounds. "Tell me, how are you feeling now?" he asked. "A lot better, thank you," purred the star in reply. "But one thing does bother me. When will I be able to resume a normal sex life?" "Oh, that's rather hard to say," said the doctor, "I've never been asked that after a tonsillectomy before."

✳✳✳✳

A man swallowed a mouse while sleeping on the couch one day. His wife quickly called the doctor and said: "Doc, Doc, please come quickly. My husband just swallowed a mouse and he's gagging and thrashing about." "I'll be right over," the doctor said. "In the meantime, keep waving a piece of cheese over his mouth to try to attract the mouse up and out of there." When the doctor arrived, he saw the wife waving a piece of smoked herring over her husband's mouth. "Er, I told you to use cheese, not herring, to lure the mouse." "I know, doctor," she replied, "but first I've got to get the bloody cat out of him."

****

Man: "Doc, Doc, my wife thinks she's a refrigerator." Psychiatrist: "Don't worry, it will pass." Man: "But, doctor, when she sleeps with her mouth open, the damn light keeps me awake."

****

"Congratulations, Mr Brown, you're in great shape for a man of sixty. Pity you're only forty."

****

Patient: "Tell me, doctor. Is it serious?" Doctor: "Well, I wouldn't advise you to start reading any thick books."

****

Hypnotist: "Alright, Mr Henry, when I say wake up you will no longer be shy but full of confidence and be able to speak your mind... Wake up." Patient: "Right, you! How about giving me a refund, you money-grubbing old quack?"

****

A woman has just started to play golf when she gets stung on the arm by a bee. She rushes back to the clubhouse, hoping to find a doctor. She asks: "Is anyone here a doctor?" One fairly drunk guy stands up and says: "I'm a doctor, what can I help you with?" "I've been stung by a bee." "Oh really, where?" "Between the first and second holes" "Well, clearly your stance is too wide..."

****

A man speaks frantically into the phone, "My wife is pregnant, and her contractions are only two minutes apart." "Is this her first child?" the doctor queries. "No, you idiot!" the man shouts. "This is her husband!"

****

A chap walks into a local pharmacy and walks up to the counter where a lady pharmacist is filling prescriptions. When she finally gets around to helping him he says, "I'd like 99 condoms, please." With a surprised look on her face the pharmacist says, "You want 99 condoms! Fuck me!" To which the guy replies, "Make it 100."

****

Doctor: "We need to get these people to a hospital." Nurse: "What is it?" Doctor: "It's a big building with a lot of doctors in it. Why do you ask?"

****

Patient: "Doc, Doc, I've got five penises." Doctor: "Well, how do your pants fit?" Patient: "Like a glove."

****

Patient walks into a doctor's office. Patient: "Doc, Doc, people ignore me." Doctor: "Next."

****

Patient: "Doctor, doctor. My hair keeps falling out. What can you give me to keep it in?" Doctor: "A shoebox."

****

A psychiatrist, who was just starting out, advertised his clinic as follows: "Satisfaction guaranteed or your mania back."

****

"Doctor, I don't understand what's going on with me. It's really strange, sometimes I feel like a teepee." The doctor thinks about it for a while and then urges the man to continue. So, the man continues, "and sometimes I feel like a wigwam." To which the doctor says: "I wouldn't worry about it, Fred, you're just two tents."

****

A man walked into a psychiatrist's office, sat down and took out a pack of cigarettes. He removed a cigarette from the pack, unrolled it, and stuffed the tobacco up his nose. The shrink frowned and said, "I see you need my help." The guy said, "Yeah doctor. Got a match?"

****

A man goes to the doctor's office one day. The attractive nurse says: "The doctor is over at the hospital right now. He won't be back for about an hour. Could you tell me your symptoms, please?" He tells her. She looks at him appraisingly and decides he's just tense. She offers: "Well, um, for £50, I've got just the thing for you." He agrees, and she takes him into an examining room and screws the daylights out of him. About a week later, he returns, only to find that the doctor is there. The doctor listens to the man's symptoms, examines him and decides the man is just tense. The doctor writes out a prescription for a sedative and says, "That'll be £150 for this visit." The man says, "If it's all the same to you, doctor, I'd rather have the £50 cure."

✳✳✳✳

As the doctor completed an examination of the patient, he said: "I can't find a cause for your complaint. Frankly, I think it's due to drinking." "In that case," said the patient, "I'll come back when you're sober."

✳✳✳✳

The brash young gynaecologist, fresh out of medical school, took one look at his voluptuous new patient and abandoned his professional ethics entirely. As he stroked the supple skin of her naked body, he asked: "Do you understand what I am doing?" "Yes," the patient answered. "You're checking for dermatological abrasions." "Correct," the doctor lied. Next, he fondled her breasts long and lovingly. Again, he inquired, "Do you understand what I am doing?" "You're feeling for cancerous lumps," she ventured. "Very astute," the doctor complimented, getting more excited. He placed the woman's feet in stirrups, dropped his pants, and slipped his member inside her. "And do you know what I am doing now?" "Yes, you're catching herpes."

Patient: "Doc, Doc, I think I need glasses." Teller: "You certainly do. This is a bank."

✳✳✳✳

Patient: "Doc, Doc, should I file my nails?" Doctor: "No, throw them away like everybody else."

✳✳✳✳

Mavis: "My daughter believes in preventative medicine, doctor." Doctor: "Oh, really?" Mavis: "Yes, she tries to prevent me from making her take it."

✳✳✳✳

Have you heard about the new medication that is both an aphrodisiac and a laxative? It's called "Easy Come, Easy Go."

✳✳✳✳

Patient: "Doc, Doc, you must help me. I'm under such a lot of stress, I keep losing my temper with people." Doctor: "Tell me about your problem." Patient: "I just did, you stupid bastard."

✳✳✳✳

Bill: "Doc, Doc. my wife beats me." Doctor: "Oh dear. How often?" Bill: "Every time we play Scrabble."

****

"The doctor said he would have me on my feet in two weeks." "And did he?" "Yes, I had to sell the car to pay the bill."

****

Woman: "Doc, Doc, my husband tells me my pussy's too big. So I'd like you to tell me if you find it unusual." Doctor: "Please, take off your clothes and I'll examine you. [shouting] What a giant pussy. What a giant pussy." Woman [angry]: "Did you have to say it twice?" Doctor: "I didn't."

****

Patient: "Doc, Doc, when I wasn't married I had six abortions, and now I've got married and can't get pregnant." Doctor: "Evidently you don't breed in captivity."

****

First man: "There's a guy who lives up the street from me who used to work in construction. One day last year his hand got run over by a bulldozer. Whatever those doctors did, it's really amazing – today he's a concert pianist." Second man: "That's nothing. I knew a guy in college – laziest bum I ever knew. He was really fat and out of shape. He was trying to hitch a ride one day and got hit by a truck. Broke nearly every damn bone in his body. Somehow they put him back together better than he was before. Now he's a triathlete and he's planning to try out for the Olympics." Third man:"Yeah, well I knew this poor retarded kid. He couldn't do a whole lot, but someone at the dynamite factory got charitable and gave him a job as a stockboy. He was working in the warehouse one day and got locked in. It was dark and he couldn't find the door. Not being too bright, he lit a match to try to find his way. The whole place exploded. All they could find of him was a few fingers and his eyebrows. From that little bit they were able to put him back together and today that kid is the president of the USA."

****

Doctor: "You're in good health. You'll live to be 80." Patient: "But, doctor, I am 80 right now." Doctor: "See, what did I tell you?"

****

A child psychologist for a school is asked to see a pupil who draws all his pictures with black and brown crayons. He talks to him. Nothing obvious. He gives him projective tests. Nothing shows up. Finally, in desperation, he gives him some paper and a box of crayons. "Oh goody," says the boy, "I got an old box in school and only black and brown were left."

****

One night in the pub, the landlord is lamenting the fact that business is so quiet on Mondays, Tuesdays and Wednesdays. As he moans to some of the regulars a stranger, dressed in a tweed jacket and wearing glasses, wanders over and says: "I'm sorry, but I couldn't help overhearing your conversation. I'm a doctor at the lunatic asylum up the road and I'm trying to integrate some of the more sane individuals into the community. Why don't I bring some of my patients along, say next Tuesday.? You'll have some customers and my patients will have a night out." Well, the publican isn't sure but the thought of more paying customers on a quiet night appeals, so he agrees. So, the following Tuesday the guy in the tweed jacket and glasses shows up with about ten lunatics. He says to the publican: "Give them whatever they want, let them practise paying with milk bottle tops, put it on a tab and I'll settle up at closing time." The publican has a great time selling loads of drinks and encouraging the loonies to eat crisps and peanuts. The loonies have a great time getting drunk but they behave themselves and hand over bottle-top money for their drinks. At closing time the publican adds up the bill and it comes to just over a hundred pounds. The guy with the glasses and the tweed jacket starts to organize the loonies ready to take them back to the asylum. Finally he comes over and asks for the bill. The publican, feeling that he's charged them rather a lot and he should do his bit to help these poor unfortunate people gives him a discount. "It's 80 quid," he says. The guy in the tweed jacket smiles and says: "That's fine. Have you got change for a dustbin lid?"

****

A man working at a lumberyard is pushing a tree through a bandsaw when he accidentally shears off all his fingers and thumbs. He rushes to the emergency entrance of a nearby hospital where the awaiting doctor takes a look and says. "Yuck! Well, give me the fingers and I'll see what I can do." "I haven't got the fingers." The doctor says, "What do you mean, you haven't got the fingers? This is the age of medical advances. We've got microsurgery and all sorts of incredible techniques. Why didn't you bring me the fingers?" "Well, heck, doctor,. I tried, but I couldn't pick 'em up."

****

The patient shook his doctor's hand in gratitude and said: "Since we are the best of friends, I would not want to insult you by offering payment. But I would like you to know that I have mentioned you in my will." "That is very kind of you," said the doctor emotionally, and then added, "Can I see that prescription I just gave you? I'd like to make a little change..."

How do you tell which nurse is the head nurse? The one with scuffed knees.

****

Proctology is the rare profession in which the doctor starts out at the bottom and stays there.

****

The crofter's wife went into labour in the middle of the night, and the doctor was called out to assist in the delivery. To keep the father-to-be busy, the doctor handed him a lantern and said: "Here, you hold this high so I can see what I'm doing." Soon, a lusty baby boy was brought into the world. "Och!" said the doctor. "Don't be in a rush to put the lantern by...I think there's yet another wee bairn to come." Sure enough, within minutes he had delivered a bonnie lass. "Na, dinna be in a great hurry to be putting down that lantern, lad...It seems there's yet another one besides," cried the doctor. The crofter scratched his head in bewilderment, and asked the doctor: "Well, now, mon. Do ye suppose the light's attracting them?"

****

Patient: "Doc, Doc, I keep thinking I'm a pair of curtains."
Psychiatrist: "Pull yourself together."

Patient: "Doc, Doc, I keep thinking I'm invisible." Psychiatrist: "Who said that?"

****

Patient: "Doc, Doc, I keep thinking I'm a dustbin." Psychiatrist: "Don't talk such rubbish."

****

Patient: "Doc, Doc, I keep thinking I'm a billiard ball." Psychiatrist: "Get to the end of the queue."

****

Patient: "Doc, Doc, my wife thinks I'm crazy because I like sausages." Psychiatrist: "Nonsense! I like sausages too." Patient: "Good, you should come and see my collection. I've got hundreds."

****

Patient: "Doc, Doc, people tell me I'm a wheelbarrow." Psychiatrist: "Don't let them push you around."

****

Doctor: "Did you take those pills I gave you to improve your memory?" Patient: "Pills?"

****

I was 12 years old before I realized I could cough without having a doctor holding my bollocks.

****

A somewhat advanced society has figured how to package basic knowledge in pill form. A student, needing some learning, goes to the pharmacy and asks what kind of knowledge pills are available. The pharmacist says: "Here's a pill for English literature." The student takes the pill and swallows it and has new knowledge about English literature. "What else do you have?" asks the student. "Well, I have pills for art history, biology, and world history," replies the pharmacist. The student asks for these, and swallows them and has new knowledge about those subjects. Then the student asks: "Do you have a pill for maths?" The pharmacist says, "Wait just a moment," goes back into the storeroom, brings back a whopper of a pill and plonks it on the counter. "I have to take that huge pill for maths?" inquires the student. The pharmacist replied, "Well, you know maths always was a little hard to swallow."

****

A pipe burst in a doctor's house. He called a plumber. The plumber arrived, unpacked his tools, did mysterious plumber-type things for a while and handed the doctor a bill for £600. The doctor exclaimed: "This is ridiculous. I don't even make that much as a doctor." The plumber waited for him to finish and quietly said: "Neither did I when I was a doctor."

****

A man is having problems with his dick, which certainly has seen better times. He consults a doctor who, after a couple of tests, says: "Sorry, but you've overdone it the last 30 years, your dick is burned out. You won't be able to make love more than 30 times." The man walks home deeply depressed; his wife is already expecting him at the front door and asks him what the doctor said concerning his problem. He tells her what the doctor told him. She says: "Oh my God, only 30 times. We should not waste that; we should make a list." He replies, "Yes, I already made a list on the way home. Sorry, your name's not on it."

****

A Jewish boy was walking with his girlfriend in the grounds of his father's house. His father was a successful doctor, and was carrying out a circumcision in the on-site surgery. As they were walking, they heard a scream and a foreskin flew out of the window and landed at the girl's feet. "What's this?" she asked. "Taste it," he replied, "If you like it, I'll give you a whole one."

✱✱✱✱

Wife: "Doc, Doc, my husband thinks he's a horse." Psychiatrist: "He is just probably a little stressed out and needs some rest." Wife: "But he kicks chairs and eats grass and doesn't even sleep in the bed." Psychiatrist: "Well, in that case, it looks like he may need a lot of help, but it may cost quite a lot of money for prolonged treatment." Wife: "Oh, you don't have to worry about the money part. Last Sunday he won the Grand National."

✱✱✱✱

"I'm worried," said the woman to her sex therapist. "I happened to find my daughter and the boy next door both naked and examining each other's bodies." "That's not unusual," smiled the therapist. "I wouldn't worry about it." "But I am worried, doctor," insisted the woman, "and so is my son-in-law."

✱✱✱✱

Patient: "Doc, Doc, you've got to help me. Every time I sneeze, I have an orgasm." Doctor: "Really? What are you taking for it?" Patient: "Black pepper."

Patient: "Doc, Doc, you've got to help me. I eat apples, apples later come out into the toilet. I eat bananas, bananas come out." Doctor: "That's easy. Eat shit."

✶✶✶✶

Patient: "Doc, Doc, you've got to help me. Every night I get the uncontrollable urge to go downstairs and stick my dick into the biscuit tin. Do you know what's wrong with me?" Doctor: "Yes... You're fucking crackers."

✶✶✶✶

What do puppies and near-sighted gynaecologists have in common? They both have wet noses.

✶✶✶✶

Patient: "Doc, Doc, I have yellow teeth. What do I do?" Dentist: "Wear a brown tie..."

✶✶✶✶

There are two businessmen, whose names happen to be Mr Turtle and Mr Carrot and, one day, as they were coming back from lunch, Mr Turtle says to Mr Carrot: "You know, you're getting fat." To which

Mr Carrot says, "You're not so slim yourself." So Mr Turtle says, "Okay, we'll see who is the least fit; race you back to the office." So the race starts and they have only got about a hundred yards down the street when Mr Turtle crosses the road in front of a car and gets knocked down. Mr Carrot sees that he's in a pretty bad way, so he rushes to the phone and calls Mr Cabbage, the ambulance driver. Mr Cabbage duly arrives and piles Mr Turtle into the ambulance and rushes to a hospital. Mr Turtle follows and as soon as he gets to the hospital he asks the nurse, Miss Cauliflower, whether he will be alright. "Miss Cauliflower, Miss Cauliflower, will Mr Turtle be alright?" She replies, "Well, I couldn't really say, you'll have to ask Dr Bean." So he rushes over to Dr Bean and says, "Dr Bean, Dr Bean, will Mr Turtle be alright?" And the doctor says, "Well, I wouldn't like to say, you'd best ask the specialist, Dr Pea." So of course, Mr Carrot rushes over to Dr Pea and says, "Dr Pea, Dr Pea, will Mr Turtle be alright?" And Doctor Pea says, "I've done all I can for him, it's all in the hands of the surgeon, Dr Turnip." So Mr Carrot waits outside the surgery for three hours until they have finished the operation and rushes up to Dr Turnip and says, "Dr Turnip, Dr Turnip, will Mr Turtle be alright?" Dr Turnip turns to him and says, "We did all we could, but I'm afraid he'll be a vegetable for the rest of his life..."

✱✱✱✱

Once I was sick and I had to go to an ear, nose, and throat specialist. There are ear doctors, nose doctors, throat doctors, gynaecologists, proctologists. Any place you have a hole, there's a guy who specializes in your hole. They make an entire career out of that hole. And if the ear doctor, nose doctor, throat doctor, gynaecologist, or proctologist can't help you, he sends you to a surgeon. Why? So he can make a new hole.

✱✱✱✱

What do you call a gynaecologist who specializes in geriatric care? A spreader of old wives' tails.

✱✱✱✱

A proctologist pulls out a thermometer from his shirt pocket. He looks at it and says: "Shit, some arsehole has my pen."

✱✱✱✱

What is the proper medical term for the circumcision of a rabbit? A hare cut.

✱✱✱✱

A guy hasn't been feeling well for a while, so he goes to the doctor for a check-up. After he sees the doctor, the doctor tells him he has a very serious condition and says that he would like to talk to the man's wife. So the man leaves and sends his wife in. The doctor tells the wife that her husband has a very serious condition and that he is going to die. However, the doctor tells her that there is one way she can save his life – she must cook him three meals a day and have sex with him every night for six months and then he'll be okay. When the wife leaves the office her husband asks her what the doctor said. She looks at her husband and tells him: "He said you're gonna die."

****

This guy goes to the doctor for a vasectomy. Unlike the usual patients, he shows up in a Rolls Royce, and sits in the doctor's office in a tuxedo with black tie. The doctor says, "I've done a lot of these, but I've never seen a Rolls and tuxedo before. What's the story?" To which the fellow responds, "If I'm gonna BE impotent, I'm going to LOOK impotent."

****

A man is talking to the family doctor. "Doctor, I think my wife's going deaf." The doctor answers, "Well, here's something you can try on her to test her hearing. Stand some distance away from her and ask her a question. If she doesn't answer, move a little closer and ask again. Keep repeating this until she answers. Then you'll be able to tell just how hard of hearing she really is." The man goes home and tries it out. He walks in the door and says: "Honey, what's for dinner?" He doesn't hear an answer, so he moves closer to her. "Honey, what's for dinner?" Still no answer. He repeats this several times, until he's standing just a few feet away from her. Finally, she answers: "For the eleventh time, I said we're having MEATLOAF."

****

An elderly woman went into the doctor's office. When the doctor asked why she was there, she replied: "I'd like to have some birth control pills." Taken aback, the doctor thought for a minute and then said, "Excuse me, Mrs Smith, but you're 75 years old. What possible use could you have for birth control pills?" The woman responded, "They help me sleep better." The doctor thought some more and continued, "How in the world do birth control pills help you to sleep?" The woman said: "I put them in my granddaughter's orange juice and I sleep better at night."

****

Patient: "What's good for excessive wind, doctor?" Doctor: "A kite."

****

A woman went to her new doctor for a check-up. He turned out to be absolutely gorgeous. He told her he was going to put his hand on her back and he wanted her to say "Eighty-eight." "Eighty-eight," she purred. "Good. Now I'm going to put my hand on your throat and I want you to again say 'Eighty-eight.'" "Eighhty...eighhhhtttt." "Fine. Now I'm going to put my hand on your chest and I want you one more time to say 'Eighty-eight.'" "One, two, three, four, five..."

****

A man goes to see his doctor. He pokes himself in the arm, leg, and torso, complaining that it hurts when he does this. The doctor asks him if he is Irish. The man replies that he is, to which the doctor replies that the man's finger is broken.

****

An extremely old man visits his doctor and tells him, "I need my sex drive lowered." The doctor, incredulous, says, "What? You want your sex drive lowered?" To which the old man replies: "It's all in my head; I need it LOWERED."

****

Doctor: "Does it hurt when you do this?" Patient: "Yes." Doctor: "Well, don't do it, then."

****

Patient: "Doc, Doc what should I do if my temperature goes up a point or more?" Doctor: "Sell!"

****

After much soul-searching and having determined the husband was infertile, the childless couple decided to try artificial insemination. When the woman showed up at the clinic, she was told to undress from the waist down, get on the table and place her feet in the stirrups. She was feeling rather awkward about the entire procedure when the doctor came in. Her anxiety was not diminished by the sight of him pulling down his pants. "Wait a minute. what the hell is going on here?" yelled the woman, pulling herself into a sitting position. "Don't you want to get pregnant?" asked the doctor. "Well, yes, I do," answered the woman. "Then lie back and spread 'em," replied the doctor. "We're all out of the bottled stuff. You'll just have to settle for what's on tap."

****

Dentist: "Could you help me? Could you give me a few of your loudest, most agonised screams?" Patient: "Why? It isn't that bad." Dentist: "Well, there are loads of people in the waiting room, and I'm playing golf at four."

****

Did you hear about the two blood corpuscles named Romeo and Juliet? They loved in vein.

****

Three doctors are in a duck blind and a bird flies overhead. The GP looks at it and says: "Looks like a duck, flies like a duck...it's probably a duck," and shoots at it, but he misses and the bird flies away. The next bird flies overhead and the pathologist looks at it, then looks through the pages of a bird manual, and says: "Hmmmm...green wings, yellow bill, quacking sound...might be a duck." He raises his gun to shoot it, but the bird is long gone. A third bird flies over. The surgeon raises his gun and shoots almost without looking, brings the bird down, turns to the pathologist and says: "Go and see if that was a duck, would you, old chap?"

****

Doctor: "Have you ever had this before?" Patient: "Yes." Doctor: "Well, you've got it again."

****

A woman starts dating a doctor. Before too long, she becomes pregnant and they don't know what to do. About nine months later, just about the time she is going to give birth, a priest goes into the hospital for a prostate gland infection. The doctor says to the woman: "I know what we'll do. After I've operated on the priest, I'll give the baby to him and tell him it was a miracle." "Do you think it will work?" she asks the doctor. "It's worth a try," he says. So the doctor delivers the baby and then operates on the priest. After the operation he goes in to the priest and says, "Father, you're not going to believe this." "What?" says the priest. "What happened?" "You gave birth to a child." "But that's impossible." "I just did the operation," insists the doctor. "It's a miracle! Here's your baby." About 15 years go by, and the priest realizes that he must tell his son the truth. One day he sits the boy down and says, "Son, I have something to tell you. I'm not your father." The son says, "What do you mean, you're not my father?" The priest replies, "I'm your mother. The archbishop is your father."

✵✵✵✵

The new mother got out of bed for the first time since giving birth, dressed in her robe and walked down the hospital hallway to the nurse's desk where she asked for a phone book. "What are you doing out here? You should be in your room resting," the nurse exclaimed. "I want to search through the phone book for a name for my baby," the new mother replied. "You don't have to do that here. The hospital furnishes a booklet to all new mothers to assist them in picking a first name for their baby." "You don't understand," the woman said and frowned, "My baby already has a first name."

A man comes to a doctor because of a sore throat. The doctor tells him to pull down his pants and to swing his genitals out of the window. "What does this have to do with my throat?" "Nothing, I just hate the neighbours."

****

A sex therapist was doing research at the local college when one of the male volunteers told him: "When I get it in part-way, my vision blurs. And when I get it all the way in, I can't see a thing." "Hmmm...that's an interesting optical reaction to sex," said the researcher. "Would you mind if I had a look at it?" So the volunteer stuck out his tongue.

****

The head doctors in a lunatic asylum have a meeting and decide that one of their patients is potentially well. So they decide to test him and take him to the movies. When they get to the movie theatre, there are 'Wet Paint' signs pointing to the benches. The doctors just sit down, but the patient puts a newspaper down first and then sits down. The doctors get all excited because they think he may be in touch with reality now. So they ask him: "Why did you put the newspaper down first?" He answers: "So I'd be higher and have a better view."

****

Guys & Dolls

Jokes About Men, Women and Relationships

Choose a wife by your ear rather than by your eye.

****

Take an interest in your husband's activities: hire a detective.

****

Sex is hereditary. If your parents never had it, chances are you won't either.

****

Never try to guess your wife's size. Just buy her anything marked 'petite' and hold on to the receipt.

****

Insurance is like marriage. You pay, pay, pay, and you never get anything back.

****

Don't marry for money; you can borrow it cheaper.

****

Husband: "Darling, will you love me when I'm old and feeble?"
Wife: "Of course I do, honey."

****

Sex is like snow; you never know how many inches you are going to get or how long it is going to last.

****

Irritated wife: "What do you mean by coming home half-drunk?"
Hubby: "It's not my fault...I ran out of money."

****

Think how much fun you could have with the doctor's wife and a bucket of apples.

****

Brains x Beauty x Availability = 1.

****

It is always the wrong time of the month.

Sex is a three-letter word which needs some old-fashioned four-letter words to convey its full meaning.

****

What do men and women have in common? They both distrust men.

****

Women who love only women may have a good point.

****

Bachelors know more about women than married men; if they didn't, they'd be married too.

****

How does an older woman keep her youth? By giving him money.

****

Never argue with a woman when she's tired...or when she's rested.

****

A lady is a woman who never shows her underwear unintentionally.

****

Why did God give woman nipples? To make suckers out of men.

****

Never hit a man with glasses. Hit him with a baseball bat.

****

Women! You can't live with them, you can't do most positions without them.

****

Men are those creatures with two legs and eight hands.

****

A woman was chatting with her next-door neighbour. "I feel really good today. I started out this morning with an act of unselfish generosity. I gave a fiver to a dosser." "You mean you gave a dosser five quid? That's a lot of money to give away like that. What did your husband say about it?" "He said 'Thanks'."

If only women came with pull-down menus and online help...

****

Women! You can't live with them, and you can't get them to dress up in a skimpy Nazi costume and beat you with a warm courgette.

****

Why are men endowed with half an ounce more brains than dogs? So they know not to embarrass themselves by humping women's knees at parties.

****

A young couple met their priest to set a date for their wedding. When he asked whether they preferred a contemporary or a traditional service, they opted for the contemporary. On the big day, a major storm forced the groom to take an alternate route to the church. The streets were flooded, so he rolled up his trouser legs to keep them dry. When he finally reached the church, his best man rushed him into the sanctuary and up to the altar, just as the ceremony was starting. "Pull down your trousers," whispered the priest "Er, Reverend, I've changed my mind," the groom responded. "I think I want the traditional service."

My opinions are my wife's, and she says I'm damn lucky to have them.

****

Whenever a husband and wife begin to discuss their marriage, they are giving evidence at an inquest.

****

A husband and his wife advertised for a live-in maid to cook and do the housework. A likely-looking girl came in from the country, and they hired her. She worked out well, was a good cook, was polite, and kept the house neat. One day, after about six months, she came in and said she would have to quit. "But why?" asked the disappointed wife. She hummed and hahed and said she didn't want to say, but the wife was persistent, so finally she said: "Well, on my day off a couple of months ago I met this good-looking fellow from over in the next county, and - well, I'm pregnant." The wife said: "Look, we don't want to lose you. My husband and I don't have any children, and we'll adopt your baby if you will stay." She talked to her husband; he agreed, and the maid said she would stay. The baby came, they adopted it, and all went well. After several months, though, the maid came in again and said that she would have to quit. The wife questioned her, found out that she was pregnant again, talked to her husband and offered to adopt the baby if she would stay. She agreed, had the baby, they adopted it, and life went on as usual. In a few months, however, she again said she would have to leave. Same thing – she was pregnant. They made the same offer, she agreed, and they adopted the third baby. She worked for a week or two, but then said, "I am definitely leaving this time." "Don't tell me you're pregnant again?" asked the lady of the house. "No," she said, "there are just too many damn kids here to tidy up after."

****

It doesn't much signify who one marries, for one is sure to find out next morning it was someone else.

****

Marriage: A ceremony in which rings are put on the finger of the lady and through the nose of the gentleman.

****

How can you tell which bottle contains the PMT medicine? It's the one with bite marks on the cap.

****

A man and woman are on their honeymoon after a long and very happy courtship. On their honeymoon, they decide to take their horses through the beautiful mountain passes of Europe. The horses are crossing a small stream when the woman's horse stumbles and jostles the man's wife. Once across the stream the man dismounts, walks over to the horse and stares into its eyes. Finally, he states: "That's one." The man remounts his horse and they continue their ride. A bit further down the path, the woman's horse stumbles when stepping over a fallen tree. The man dismounts, stares the horse in the eyes, and boldly states: "That's two!" He returns to his saddle and they move on. As the afternoon sun began to set, the woman's horse loses its footing on a mossy slope. The man dismounts, moves to the woman's horse and helps his wife out of the saddle. The man, moving to the front of the horse, stares it in the eyes and firmly says: "That's three." He removes a pistol from his coat, and shoots the horse dead. The woman, quite upset at seeing the beautiful horse killed, says to her husband, "That's terrible, why would you do such a thing." The man stares at his wife and firmly says: "That's one!"

****

If you meet somebody who tells you that he loves you more than anybody in the whole wide world, don't trust him; it means he experiments.

****

If a man hears what a woman says, she is not beautiful.

During the wedding ceremony, when the minister comes to the part about, "If anyone knows any reason why these two people should not marry, speak up now or for ever hold your peace," have a four-year-old boy run up the aisle yelling, "Daddy, Daddy..."

****

Why do men snore? When they fall asleep, their balls cover their arseholes and they get blow-back.

****

Besides "I love you", what three words does a wife want to hear most? "I'll fix it."

****

In olden times, sacrifices were made at the altar, a custom which is still very much practised.

****

If the effort that went into research on the female bosom had gone into the space program, we would now be running hot-dog stands on the moon.

A woman may very well form a friendship with a man, but for this to endure, it must be assisted by a little physical antipathy.

✱✱✱✱

If one man can wash one stack of dishes in one hour, how many stacks of dishes can four men wash in four hours? None. They'll all sit down together and watch football on television.

✱✱✱✱

In marriage, as in war, it is permitted to take every advantage of the enemy.

✱✱✱✱

No man should marry until he has studied anatomy and dissected at least one woman.

✱✱✱✱

A man and woman were lying in bed one night and the woman said to the man: "I really wish I had bigger tits." The man responded by saying she should rub toilet paper all over them. The woman looked at him and asked: "Toilet paper? What will that do?" The man said, "I don't know, but look what it's done for your arse."

Why are some men uncircumcised? The doctors were afraid of causing brain damage to the infant.

****

How are men like UFOs? You don't know where they come from, what their mission is, or what time they're going to take off.

****

What is a wedding tragedy? To marry a man for love, and then find out he has no money.

****

What's the best thing to come out of a penis? The wrinkles.

****

Most men prefer looks to brains, because most men see better than they think.

****

It destroys one's nerves to be amiable every day to the same human being.

Adam was created first to give him a chance to say something.

****

"I'd like my wife to be beautiful, well-behaved, smart and rich," the bachelor said. "Oh, well," his friend replied, "then you have to get married four times."

****

Women! If you want to know why they are called the 'opposite sex', express an opinion.

****

A woman was complaining to her best friend over lunch. "Every time my husband climaxes, he lets out an ear-splitting yell." "That doesn't sound all that bad to me," said her friend. "As a matter of fact, that would kind of turn me on." "It would me, too," said the first woman, "if it didn't keep waking me up."

****

Where do you have to go to find a man who is truly into commitment? A mental hospital.

The newlywed wife said to her husband when he returned from work: "I have great news for you. Pretty soon, we're going to be three in this house instead of two." The husband glowed with happiness and kissed his wife until she added: "I'm glad that you feel this way, as tomorrow morning my mother moves in with us."

****

What's the best way to have your husband remember your anniversary? Get married on his birthday.

****

It now costs more to amuse a child than it once did to educate his father.

****

A man was complaining to a friend: "I had it all – money, a beautiful house, a big car, the love of a beautiful woman; then, pow! it was all gone." "What happened?" asked the friend. "My wife found out..."

****

"We have a terrible time making ends meet on Bob's income," his wife told her best friend. "How do you two manage? And you even have kids." "We get along okay," her friend said. "You see, we work on our budget every evening. That saves us lots of money." "Really? How can that be?" "Well, by the time we get it all balanced, it's too damn late to go anywhere and do anything."

****

No matter how many times you've had it, if it's offered, take it, because it'll never be quite the same again.

****

What could men do to make their marriages last longer? Pay less attention to prenuptial agreements and more to postnuptual affection and sex.

****

A beggar walks up to a well-dressed woman who is shopping in Knightsbridge and says: "I haven't eaten anything in four days." She looks at him and says: "God, I wish I had your willpower."

****

Most husbands don't like to hear their wives struggling with housework - so they turn up the volume on the television.

Two bits of advice to the new bride: 1) tell your new husband that you have to have one night a week out with the girls, and 2) don't waste that night with the girls.

****

"It's just too hot to wear clothes today," said Jack as he stepped out of the shower. "Honey, what do you think the neighbours would think if I mowed the lawn like this?" "That I married you for your money."

****

What is the only time a man thinks about a candlelit dinner? When the power goes off.

****

What do most men think mutual orgasm is? An insurance company.

****

What is the one thing that all men at singles bars have in common? They're married.

****

Behind every great man, there is a surprised woman.

****

Three honeymoon couples find themselves in adjacent rooms in a hotel. As they are getting undressed, the first man says to his wife: "What huge buttocks!" Much offended, she throws him into the corridor. The second man, also undressing, says to his wife: "Christ! What huge tits!" She is also greatly offended and throws him out into the corridor. Several minutes later, the third newlywed husband arrives in the corridor as well. The other two ask: "What happened? Did you put your foot in it?" "No, but I could have," the third man replied.

****

Why do women change their minds so often? To keep them clean.

****

Why is it never the cold girl who gets given the fur coat?

****

Fred and Jane were relating their holiday experiences to a friend. "It sounds as if you had a great time in Cornwall," the friend observed, "but didn't you tell me you were going to Scotland?" "Yes, it's just ridiculous," said Jane, "Fred simply will not ask for directions."

****

Why do women rub their eyes when they wake up in the morning? Because they don't have any balls to scratch.

****

Why do men name their penises? Because they don't like the idea of having a stranger make 90 per cent of their decisions.

****

Do it only with the best.

****

Don't keep him in the doghouse too often or he might give his bone to the woman next door.

****

Love is an ideal thing, marriage is a real thing. A confusion of the real with the ideal never goes unpunished.

Did you hear about the scientist whose wife had twins? He baptized one and kept the other as a control.

****

Women are one of the Almighty's enigmas, created to prove to men that He knows more than they do.

****

What matters is not the length of the wand, but the magic in the stick.

****

Have you heard about the couple who got married in a nudist colony? They wanted everyone to be sure who the best man was.

****

If life were fair, the acquisition of a large bosom or a massive inheritance would have no bearing on your ability to attract the opposite sex.

****

Love is the delusion that one man or woman differs from another.

Marriage is a ceremony that turns your dreamboat into a barge.

****

I told my wife that a husband is like a fine wine; he gets better with age. The next day, she locked me in the cellar.

****

The bachelor who complained that the women he selected would not remain his friend for more than a few weeks was told: "Your problem is that you are looking for a particular kind of woman. You ought to be looking for the kind of woman who is not particular."

****

Every mother generally hopes that her daughter will snag a better husband than she managed to do...but she's certain that her boy will never get as great a wife as his father did.

****

A recent survey shows that the commonest form of marriage proposal these days consists of the words: "You're WHAT?"

****

When do men insist that women are illogical? When a woman doesn't agree with them.

****

Marriage has driven more than one man to sex.

****

Women truly are better than men. Otherwise, they'd be intolerable.

****

Why is food better than men? Because you don't have to wait an hour for seconds.

****

I don't worry about terrorism. I was married for two years.

****

How can a woman tell if she is having a super orgasm? Her husband wakes up.

****

A person receives a telegram informing him of his mother-in-law's death. It also enquires whether the lady should be buried or burnt. He replies: "Don't take chances. Burn the body and bury the ashes."

****

Bachelors should be heavily taxed. It is not fair that some men should be happier than others.

****

The definition of a husband: A man who stands by his wife in troubles she'd never have been in if she hadn't married him.

****

Why are men and spray paint alike? One squeeze and they're all over you.

****

"I'd like to buy some gloves for my wife," the young man said, eyeing the attractive salesgirl, "but I don't know her size." "Will this help?" she asked sweetly, placing her hand in his. "Oh, yes," he answered. "Her hands are just slightly smaller that yours." "Will there be anything else?" the salesgirl queried as she wrapped the gloves. "Now that you mention it," he replied, "she also needs a bra and knickers."

****

My latest Freudian slip came just as my wife arrived back from a week-long business trip. As she grabbed her luggage and we headed off, she asked, "Did you miss me?" I replied quite innocently, "It's been so hard without you."

****

Why don't men often show their true feelings? Because they don't have true feelings.

****

A best man's speech should be like a mini-skirt – short enough to be interesting, but long enough to cover the bare essentials.

****

Watching her mother as she tried on her new mink coat, the daughter protested, "Mum, do you realize some poor, dumb beast suffered so you could have that coat?" Her mother glared back at her and said, "Don't talk about your father that way."

My wife has a split personality, and I hate both of them.

****

The three different stages of sex in marriage: tri-weekly; try weekly; try weakly.

****

Two men who hadn't seen each other in years met on the street. While they were talking and trying to catch up on all those intervening years, one asked the other if he had got married. "No," the other man replied. "I look this way because someone just spilled a cup of coffee on me."

****

Marriage is the high sea for which no compass has yet been invented.

****

If you want to sacrifice the admiration of many men for the criticism of one, go ahead, get married.

****

Marriage is a three-ring circus: engagement ring, wedding ring and suffering.

****

Being a woman is quite difficult, since it consists mainly of dealing with men.

****

A husband is living proof that a wife can take a joke.

****

Why are men like popcorn? They satisfy you, but only for a little while.

****

Men always want to please women, but these last 15 years women have been hard to please. If you want to resist the feminist movement, the simple way to do it is to give them what they want and they'll defeat themselves. Today, you've got endless women in their twenties and thirties who don't know if they want to be a mother, have lunch or be Secretary of State.

Marry not a tennis player. For love means nothing to them.

****

A truck stops to pick up a female hitchhiker. The driver opens the door and says: "Come on in. I'm not like the other ones that only let the good-looking girls have a ride."

****

Marriage is a rest period between romances.

****

Why is being a penis not all it's cracked up to be? Because you have a head, but no brains. There's always a couple of nuts following you around. Your neighbour's an arsehole and your best friend's a cunt.

****

Fidelity is a virtue peculiar to those who are about to be betrayed.

****

Why are men like paper cups? They're disposable.

Hot dogs come in packs of ten, buns in packs of eight, beer in packs of six, ham comes in packs of 16 slices, condoms come in packs of three. Why can't they get it straight? Nowadays, a man needs a calculator just to have a weekend...

****

When the lights are out, all women are beautiful.

****

They say that men only think about sex. That's not exactly true. They also care a lot about power, world domination, money and beer.

****

A successful man is one who makes more money than his wife can spend. A successful woman is one who can find such a man.

****

An ideal wife is one who remains faithful to you but tries to be just as charming as if she weren't.

****

One night, while a woman and her husband were making love, she suddenly noticed something sticking in his ear. When she asked him what it was, he replied: "Be quiet, woman. I'm listening to the cricket."

****

I was engaged myself , once. To a contortionist. But she broke it off.

****

Sow your wild oats on Saturday night – then on Sunday, pray for crop failure.

****

A young couple were on their honeymoon. The husband was sitting in the bathroom on the edge of the bathtub saying to himself, "Now how can I tell my wife that I've got really smelly feet and that my socks absolutely stink? I've managed to keep it from her while we were dating, but she's bound to find out sooner or later that my feet stink. Now, how do I tell her?" Meanwhile, the wife was sitting in the bed saying to herself, "Now how do I tell my husband that I've got really bad breath? I've been very lucky to keep it from him while we were courting, but as soon as he's lived with me for a week, he's bound to find out. Now, how do I tell him gently?" The husband finally plucked up enough courage to tell his wife and so he walked into the bedroom. He walked over to the bed, climbed over to his wife, put his arm around her neck, moveed his face very close to hers and said, "Darling, I've a confession to make." And she said, "So have I, love." To which he replied, "Don't tell me, you've eaten my socks."

****

Love: a temporary insanity often curable by marriage.

****

Women sometimes make fools of men, but most guys are the DIY type.

****

Love is the triumph of imagination over intelligence.

****

The doctor came out of the operating room to talk with the man's wife. "I don't like the look of your husband," he said. "Neither do I," said the wife, "but he's not home much, and he's great with the kids."

****

What's a man's idea of helping with the housework? Lifting his legs so you can vacuum.

****

Marriage is the process of finding out what kind of person your spouse would have really preferred.

****

The next-door neighbour of a middle-aged wife came over to inform her that her retired husband was chasing around after young prostitutes. The woman smiled. "So what?" The neighbour was surprised: "It doesn't bother you that he's running around with those women?" The woman replied, "I have a dog who chases cars and buses, too."

****

Being a woman is of special interest to aspiring male transsexuals. To actual women it is simply a good excuse not to play football.

****

There are five types of sex involved in a marriage. The first is Smurf Sex. This happens during the honeymoon; you both keep doing it until you're blue in the face. The second is Kitchen Sex. This is at the beginning of the marriage; you'll have sex anywhere, any time. Hence, also in the kitchen. The third kind is Bedroom Sex. You've calmed down a bit, perhaps have kids, so you have to do it in the bedroom. The fourth kind is Hallway Sex. This is where you pass each other in the hallway and say: "Fuck you!" The fifth kind is Courtroom Sex. This is when you get divorced and your wife fucks you in front of everyone in court.

✳✳✳✳

On the first evening of their honeymoon, they were sitting on the balcony of the hotel while the sun was setting. "Honey," she said, "now that we're married, will you tell me what a penis is?" He almost fell off the chair. Being her husband, he led her into their room and took his pants off. "This, my love, is a penis," he told her. "Oh!" she exclaimed, "it looks like a cock, only smaller."

✳✳✳✳

A psychiatrist visited a Norwich mental institution and asked a patient, "How did you get here? What was the nature of your illness?" He got this reply... "Well, it all started when I got married, and I reckon I should never have done it. I married a widow with a grown daughter who then became my stepdaughter. My dad came to visit us, fell in love with my lovely stepdaughter, then married her. And so my stepdaughter was now my stepmother. Soon, my wife had a son who was, of course, my daddy's brother-in-law, since he is the half-brother of my stepdaughter, who is now, of course, my daddy's wife. So, as I told you, when my stepdaughter married my daddy, she was at once my stepmother. Now, since my new son is brother to my stepmother, he also became my uncle. As you know, my wife is my step-grandmother since she is my stepmother's mother. Don't forget that my stepmother is my stepdaughter. Remember, too, that I am my wife's grandson. But hold on just a few minutes more. You see, since I'm married to my step-grandmother, I am not only the wife's grandson and her hubby, but I am also my own grandfather. Now can you understand how I got put in this place?"

****

How are men like noodles? They're always in hot water, they lack taste and they need dough.

****

My mother-in-law broke up my marriage. My wife came home from work one day and found me in bed with her.

****

Nothing astonishes men so much as common sense and plain dealing.

Why are women so much more interesting to men than men are to women?

****

One good turn gets most of the duvet.

****

A man needs a mistress, just to break the monogamy.

****

Love is a thousand miles long, but comes in six-inch instalments.

****

Sometimes I wonder if men and women really suit each other. Perhaps they should live next door and just visit now and then.

****

I've sometimes thought of marrying, and then I've thought again.

****

A woman was getting married. She entered the church wearing a black wedding gown that surprised everyone. The pastor was a bit annoyed and asked her: "Why are you dressed up in black?" The woman replied: "Well, that's because I'm not a virgin."

✳✳✳✳

When a woman gets married, she wants the three Ss: Sensitivity; Sincerity; and Sharing. What does she get? The three Bs: Belching; Body odour; and Bad breath.

✳✳✳✳

You know you've been married too long when a 'quickie' before dinner now means a drink.

✳✳✳✳

It's sad that a married couple can be torn apart by something as simple as a pack of wild dogs.

✳✳✳✳

It's not true that married men live longer than single men. It only seems longer.

A young couple get married and they've never made love before. On their wedding night, the new bride is quite anxious to get things going, but the man seems to be having some difficulty. Finally, he starts to undress. When he takes off his pants, she notices that his knees are deeply pockmarked and scarred. So his wife says, "What happened to you?" The man says, "When I was young, I had the kneesles." He then takes off his socks and his wife sees that his toes are all mangled and deformed. "Hmmm, well what happened to your feet?" inquires the wife. "When I was a young boy, I had tolio." So, finally, the man takes off his shorts and the woman says: "Don't tell me. Smallcox, right?"

✱✱✱✱

This guy is getting married and he is a bit nervous since he is not too experienced. So he asks his best man to come along on the honeymoon and give a few pointers. The best man exclaims, "Come on man, its your honeymoon, you're supposed to be spending time with your wife, not your best friend." To which the groom replies that he has already paid for a room next-door to his for the best man. After much coercion, the best man give in and decides to go along. They work out a system where the best man will pound on the wall and shout advice if he hears anything going wrong. So the honeymoon arrives, and the bride and groom go to the honeymoon suite of the hotel, and the best man goes to his room next door. After a few moments, the bride gets undressed, but the groom gets so nervous he runs into the bathroom and locks the door. After about five minutes of waiting, the bride says, "Honey, are you coming out? I have to go to the bathroom." The groom replies, "I will be out in a few minutes, Hon, I'll be ready soon." After a few more minutes, the bride can't take it any longer, so she rummages under the bed where all the wedding gifts are stashed, grabs a box, unwraps it, pulls out the fondue pot, shits in it, wipes with the tissue paper, closes it and shoves it under the bed. Just then the groom, having summoned his manly nerve walks out of the bathroom. The bride, being feminine and all, goes into the bathroom to stall for a few minutes so the groom won't know what she did. The groom, sitting on the bed, notices this awful smell. What can that be? He looks under the bed, finds the box, pulls it out and exclaims: "Honey, there's shit in your box." Boom! Boom! Boom! (There's pounding on the wall...) The best man yells from the other room, "Turn her over, turn her over!"

****

Six months into a marriage, a man was asked by his best friend how everything was going. He replied: "Oh, just fine. We practically never have any arguments. In the morning, she does what she wants. In the afternoon, I do what she wants. And at night, we both do what we both want."

****

The days just before marriage are like a snappy introduction to a tedious book.

****

Anybody who claims that marriage is a 50/50 proposition doesn't know the first thing about women - or fractions.

****

One cardinal rule of marriage should never be forgotten: "Give little, give seldom, and above all, give grudgingly." Otherwise, what could have been a proper marriage could become an orgy of sexual lust.

****

Ever notice how so many of women's problems can be traced to the male gender? MENstruation, MENopause, MENtal breakdown, GUYnaecology, HIMmorrhoids...

****

What happens when a man tries to hide his baldness by combing his hair across his head? The truth comes shining through.

****

The Great White Telephone to God

5

Jokes About Religion

A Swedish bishop was getting ready to visit America. Some of his close associates advised him to be careful when responding to reporters on his arrival in New York. The bishop, however, was overconfident and paid little heed to the advice. During a press conference, held on his arrival at JFK Airport, one reporter asked the bishop if he was planning on visiting any nightclubs in New York. The bishop replied "Are there any nightclubs in New York?" suggesting that he was ignorant of anything like night clubs in New York. To his surprise, the next morning's papers had the following banner headlines: "While still on tarmac at JFK, Swedish bishop asks, 'Are there any nightlubs in New York?'"

✱✱✱✱

Two brothers went to confession; the younger one went in first. The priest always liked to ask questions of the children before their confession, so the priest asked the little boy: "Do you know where God is?" The little boy ran out and told his brother, "Let's get the hell out of here, the priest has lost God and wants to blame it on me."

✱✱✱✱

A rabbi went to heaven and met God for the first time. A thought hit him and he asked God about what souls eat when they go to hell. God told him to look at what was being served. So the rabbi peeked down below the clouds and, behold, it was mealtime in hell. The souls there were being offered a seven-course meal with steak, mashed potatoes, tossed salad and a blue cheese sauce, and a bottle of wine was being passed round. Meanwhile God informed the rabbi that it was time for his meal – a peanut butter sandwich. The rabbi asked God why the guys down there were getting the royal treatment while he had to eat sandwiches. God replied: "It simply does not pay to cook for two."

****

A Nuncio, where they exist, has the rank of an ambassador. While in Paris, Roncalli once said: "You know, it's rough being a Papal Nuncio. I get invited to these diplomatic parties where everyone stands around with a small plate of canapés trying not to look bored. Then, in walks a shapely woman in a low-cut, revealing gown, and everyone in the whole place turns around and looks – AT ME."

****

A man in the Middle Ages became fed-up with humanity and decided to spend the rest of his life in a monastery. The abbot warned him that he would have to take a vow of silence and live the rest of his life as a scribe, to which the man replied, "No problem. I'm sick of talking." Ten years went by, and the abbot called for the man. He told him that he was a model monk and perfect scribe, and that they were very happy to have him. As per their tradition, he was allowed to say two words. Asked if he had anything to say, the man nodded and said:

"Food cold." The abbot sent him on his way. Ten years later, he was brought before the abbot again and once again told how pleased they were with his performance, and that he was again allowed two more words if he so chose. The man said: "Bed hard," and was sent back to work. Another ten years went by and again the abbot sent for the man, telling him that he was the best monk they had ever had, and that he was allowed another two words. The man nodded and said: "I quit." To this, the abbot replied in a disgusted tone: "Doesn't surprise me. You've done nothing but whinge since you got here."

****

A busload of priests have an accident and all of them are killed instantly. On arriving at the Pearly Gates, they find there's a terrible queue. St Peter is there looking at a big book, jotting down notes, mumbling occasionally. There is a person standing in front of his desk being processed. After some time St Peter says, "Next", and another person steps up. The wait seems to take for ever and there are an enormous number of people waiting, but St Peter doesn't seem to be hurrying. People are arriving all the time, some in mangled states, some famished and some looking 'normal'. Then a dishevelled man comes in, cigarette butt hanging from his lips like it has taken root. The stubble on his chin looks as though it could sand diamonds. He stands at the back of the queue like everyone else. St Peter, however, spies him and hurries over to him. "Oh come in, come in. Welcome! No need to queue, we have you already processed. Your residence is in order. There's special treatment for you." The priests have something to say about that. "Hey," says their spokesman, "how come he gets the special treatment? We are, after all, men of God." "That man," says St Peter, "was a taxi driver. He has scared the hell out of far more people than any of you lot."

✳✳✳✳

A Catholic priest felt despondent about being posted to a very rural parish in the middle of a forest. He wrote letters to his bishop constantly, requesting that he be posted somewhere more hospitable. No reply to his letters ever came, and soon the letters stopped. Some time later, when the archbishop was making the rounds of the rural churches, he dropped in to see how the unhappy priest was doing. He found a pleasant man, in an air-conditioned church. There were no parishioners, since the closest neighbours were many miles away. The archbishop admitted to some confusion, since the priest did not look like the desperate writer of so many letters. He asked the priest how he liked it out in the woods. "At first I was unhappy. But thanks to two things I have grown to love it out here." "And they are?" the archbishop inquired. "The first is my rosary. Without my rosary I wouldn't make it a day out here." "And the second?" At this the priest looked askance. "Well, to be honest, I have developed a taste for Martinis in the afternoon. They help to alleviate the boredom during the worst part of the day." He looked sheepish at this admission, but the archbishop just smiled. "Martinis, eh? Well, that's not so bad. In fact, I'd be glad to share one with you right now, if you don't mind that is." "Not at all!" the priest exulted. "Let me get one for you right away." Turning to the back of the church, the priest shouted, "Oh, Rosie?... Marti?"

****

Why were most of Jesus' apostles fishermen and not cabinet-makers? If they were cabinet-makers, Jesus would have had to say: "Drop your drawers and follow me."

****

A group of new arrivals were sitting in the foyer in heaven, waiting for their turn to see St Peter. On the walls of the reception room were hundreds of clocks all ticking away. Every once in a while, however, a clock would suddenly move ahead several minutes in one jump. Curious, one fellow who was waiting turned to the receptionist and said: "Excuse me, but why do some of those clocks jump ahead now and then?" The receptionist answered: "Oh, those are the clocks that keep track of the days that people still have to live on Earth. Each person has a clock. Every time they do something sneaky or bad, they lose some of their allotted time on Earth and their clock jumps ahead a few minutes." Interested, the man asked, "Can I see my little daughter's clock?" "Sure, said the receptionist," and showed him a clock that ticked calmly and steadily along. "Now, can I see my wife's clock, please?" asked the man. "Why not?" said the receptionist and showed him a clock that for the most part ran smoothly, once in a great while jumping ahead two or three minutes at once. The man said, "You know, I was a Democrat back there on Earth, can I see Bill Clinton's clock?" "I'm afraid not," said the receptionist. "It's down in the accounting department. Their air conditioning broke this morning and they're using it for an electric fan."

****

Who is the most elastic man in the Bible? Balaam. He tied his ass to a tree and walked two miles into town.

****

A woman is nearly caught with her lover when her husband comes home early. To hide the man she puts him in the closet, but the lover soon discovers that he is not alone. The breathing he hears belongs to the woman's young son. "Gosh, it's dark in here," says the boy. "Bloody hell, child, please shut up," replies the nervous man. "Well, mister, I think I'm going to scream." "Please, kid, don't scream." "Can I have some money?" asks the boy. "Well, here, - here's five quid, it's all I've got." The boy, sensing that the man is lying, presses on. "I really feel like screaming." "No, kid, look, here's 50 quid, just don't scream." "Well, I don't know." "Here's the last of my money, just don't scream." The boy, satisfied, agrees to be quiet. Later, he goes with his mother to a store where a brand new bike is on sale. When he tries to buy it with his new-found cash, his mother becomes suspicious of the source of this money. So, being a good Catholic, she takes him to see the local priest in confession. "Gosh," says the boy, not used to being in the confessional, "it's dark in here." "Don't start with that again," says the priest.

****

Who is the most constipated man in the Bible? David – on the throne for 40 years.

****

How can you make God laugh? Tell Him your plans for the future.

****

A pious man lived right next door to an atheist. While the religious one prayed, day in, day out, and was constantly on his knees in communion with his Lord, the atheist never even looked twice at a church. However, the atheist's life was good; he had a well-paying job and a beautiful wife, and his children were healthy and good-natured. The pious man's job was strenuous and his wages were low, his wife was getting fatter every day and his children wouldn't give him the time of day. So one day, deep in prayer as usual, he raised his eyes towards heaven and asked: "Oh God, I honour you every day, I ask your advice for every problem and confess to you my every sin. Yet my neighbour, who doesn't even believe in you and certainly never prays, seems blessed with every happiness, while I go poor and suffer many an indignity. Why is this?" And a great voice was heard from above: "BECAUSE HE DOESN'T BOTHER ME ALL THE TIME!"

****

A Catholic, a Jew, and an Episcopalian reach the Pearly Gates. The Catholic asks to get in and St Peter says, "No, sorry." "Why not?" says the Catholic, "I've been good." "Well, you ate meat on a Friday in Lent, so I can't let you in." The Jew walks up and again St Peter says no. The Jew wants an explanation so St Peter replies, "There was that time you ate pork...sorry, you have to go to the other place." Then the Episcopalian goes up and asks to be let in and St Peter again says no. "Why not?" asks the Episcopalian, "What did I do wrong?" "Well," says St Peter, "you once ate your *entrée* with the salad fork."

****

A man who is an avid golfer finally gets a once-in-a-lifetime chance for an audience with the Pope. After standing in line for hours, he gets to the Pope and says, "Holiness, I have a question that only you can answer. You see, I love golf, and I feel a real need to know if there is a golf course in heaven. Can you tell me if there is?" The Pope considers for a moment, and says, "I do not know the answer to your question, my son, but I will talk to God and get back to you." The next day, the man is called for another audience with the Pope to receive the answer to his question. He stands before the Pope, who says, "My son, I have some good news and some bad news in relation to your question. The good news is that heaven has the most fabulous golf course that you could imagine and is in eternally perfect shape. It puts all courses on Earth to shame. The bad news is that you tee-off tomorrow morning."

✳✳✳✳

One sunny Sunday in spring, Father Fitzpatrick noticed that there was a smaller gathering than usual for the noon service. So as soon as the final hymn was sung, he slipped out the back way and went along the street to see who was out and about instead of coming to church. The first person he saw was old Mrs O'Neill, sitting on a park bench with her cane beside her. The good cleric sat down next to her and said, "Good afternoon, Mrs O'Neill, why weren't you in church today?" Mrs O'Neill replied: "Well, Father, it was just such a lovely day today I didn't want to be cooped up in that stuffy old church." The priest was a bit taken aback by this blunt answer, so he thought for a minute, then asked, "But Mrs O'Neill, don't you want to go to heaven?" To his surprise, the elderly lady shook her head vehemently and said, "No, Father." At that, the priest got to his feet indignantly and said firmly, "Then I am ashamed for you." Now it was Mrs O'Neill's turn to be surprised. She looked up at him and said, "Oh, Father, I thought you meant right now."

****

The Pope was in the middle of an audience when his principal advisor whispered in his ear: "Your Holiness, I hate to interrupt, but the Messiah is on the phone and he wants to talk to you." The Pope excused himself so he could take the call in private. A few minutes later he came back out with a sombre expression. He said, "I have some good news and some bad news. The good news is that the call was from the Messiah, the Lord Jesus, our saviour, and the time of the second coming is at hand. The bad news is that He was calling from Salt Lake City."

****

A Jew, a Hindu and a Baptist acquire a time machine. They decide that their first trip will be back to Bethlehem to witness the birth of Christ. They manage to arrive a little later than planned and find that there is only one room left at the inn and it has only one narrow bed. "It's perfectly alright," says the Hindu, "material things are unimportant. I will go and sleep in the stable." He leaves, but ten minutes later there is a knock on the door. It is the Hindu. "I'm sorry, but there is a cow in the stable. Cows are sacred and it would be quite improper for me to stay there." "Alright," says the Jew, "you are, in a manner of speaking, my guests here. I will sleep in the stable." He leaves, but ten minutes later there is a knock on the door. It is the Jew,. "I'm sorry, but there is a pig in the stable. I cannot possibly stay there." "Ah my friends," says the baptist, "was not our Lord Jesus unafraid to stay in poor lodgings? I will sleep in the stable," and he leaves. A few minutes later there's a knock on the door. It's the pig and the cow. The cow says: "Excuse me but there's a Baptist in the stable..."

****

A Jewish couple have a son who is a bit troublesome. At the age of five he starts in school, and pretty soon, his parents get to hear that things aren't going well. After a couple of months, they are asked to take him out of school, since he is not setting a good example to the other Jewish children. Things go from bad to worse: after only a month in reform school he's thrown out again, and even the state correction centre can't deal with him. Eventually, in desperation, the parents take him to the only place left: a local Catholic school. They don't hear anything concerning his performance, no reports of trouble, but their curiosity is really aroused when he comes home at the end of the term with a report card showing three Bs and the rest As. Things continue in the same vein, and at the end of the second term, he's running straight As. By the end of the school year, his performance has been so good that he is top of the class. His mother takes him aside and asks, "What's going on? We send you to your own people, and they throw you out. The reform school can't deal with you, and even the state correction centre wasn't enough. But now, with these Catholics, you're getting the best grades ever." "Well Mum," says the boy "I wasn't too bothered by those other places, but the first thing I see when I go into that Catholic school is a Jewish kid nailed to a couple of planks. I know when to back down."

****

Jesus returned and ended up by the side of the River Severn in Worcestershire. He confronted an old boy who was sat there fishing. "I am Jesus – I have come to save all from the horrors that be," exclaimed the great one. "Sod off, you're scaring the fish," answered the old one. "No, you don't understand – I have returned to save the Earth, now tell me, where should I start?" The old boy thinks for a while and tells him to perform a miracle, then he will believe that this is truly The Lord. "Walk across the river," he tells Jesus. So Jesus starts walking across the river, and the water is lapping round his ankles – then around his shins, then his knees. This starts worrying him, but he continues, knowing that he can do it. The next thing he knows, he slips and disappears under the water, and nearly drowns. He manages to claw his way back to the shore, and the old man says to him: "There you are, see, you're not Jesus, you can't walk across water." Jesus responds, "Well, I used to be able to do it until I got these nail holes in my feet."

What do you get when you cross a devil worshipper with a Jehovah's Witness? Someone who goes from door to door telling people to go to hell.

✳✳✳✳

What do you get when you cross a Mafia soldier with a Jehovah's Witness? Lots of converts.

✳✳✳✳

Who was the first computer operator in the Bible? Eve; she had an Apple in one hand and a Wang in the other.

✳✳✳✳

A well-known politician dies and goes to heaven. At the Pearly Gates he is met by St Peter and led in. St Peter speaks: "Well, you committed a few teeny-weenie sins while you were alive, didn't you? Lying is something we're a bit hot on at the moment, and, as a politician..." "Say no more," says the politician, "you've got me there." "Right, then;, since you did so much good generally for your country, we're prepared to let you in, but you'll have to do penance for two years. You will have to spend that time with this woman." At this, the most hideously deformed, smelly, gossiping woman appears. The politician appears to blanch slightly, but says: "Fair enough; I guess it's worth it for eternity in paradise." "Good man, this way now." St Peter leads them through a door into a vast chamber, filled with white-robed couples, chatting and laughing with each other. Sweet music and the aroma of rose blossom fill the air, and angels and cherubs flutter about. Suddenly, the politician notices his old rival, whose death had preceded his by a matter of weeks. Amazingly, this man is arm-in-arm with a beautiful model. "What the hell is this?" storms the politician. "That man was the worst thing to happen to my country for 200 years. He destroyed everything I stood for, and was totally dishonest in doing it. How come I get two years with this hag, while he gets to cavort with a beautiful model?" "Steady on," says St Peter, "let me explain. That's not your rival doing his penance, it's the model doing hers."

✳✳✳✳

There was an elderly Alabama widow who lived in a large mansion. She was feeling generous when it came to Thanksgiving, so she called up the local military base, and asked to speak with the lieutenant. "Please send up four nice young men to eat dinner here on Thanksgiving, but please, don't send any Jews. Please, no Jews." The lieutenant replied, "No problem ma'am, and I am sure I speak for the army when I say we all appreciate your kindness." Well, Thanksgiving rolled around, and the widow went to answer the door when the bell rang. She was surprised to see four of the blackest boys that anyone had ever seen, especially in the south. "But, but, there must be some mistake," she stammered. One of them replied: "No ma'am Lieutenant Goldstein doesn't make mistakes."

****

Two navvies were digging a ditch across from a brothel, and one noticed a rabbi walk into the place. One said to the other, "It's a sad day when men of the cloth walk into a place like that." After a little while, the other man saw a minister walk into the brothel. He stood up and said to his partner, "Did you see that? It's no wonder the children today are so confused with the example that the clergy are setting for them." After about another hour, the first man saw a Catholic priest walk in. He promptly stood up and proclaimed to his partner. "Aye, that is truly sad. One of the poor lassies must be dying."

****

M sends James Bond on a secret mission to heaven. When M doesn't hear from Bond for over a day, he gets worried and calls up heaven. The Virgin Mary picks up the phone and says, "Virgin Mary speaking." M asks her if Bond has reached there yet. She replies that he hasn't. M waits another few hours and calls heaven back again. "Virgin Mary speaking," comes the response. "Is James there yet?" asks M. Again the answer is no. M is really worried by this time, but he waits for a few more hours and then calls heaven back again. "Hello, Mary speaking..."

Where in the Bible does it describe the most people in one automobile? In The Acts of the Apostles it says that 100 people went to Jerusalem 'in one Accord'.

****

What's the difference between Jesus and a picture of Jesus? It only takes one nail to hang up the picture.

****

St Peter was at his post at the Pearly Gates and in rather a bad mood. That day, only couples were on line to get in. "Next," he called out, in a bored fashion. Up stepped a couple. "Name?" asked St Peter. "Smith," replied the husband. St Peter slowly looked up from his desk, looked them over for a moment, and finally asked with a bit of a sneer: "Says here that you were a banker in your time, Smith." St Peter then leaned forward, pointed his finger at them, and said: "You know, I don't like bankers. You're cheap. Always grubbing for money...cheating people...I don't know if I want to let you two in here today. So what's your wife's name?" "Penny," replied Mr Smith. "PENNY!" exclaimed St Peter. "Look at that, you even married a woman named after money. Get out of here, try again some other time. Next," he called out, still agitated. Up stepped the next couple. "Name?" asked St Peter. "Jones", replied the husband. Again St Peter slowly looked up from his desk, looked them over for a moment, and asked with a sneer: "Jones the Publican?" "Why, yes," said Mr Jones. St Peter again leaned forward, pointing his finger at them, and said: "You know, I don't like publicans. You drink too much. Always getting drunk on your own stock and throwing up all over the streets...beating up your wives and kids during drunken rages...I don't know if I want to let you two in here today. So what's your wife's name?" "Sherri" replied Mr Jones. "SHERRI!" exclaimed St Peter. "Look at that, you even married a woman named after a drink. Get out of here, try again some other time." Meanwhile, several couples back, a man overhearing all of this turns to his wife and says: "Let's get out of here Fanny."

****

A man dies, and finds himself in heaven. St Peter offers to give him the tour. They walk around a little, and the man sees Samoans worshipping God in a Samoan way, and Zoroastrians worshipping ina Zoroastrian way, and Eskimos worshipping in an Eskimo way, and so on...on and on, till at one point they come to an enormous fortress made of stone, completely sealed off, with no windows or doors. Dimly, from within, they can hear the sound of wild partying. "Shhh," says St Peter. "Be very quiet." The two tiptoe past the fortress in utter silence, and when they have left it a way behind, the man turns to St Peter and says, "Why did we have to be so quiet back there? Who's in the fortress?" St Peter answers, "Oh, those are the Jehovah's Witnesses. They don't know anyone else is here."

A pastor was addressing the children during the Christmas service. "Who is the mother of Jesus?" he asked them. Without hesitation, dozens of tiny voices chorused back "Mary." "That's right. Now who can tell me who is the father of Jesus?" There was quiet and fidgeting. After all, no one had told them there was going to be a quiz. Then a young girl spoke up. With assurance, she boldly announced: "I know. It's Virg." After two more seconds of silence the entire community erupted in laughter. Of course – we all know it was Virg an' Mary.

✳✳✳✳

The pastor of a small congregation was trying to find a contractor to paint his church. Because the church fund was low and he couldn't pay very much, he selected the lowest bidder. The contractor decided to make the job pay better by skimping on materials. He thinned the paint with solvent and then only applied one coat. Within months, the poor paint job began to flake away and the church looked worse than it had before the work was done. The pastor sent a note to the contractor that said: "Repaint, repaint – thin no more!"

✳✳✳✳

Jesus walked into a bar in Balham. He approached three sad-faced gentlemen at a table, and greeted the first one: "What's troubling you, brother?" he said. "My eyes. I keep getting stronger and stronger glasses, and I still can't see." Jesus touched the man, who ran outside to tell the world about his, now, 20-20 vision. The next gentleman couldn't hear Jesus' questions, so the Lord just touched his ears, restoring his hearing to perfection. This man, too, ran out the door, praising God. The third man leapt from his chair and backed up against the wall, even before Jesus could greet him. "Don't you come near me, man. Don't touch me!" he screamed. "I'm on disability benefit!"

****

Did you hear about the child who thought Jesus was a giant teddy bear called Gladly, who had something wrong with his eyes, because every time she went to church they would sing ,"Gladly the cross I'd bear."

****

Blessed is he who expects no gratitude, for he shall not be disappointed.

****

A priest and a rabbi found themselves seated together on a long trans-Atlantic flight. They started talking and became quite friendly. The priest slyly said to the rabbi: "Tell me the truth rabbi. Have you ever tried a ham sandwich?" The rabbi confessed that he had once tried a ham sandwich. Then the rabbi asked the priest: "You chaps are supposed to be celibate. Have you ever had sex with a woman?" The priest confessed that he had. "Beats the hell out of a ham sandwich, doesn't it?" said the rabbi.

****

The man died. Having not lived an all-that-honest life he found himself at the gates of hell. "Welcome to hell" announced the Devil greeting him warmly. "Glad you could join us. As your last taste of free will, you are allowed to choose which of three possible places in which you will spend the rest of eternity." There were three doors behind the Devil. He opened the first door. Flames shot into the room and the man could see thousands of people in the fire. "No," said the man, "not this one." The Devil opened the second door. The man could see thousands of people slaving away at a large rock pile. They were all being whipped as they hammered the large boulders into smaller boulders. "No," said the man again. Finally, the Devil opened up that last door which showed thousands of people in an incredibly large lake with vomit up to their chins. All of them were chanting: "Don't make waves, don't make waves..." "That's awful!" commented the man in revulsion. "You think that's bad?" asked the Devil. "You should see it when the angels spend the weekend here water-skiing."

****

Assorted Crisps & Snacks

Gags, One-Liners, Limericks and Other Variations on Books, Mothers, Chickens, Seven-Course Dinners and Other Strangenesses

Have you heard about the new book, *Care For Your Lawn*? It's by Ray King.

****

Have you heard about the new book, *Speeding Up Your Work*? It's by Sheik Aleg.

****

"Mum, Mum! What's a werewolf?" "Shut up and comb your face."

****

What's the difference between a cat and a bagel? You can put a bagel in the toaster, but you have to put the cat in the oven.

****

Have you heard about the new book, *Be a Winner*? It's by Vic Trees.

****

Have you heard about the new book, *The Day We Bunked Off*? It's by Marcus Absent.

There was an old girl of Kilkenny
Whose usual charge was a penny.
For half of that sum,
You could finger her bum;
T'was a source of amusement for many.

****

Why did the graduate student cross the road? He was writing a dissertation on chickens.

****

Why did the second chicken cross the road? He was stapled to the first chicken.

****

There was a young lady from Kew
Who filled her vagina with glue.
She said with a grin,
"If they pay to get in,
They'll pay to get out of it too!"

****

Have you heard about the new book, *A Long Walk Home*? It's by Miss D Buss.

✳✳✳✳

There was a young man of St John's
Who wanted to bugger the swans.
But the loyal hall porter
Said, "Pray take my daughter,
Those birds are reserved for the dons."

✳✳✳✳

What is a politician's seven-course dinner? A piece of essential vote-winning employment for catering staff.

✳✳✳✳

"Mum, Mum! Why is my hair so slimey?" "Shut up, you little snot."

✳✳✳✳

Have you heard about the new book, *An African Trek*? It's by Dusty Rhodes.

✳✳✳✳

Have you heard about the new book, *Saudi Arabian Transport*? It's by I Rhoda Camel.

****

How many Country and Western singers does it take to change a light bulb? Four: one to change it; one to sing about how heartbroken he is at the loss of the old one; one to sing about how madly in love she is with the new one; and one to go "Yeeeee-Hah!" and throw his hat in the air.

****

Have you heard about the new book, *A Guide to Causing Chaos*? It's by Ken Fusion.

****

Have you heard about the new book, *A Guide to Japanese Fashion*? It's by Kim Ono.

****

Have you heard Broadmoor's answering machine? It says: "Welcome to the Psychiatric Hotline. If you are obsessive-compulsive, please press 1 repeatedly. If you are co-dependent, please ask someone to press 2. If you have multiple personalities, please press 3, 4, 5 and 6. If you have paranoid delusions, we know who you are and what you want; just stay on the line until we can trace your call. If you are schizophrenic, listen carefully and a little voice will tell you which number to press. If you are depressed, it doesn't matter which number you press. No one will listen to your message."

****

Have you heard about the new book, *From Highwayman to Mugger*? It's by Andy Tover.

****

Have you heard about the new book, *Everyman's Guide To Emergency Repair*? It's by Jerry Rigg.

****

Have you heard about the new book, *A Guide To Basingstoke*? It's by Helen Earth.

****

How many Jewish mothers-in-law does it take to change a light bulb? None: they'll just sit in the dark, knowing full well you can't be bothered to do a simple thing like change a light bulb for them, and after all they've done for you...

****

Do you know how many jazz musicians it takes to change a light bulb? No, but hum a few bars and I'll fake it.

****

Have you heard about the new book, *The Hero Through History*? It's by Ben Evolence.

****

A Scotsman who lived on the loch
Had holes down the length of his cock.
He could get an erection,
And play a selection
Of Johann Sebastian Bach.

****

Have you heard about the new book, *Give Him The Push*? It's by Eve Ho.

Have you heard about the new book, *No Bovver, the Story of Hover*? It's by Lorne Moor.

****

There once was a man from Cape Horn
Who wished that he'd never been born.
He wouldn't have been
If his father had seen
That the end of his condom was torn.

****

Have you heard about the new book, *Locked In The Safe*? It's by Xavier Breath.

****

Why did the chicken cross the road? To show the hedgehog it was possible.

****

"Mum, Mum! Why are we pushing the car off the cliff?" "Shut up, you'll wake your father."

How many Seventies disco dancers does it take to change a light bulb? Two: one to boogie up the ladder and one to say "Get daaoowwn!"

****

How many members of the royal family does it take to screw in a light bulb? "Actually, none. As your queen I would like to reassure the people of the Commonwealth that while our family may have had our Annus Horribilis and while some of us may have screwed in the stables or in the mud, none of us, to my knowledge, has actually screwed in a light bulb."

****

There once was a man from Nantucket
Whose dick was so long he could suck it.
He said with a grin,
As he wiped off his chin,
"If my ear was a cunt, I would fuck it."

****

How many inner-city gang members does it take to screw in a light bulb? Four: one to rob the off-licence to get money for the bulb; one to drive the getaway car; one to screw it in; and one to hold his crack pipe while he does it.

Have you heard about the new book, *The Naughty Schoolboys*? It's by Tanya Hydes.

****

Have you heard the English Foundation's answering machine? It says: "This is the literacy self-test hotline. After the tone, leave your name and number, and recite a sentence using today's vocabulary word. Today's word is 'supercilious'."

****

Have you heard the disorganized girl's answering machine? It says: "Hello. I'm home right now but cannot find the phone. Please leave a message and I will call you back as soon as I find it."

****

Have you heard the mad scientist's answering machine? It says: "The machine answering this message is connected to a 5000-volt power supply and a relay, which is wired to this small kitten. (Sound of a kitten meowing). If you hang up before you leave a message, it will complete the circuit and fry the kitty. The choice is yours."

****

Have you heard the MI6 agent's answering machine? It says: "This is John's answering machine. Please leave your name and number, and after I've doctored the tape, your message will implicate you in a serious crime and be brought to the attention of Scotland Yard."

****

Have you heard the suicidal bloke's answering machine? It says: "Sorry, I'm far too depressed to come to the phone. If you can be bothered, leave a message after the sound of the gunshot, and maybe somebody will call you, I guess..."

****

Have you heard the Psychic Hotline's answering machine? It says: "This is not an answering machine – this is a telepathic thought-recording device. After the tone, think about your name, your reason for calling, and a number where I can reach you, and I'll think about returning your call."

****

Have you heard about the new book, *The Fabrics Revolution*? It's by Polly Ester.

✳✳✳✳

Have you heard about the new book, *The Population Problem in North-West France*? It's by Francis Crowded.

✳✳✳✳

Have you heard about the new book, *Modern Business Practice*? It's by Hiram Cheep.

✳✳✳✳

What's worse than finding a dead cat on your pillow in the morning? Realizing you were drunk and made love to it the night before.

✳✳✳✳

What's pink and spits? A cat in a frying pan.

✳✳✳✳

What is a Canadian seven-course dinner? A six-pack of Molson and a moose.

****

What is a student's seven-course dinner? A six-pack of Red Bull and a slice of pizza.

What is an American seven-course dinner? A six pack of Bud Lite and a Big Mac.

****

Have you heard about the new book, *Prepare Your Own Will*? It's by Paul Bearer.

****

How many antelopes does it take to change a light bulb? None: they are herbivorous animals who live in a primarily grassland habitat and therefore have no need for artificial light sources.

****

What is a Scottish seven-course dinner? Six crumbs of stale bread and a case of whisky.

****

Have you heard about the new book, *Hymns for Our Time*? It's by Allie Louyah.

****

"Mum, Mum! I keep running in circles." "Shut up or I'll nail your other foot to the floor."

****

There once was a juggler named Drops,
Who couldn't hang on to his props.
He tossed 'em and heaved 'em,
Then dropped and retrieved 'em,
Till the audience told him to stop.

What is a Chinese seven-course dinner? Six bowls of rice and a cooked rat.

****

What is a Japanese seven-course dinner? A bowl of rice and six raw fish.

****

What is a Russian seven-course dinner? A litre of vodka and six turnips.

****

What is a Mexican seven-course dinner? A bottle of tequila and six cockroaches.

****

What is an Eskimo seven-course dinner? Six lumps of snow and a baby seal.

****

How many proofreaders does it take to change a light bulb? Proofreaders aren't supposed to change light bulbs. They should just query them.

****

How many armies does it take to change a light bulb? At least six: the Germans to start it; the French to give up really easily after only trying for a little while; the Italians to make a start, get nowhere and then run away; the English to stand firm back home but not get anywhere near the bulb; the Americans to turn up late, finish it off and take all the credit; and the Swiss to pretend nothing out of the ordinary is happening.

****

What is an Argentine seven-course dinner? Six cuts of beef and a sprig of parsley.

****

How many sheep does it take to change a light bulb? Twenty-one: one to change it and twenty to follow him round while he looks for a new one.

****

What is an English seven-course dinner? Three pints of lager, two packs of crisps, a bag of chips and a doner kebab.

****

What is an Irish seven-course dinner? A four-pack of Guinness and a potato.

****

Have you heard about the new book, *A Map of the Brain*? It's by Sarah Bellum.

****

Have you heard about the new book, *Nudist Beaches of the South Coast*? It's by Seymour Butts.

****

Have you heard about the new book, *Real Ales of the United Kingdom*? It's by Bart Enda.

****

Have you heard about the new book, *The Case Of The Missing Will*? It's by Benny Fishery.

****

How many MPs does it take to change a light bulb? Twenty-one: one to change it and twenty to take a six-week fact-finding trip to the Bahamas to learn more about how it's done.

****

Have you heard about the new book, *The Encyclopaedia of Mixers*? It's by Ginger Aile.

****

Have you heard about the new book, *Beating The Mortgage Trap*? It's by Bill Jerome Holmes.

****

"Mum, Mum! The milkman's here. Have you got the moncy or should I go out and play?"

****

How many lawyers does it take to change a light bulb? Three: one to sue the power company for insufficiently supplying power, or negligent failure to prevent the surge that made the bulb burn out in the first place; one to sue the electrician who wired the house; and one to sue the bulb manufacturers.

****

"Mum, Mum! What's a nymphomaniac?" "Shut up and help me get Gran off the doorknob!"

****

Have you heard about the new book, *The Pizza Man*? It's by Pepe Rooney.

Have you heard about the new book, *Italian Cookery Made Simple*? It's by Les Anya.

****

How many trainspotters does it take to change a light bulb? Three: one to change it; one to write down its serial number; and one to bring the anoraks and the flask of soup.

****

Have you heard about the new book, *Savaged by Lions – A Survival Story*? It's by Claudia Armoff.

****

"Mum, Mum! Why don't I have a big thing like Dad's between my legs?" "You will when you're older, Lucy!"

****

How many Belgians does it take to change a light bulb? Two: one to change it and one to serve it with chips and mayonnaise.

****

How many divorcees does it take to change a light bulb? None: the sockets all went with the house.

****

How many gardeners does it take to change a light bulb? Three: one to change it and two to have a debate about whether they should be putting in light bulbs or crocus bulbs.

****

How many thieves does it take to change a light bulb? None, but you lose a lot of light bulbs.

****

How many Italians does it take to change a light bulb? Two: one to change it and one to sprinkle it with Parmesan.

****

How many New-Agers does it take to change a light bulb? Two: one to change it and one to check the Feng Shui of the new one.

****

How many politicians does it take to change a light bulb? Four: one to change it and the other three to deny it was ever changed.

****

How many sexists does it take to change a light bulb? None: let the bitch cook in the dark.

****

How many Thatcherites does it take to change a light bulb? None: it's up to the private sector to change it.

****

There was a young man from Bel Air
Who was screwing his girl on the stair.
But the bannister broke,
So he doubled his stroke,
And he finished her off in mid-air.

****

How many Trotskyites does it take to change a light bulb? It's no use trying to CHANGE it, brothers; it's got to be SMASHED.

How many Christians does it take to change a light bulb? Three: but they're really only one, so that's okay.

****

How many consultants does it take to change a light bulb? Only one: but it takes eight months at £150 a day.

****

How many dogs does it take to change a light bulb? Two: one to change it, and one to sniff the first one's arse.

****

How many firemen does it take to change a light bulb? Four: one to change the bulb and three to cut a hole in the roof.

****

How many jugglers does it take to change a light bulb? Only one: but it takes at least three light bulbs.

****

Why did the Mormon groom cross the road? To get to the other bride.

"Mum, Mum! Are you sure this is how to learn to swim?" "Shut up and get back in the sack."

****

"Mum, Mum! What's an Oedipus complex?" "Shut up and kiss me."

****

"Mum, Mum! Why can't I play with the other kids?" "Shut up and deal."

****

Have you heard about the new book, *Without Warning*? It's by Oliver Sodden.

****

Have you heard about the new book, *Great Presents*? It's by Sue Pryse.

****

Have you heard about the new book, *Tending Lawns*? It's by Leif Raker.

Have you heard about the new book, *Beating Stress*? It's by Neddy Tate.

****

Have you heard about the new book, *Medieval Music*? It's by Manda Lynn.

****

Have you heard about the new book, *Medical Process*? It's by Steffi Scope.

****

Have you heard about the new book, *Spanish Bloodsports*? It's by Matt Adore.

****

Have you heard about the new book, *Prediction Explained*? It's by Claire Voiant.

****

How did the priest make the road a cross? He painted another line.

Have you heard about the new book, *Fitted Carpets*? It's by Walter Wall.

****

Have you heard about the new book, *Daylight Robbery*? It's by Hans Zupp.

****

Have you heard about the new book, *Dangerous Maniacs*? It's by Si Cosis.

****

Have you heard about the new book, *Being Prepared*? It's by Everett D Reddy.

****

Have you heard about the new book, *Breakfast Cookery*? It's by Hammond Degs.

****

Have you heard about the new book, *After Life*? It's by Doug Graves.

Have you heard about the new book, *Helping Others*? It's by Linda Hand.

****

Have you heard about the new book, *Fitness Explained*? It's by

Jim Nasium.

****

How do you spoil a cat? Leave it out in the sun.

****

Have you heard about the new book, *Mortgages Explained*? It's by Owen Moony.

****

Have you heard about the new book, *Security Measures*? It's by Barb Dwyer.

****

Have you heard about the new book, *Police Brutality*? It's by Lauren Order.

Have you heard about the new book, *Buying Music*? It's by Chopin Liszt.

****

Have you heard about the new book, *Perfect Parties*? It's by Greg Arius.

****

Have you heard about the new book, *Religious Governments*? It's by Dick Tater.

****

Why did the chicken cross the road? To see his friend Gregory Peck.

****

"Mum, Mum! I don't want to empty the compost heap." "Shut up and keep eating."

****

Have you heard about the new book, *The Worker's Guide to Shirking*? It's by Hans Doolittle.

Have you heard about the new book, *New Age Gemstones*? It's by Chris Tall.

****

"Mum, Mum! Grandpa's going out!" "Well, throw some more petrol on him, then."

****

What is worse than a dead cat in a dustbin? Ten dead cats in a dustbin.

****

Have you heard about the new book, *Free Yourself From Pain*? It's by Ann L Gesick.

****

"Mum, Mum! What happened to all that dog food Fido wouldn't eat?" "Shut up and eat your meatloaf."

****

Have you heard about the new book, *The Long Fall*? It's by Eileen Dover and Phil Down.

Have you heard about the new book, *Nuclear Fission Explained*? It's by Adam Bohm.

****

Have you heard about the new book, *Heroin: The Evil Pleasure*? It's by Anita Fyx.

****

"Mum, Mum! When are we going to have Aunt Edna for dinner?" "Shut up, we haven't finished your grandmother yet."

****

"Mum, Mum! Dad just poisoned my kitten!" "Never mind, dear. Perhaps he had to do it." "No, he didn't; he promised me I could!"

****

Which is easier to unload, a truck full of dead cats or a truck full of bowling balls? Dead cats, because you can use a pitchfork.

****

What's more fun than nailing a cat to a fence? Ripping it back off.

A popular girl is Miss Cholmondeley,
She's youthful, attractive and comely,
And never objects
To suggestions of sex,
But simply cooperates dumbly.

****

Why did the rabbit cross the road? Because the chicken retired and moved to Florida.

****

What is a German seven-course dinner? Six different beers and a kilo of raw sausage.

****

Why did the koala fall out of the tree? Because it was dead.

****

"Mum, Mum! Sally won't come skipping with me." "Don't be cruel, dear, you know it makes her stumps bleed."

****

What goes plink, plink, fizz? Kittens in an acid bath.

****

Why did the chicken cross the road? To get away from Colonel Sanders.

****

The sea captain's tender young bride
Fell into the sea at low tide.
You could tell by her squeals
That one of the eels
Had found her the best place to hide.

****

"Mum, Mum! What's a vampire?" "Shut up and eat your soup before it clots."

****

"Mum, Mum! What's an orgasm?" "I don't know, dear, ask your father."

****

There was an old man from Australia
Who painted his arse like a dahlia.
The colours were fine,
Likewise the design,
But the smell, alas, was a failure.

****

"Mum, Mum! Dad's running down the street!" "Shut up and step on the accelerator!"

****

How many aerospace engineers does it take to change a light bulb? None: it's not rocket science, you know.

****

How many art directors does it take to change a light bulb? Does it have to be a light bulb?

****

"Mum, Mum! Why do I have to hop everywhere?" "Shut up or I'll chop off the other leg!"

How many social workers does it take to change a light bulb? Four: one to remove the bulb from the socket and take it away without checking whether or not there was actually anything wrong with it: one to accuse its owners of mistreating it: one to find somewhere else to screw it in for the next six months: and one to eventually bring it back and say it was all done with the light bulb's best interests at heart.

✳✳✳✳

What is the difference between a pregnant woman and a light bulb? You can unscrew a light bulb.

✳✳✳✳

What do you do with four dead cats and a sheet of glass? Make a coffee table.

✳✳✳✳

"Mum, Mum! Can I wear a bra now I'm 16?" "Shut up, Albert."

✳✳✳✳

Have you heard the hypnotist's answering machine? It says: "You're growing tired. Your eyelids are getting heavy. You feel very sleepy now. You are gradually losing your willpower and your ability to resist suggestions. When you hear the tone you will feel helplessly compelled to leave your name, number, and a message."

✳✳✳✳

What is an anorexic seven-course dinner? Six peas and a sip of water.

✳✳✳✳

"Mum, Mum! I don't want to see Niagara Falls!" "Shut up and get back in the barrel!"

✳✳✳✳

"Mum, Mum! I don't want to go to Australia." "Shut up and keep swimming."

✳✳✳✳

Have you heard the lunatic's answering machine? It says: "Hi, I'm not sane right now, but if you leave your name, number and shoe size at the sound of the tone, I'll get back to you when and if I return to my senses."

****

Anything that doesn't eat you today is saving you for tomorrow.

****

A short cut is the longest distance between two points.

****

If you don't care where you are, then you aren't lost.

****

One of those days? I have one of those lives.

****

Beware of altruism. It is based on self-deception, the root of all evil.

****

After things have gone from bad to worse, the cycle will repeat itself.

****

When it's you against the world, bet on the world.

All I ask is the chance to prove that money cannot make me happy.

****

Anyone can admit they were wrong; the true test is admitting it to someone else.

****

You Know You're Getting Old When...a fortune-teller offers to read your face.

****

Old age and treachery shall overcome youth and talent.

****

Eat the rich. The poor are tough and stringy.

****

He who dies with the most toys is still dead.

****

What is orange and sleeps five? A council road-repair van.

****

You can fool some of the people and really piss them off.

****

The race is not always to the swift nor the battle to the strong, but that's the way to bet.

****

You Know You're Getting Old When... you feel like the morning after but there was no night before.

****

Information travels more surely to those with a lesser need to know.

****

The sun goes down just when you need it the most.

****

Pessimists have already begun to worry about what is going to replace automation.

****

Almost everything in life is easier to get into than to get out of.

****

You Know You're Getting Old When...the gleam in your eyes is from the sun hitting your bifocals.

****

If at first you do succeed, try to hide your astonishment.

****

If everything seems to be going well, you have obviously overlooked something.

****

If there is a possibility of several things going wrong, the one that will cause the most damage will be the one to go wrong.

Never do anything you wouldn't be caught dead doing.

****

You Know You're Getting Old When...your birthday cake collapses from the weight of the candles.

****

It's always darkest just before it goes pitch-black.

****

If ignorance is bliss, most of us must be orgasmic.

****

Left to themselves, things tend to go from bad to worse.

****

Money is better than poverty, if only for financial reasons.

✱✱✱✱

The idea is to die young as late as possible.

You Know You're Getting Old When...you regret all those mistakes resisting temptation.

✱✱✱✱

Don't be so open minded that your brain falls out.

✱✱✱✱

Some come to the fountain of knowledge to drink, some prefer just to gargle.

✱✱✱✱

Blessed are those who go around in circles, for they shall be known as wheels.

✱✱✱✱

It is impossible to make anything foolproof, because fools are so ingenious.

✳✳✳✳

If anything just cannot go wrong, it will anyway.

For every action, there is a corresponding over-reaction.

✳✳✳✳

Anybody can win, unless there happens to be a second entry.

✳✳✳✳

Everything tastes more or less like chicken.

✳✳✳✳

Beware the fury of a patient man.

✳✳✳✳

Common sense is not so common.

****

Assumption is the mother of all foul-ups.

****

Two heads are more numerous than one.

Don't lend people money...it gives them amnesia.

****

A penny saved is virtually worthless.

****

Everything in moderation, including moderation.

****

No good deed goes unpunished.

****

Friends come and go, but enemies accumulate.

****

A closed mouth gathers no foot.

****

When all else fails, read the instructions.

Change is inevitable, except from a vending machine.

****

Even paranoids have enemies.

****

Sometimes too much drink is not enough.

****

Winning isn't everything, but losing isn't anything.

****

The bigger they are, the harder they hit.

****

I think...therefore I am confused.

****

Familiarity breeds children.

Around the Pub

7

Jokes About Food, Music, Sport and Old People in the Corner

IN THE RESTAURANT

A family of three tomatoes are walking downtown one day when the little baby tomato starts lagging behind. The big father tomato walks back to the baby tomato, stomps on her, squashing her into a red paste, and says, "Ketchup!"

****

One day, Bill and Tom went to a restaurant for dinner. As soon as the waiter brought out two steaks, Bill quickly picked out the bigger steak for himself. Tom wasn't happy about that, asking: "When are you going to learn to be polite?" Bill replied "If you had the chance to pick first, which one would you pick?" Tom said: "The smaller piece, of course." Bill sneered: "What are you mumbling about then? Then the smaller piece is what you want, right?"

****

"Here, waiter, my plate's wet!" "That's not wet, sir – that's the soup!"

****

A customer was bothering the waiter in a restaurant. First, he asked that the air conditioning be turned up because he was too hot, then he asked it be turned down because he was too cold, and so on for about half an hour. Surprisingly, the waiter was very patient. He walked back and forth and never once got angry. So finally, a second customer asked him why he didn't throw out the pest. "Oh, I don't care," said the waiter with a smile, "we don't even have an air conditioner."

****

"Here, waiter, have you got asparagus?" "We don't serve sparrows and my name is not Gus!"

****

"Here, waiter, this coffee is horrible." "Don't complain, sir. You may be old and weak yourself some day."

****

One day, Johnny asked: "Daddy, are caterpillars good to eat?" His father was irritated. "I've told you not to talk about things like that during meals." "Why did you want to know?" asked his mother. Johnny said: "It's because I saw one on daddy's lettuce, but now it's gone."

****

"Here, waiter, this bun tastes of soap." "Yes, sir – it's a Bath bun."

"Here, waiter, what do you call this?" "That's bean soup, sir." "I don't care what it's been, what is it now?"

✳✳✳✳

"Here, waiter, what do you call this?" "Cottage pie, sir." "Well, I've just bitten on a piece of the door."

✳✳✳✳

"Here, waiter, there's no chicken in this chicken pie." "So what? You don't get dog in a dog biscuit, do you?"

✳✳✳✳

"Here, waiter, what's the meaning of this fly in my tea-cup?" "I wouldn't know, sir. I'm a waiter, not a fortune-teller."

✳✳✳✳

"Here, waiter, if this is plaice then I'm an idiot." "You're right, sir – it is plaice."

✳✳✳✳

What is the most common speech impediment? Chewing gum.

"Here, waiter, this egg tastes rather strong." "Never mind, sir, the tea's nice and weak."

****

"Here, waiter, this soup tastes funny." "So why aren't you laughing then, sir?"

****

"Here, waiter, how long will my sausages be?" "Oh, about three or four inches if you're lucky."

****

A man in a restaurant orders chicken noodle soup. He starts to eat the soup and chokes on a hair in it. After gagging for a minute, he calls the waitress. "I'm not paying for this soup. There was a hair in it." The waitress and customer get into a bit of an argument over the problem. The man ends up storming out of the restaurant without paying. The waitress sees him go across the street to a house of ill repute. The waitress's shift finishes and she hurries over to the house, finds out where the man is and interrupts his evening of pleasure. As she walks in, she sees the man with his face in the hooker's business area. "You wouldn't pay for the chicken noodle soup because you found hair in it. Now look where your face is." The man pulls his face out of the muff, turns to the waitress and says, "And if I find a noodle in there, I won't pay for that either."

****

"Here, waiter, does the pianist play requests?" "Yes, sir." "Then ask him to play tiddlywinks till I've finished my meal."

****

"Here, waiter, I'll have the pie, please." "Anything with it, sir?" "If it's anything like last time I'd better have a hammer and chisel."

****

Clearly it is not the lovelorn sufferer who seeks solace in chocolate, but rather the chocolate-deprived individual, who, desperate, seeks in mere love a pale approximation of bittersweet euphoria.

****

"Here, waiter, this lobster's only got one claw." "I expect he's been in a fight, sir." "Well, bring me the winner!"

****

"Here, waiter, that dog's just run off with my roast lamb!" "Yes, it's very popular, sir."

****

"Here, waiter, bring me a glass of milk and a Dover sole." "Fillet?" "Yes, to the brim."

****

"Here, waiter, bring me a fried egg with finger-marks in it, some luke-warm greasy chips and a portion of watery cabbage." "We don't do food like that, sir!" "You did yesterday..."

****

"Here, waiter, I'll pay my bill now." "I'm afraid this £10 note is bad, sir." "So what? So was the meal."

****

"Here, waiter, I'll have a chop; no – make that a steak." "I'm a waiter, sir, not a magician!"

****

"Here, waiter, there's a bird in my soup." "That's all right, sir. It's bird's nest soup."

****

"Here, waiter, there's a hair in my honey." "It must have dropped off the comb, sir!"

****

"Here, waiter, there's a fly in my soup." "That's all right, sir, he won't drink much."

****

"Here, waiter, send the chef here. I want to complain about this disgusting meal." "I'm afraid you'll have to wait, sir. He's just popped out for his dinner."

****

"Here waiter, there's a beetle in my soup. Get me the manager." "That won't do any good, sir – he's frightened of them as well!"

****

"Here, waiter, there's a fly in my soup." "Couldn't be, sir. The cook used them all in the raisin bread."

✳✳✳✳

"Here, waiter, there's a worm on my plate." "That's the sausage, sir."

✳✳✳✳

"Here, waiter, this coffee tastes like mud!" "I'm not surprised, sir, it was ground only a few minutes ago."

✳✳✳✳

"Here, waiter, bring me tea without milk." "We haven't any milk, sir. How about tea without cream?"

✳✳✳✳

"Here, waiter, have you got frogs' legs?" "Certainly, sir." "Then hop into the kitchen and get me a steak!"

✳✳✳✳

"Here, waiter, there's a fly swimming in my soup." "What do you expect me to do, call a lifeguard?"

"Here, waiter, there's a dead fly in my soup!" "Yes, sir, it's the hot water that kills them."

****

"Here, waiter, there's a dead fly in my soup." "What do you expect for £4 – a live one?"

****

"Here, waiter, this bread's got sand in it." "That's to stop the butter slipping off, sir."

****

A friend got vinegar in his ear, now he suffers from pickled hearing.

****

"Here, waiter, there is a fly in my soup." "Sorry sir, I must have missed it when I removed the other three."

****

"Here, waiter, there is a fly in my salad." "I'm sorry sir, I didn't know that you were vegetarian."

A guy goes to visit his aunt in the nursing home. It turns out she's napping so he just sits down in a chair in her room, flips through a few magazines, and munches on some peanuts sitting in a bowl on the table. Eventually, the aunt wakes up, and her nephew realizes he's absentmindedly finished the entire bowl. "I'm so sorry, auntie, I've eaten all of your peanuts!" "That's okay, dearie," the aunt replied. "After I've sucked the chocolate off, I don't care for them anyway."

****

"Here, waiter. Bring me a crocodile sandwich, and make it snappy."

****

"Here, waiter, there is a mosquito in my soup." "Yes sir, I'm afraid we've run out of flies."

****

"Here, waiter, is this a hair in my soup?" "Why, of course sir. That's rabbit stew!"

****

"Here, waiter, is this all you've got to eat?" "No, sir, I'll be having a nice shepherd's pie when I get home."

"Here, waiter, is this a fly in my soup?" "Quite possibly, sir. The chef used to be a tailor."

✱✱✱✱

"Here, waiter, I'll have soup and then fish." "I'd have the fish first if I were you, sir, it's just on the turn."

✱✱✱✱

"Here, waiter, my bill please." "How did you find your luncheon, sir?" "With a magnifying glass."

✱✱✱✱

I know about stressed...it's desserts spelled backwards.

✱✱✱✱

"Here, waiter, is this a lamb chop or a pork chop?" "Can't you tell by the taste?" "No, I can't." "Well what does it matter, then?"

✱✱✱✱

A man walks into a Chinese restaurant but is told that there will be at least a 20 minute wait and he is asked if he would like to wait in the bar. He goes into the bar and the bartender says, "What'll it be?" The man replies, "Give me a Stoli with a twist." The bartender squints at him for a few seconds, then smiles and says: "Once upon time there were four little pigs..."

****

"Here, waiter, how long have you been here?" "Six months, sir." "Ah, then it can't be you who took my order."

****

"Here ,waiter, I'd like a little game." "Draughts or tiddlywinks, sir?"

****

"Here, waiter, do you call this a three-course meal?" "That's right, sir. Two chips and a pea."

****

"Tea or coffee, gentlemen?" asked the waiter. "I'll have tea," said one bloke. "Me, too," said his mate, "and make sure the glass is clean." The waiter returned shortly afterwards, saying, "Two teas. Which of you asked for the clean glass?"

THE JUKEBOX

Two violinists make a pact that whoever dies first will contact the other and tell him what life in heaven is like. Poor Max has a heart attack and dies. He manages to make contact with Abe the next day. Abe says: "I can't believe this worked. What is it like in Heaven?" Max replies: "Well, it's great, but I've got good news, and I've got bad news. The good news is that there's a fantastic orchestra up here, and in fact, we're playing 'Sheherazade', your favourite piece, tomorrow night." Abe says: "So what's the bad news?" Max replies: "Well, you're booked to play the solo."

✶✶✶✶

Vibrato: the singer's equivalent of an epileptic seizure.

✶✶✶✶

What is the definition of a Soviet string quartet? A Soviet symphony orchestra after a tour of the USA.

✶✶✶✶

What is the range of a tuba? Twenty yards, if you've got a good arm.

A harp is a nude piano.

****

English horn: a woodwind that got its name because it's neither English nor a horn. Not to be confused with the French horn, which is German.

****

Agnus Dei was a woman composer famous for her church music.

****

Trombone: a slide whistle with delusions of grandeur.

****

Chord: usually spelled with an 's' on the end, means a particular type of trousers, eg 'he wears chords.'

****

Rubber bands are musicians who believe in safe sex.

****

Metronome: a dwarf who lives in the city.

****

Tempo: this is where a headache begins.

****

Why don't they know where Mozart is buried? Because he's Haydn.

****

Why do bagpipers walk when they play? To get away from the noise.

****

What do you get when you drop a piano down a mine shaft? A flat minor.

****

What do you get when you cross a Mafia lieutenant and a performance artist? Someone who makes you an offer that you can't understand.

****

What do you get when an army officer puts his nose to the grindstone? A sharp major.

✳✳✳✳

What do you get when you play a New-Age song backwards? Another New-Age song.

✳✳✳✳

A soprano died and went to heaven. St Peter stopped her at the gate and asked: "Well, how many false notes did you sing in your life?" The soprano answers: "Three." "Three times, fellows," says St Peter, and along comes an angel and sticks the soprano three times with a needle. "Ow! What was that for?" asks the soprano. St Peter explains, "Here in heaven, we stick you once for each false note you've sung down on Earth." "Oh," says the soprano, and is just about to step through the gates when she suddenly hears a horrible screaming from behind a door. "Oh my goodness, what is THAT?" asks the soprano, horrified. "That," says St Peter, "is a tenor we got some time back. He's just about to start his third week in the sewing machine."

✳✳✳✳

Gregorian chant: a way of singing in unison, invented by monks to hide snoring.

What do you get if Bach falls off a horse, but has the courage to get on again and continue riding? Bach in the saddle again.

****

Real musicians don't die, they just decompose.

****

Music sung by two people at the same time is called a duel.

****

Did you hear about the female opera singer who had quite a range at the lower end of the scale.? She was known as the deep C diva.

****

Have you heard about the new American radio station called WPMS? Each month, they play two weeks of love songs, one week of blues, one week of ragtime and two days of death metal.

****

It is easy to teach anyone to play the maracas. Just grip the neck and shake him in rhythm.

One evening, after a symphony rehearsal, some of the players went out to Sam's Discotheque to unwind. After several relaxing drinks, they all went their separate ways home. The next night, the harpist showed up at the concert hall and realized that he didn't have his instrument. "Oh no," he cried, "I left my harp in Sam's damn disco..."

****

Beat: what music students do to each other with their musical instruments. The down beat is performed on the top of the head, while the up beat is struck under the chin.

****

Rhythmic drone: the sound of many monks suffering with crotchet.

****

Dad, why do the singers rock left and right while performing on stage? Because, son, it is more difficult to hit a moving target.

****

Refrain means don't do it. A refrain in music is the part you had better not try to sing.

How many tenors does it take to change a light bulb? Six. One to do it and five to say, "It's too high for HIM."

****

How many altos does it take to change a light bulb? None. They can't get up that high.

****

A trumpet is an instrument when it is not an elephant sound.

****

Band members do it in front of 100,000 people.

****

Woodwind players do it in the reeds.

****

An eccentric lady was in need of a piano player for her forthcoming party. She placed ads and spread the word but could not find a suitable one. A bum knocked on her door and when she saw the state of his condition, she responded, "Go away." He said: "Please, won't you just give me a chance? I'm a piano player." She was desperate, so she let him in. After his performance, she couldn't believe her ears. "Wow! That sounded great - best I've heard in years. What was the name of that song?" The bum answered, "Oh, it's called 'I Love Me Wife So Much I Took A Big Dump'." "Oh," said the lady, "how unusual, would you play another?" He proceeded to play another tune and again she was astounded by the performance. "That was fantastic," she said. "What was the name of that tune?" "That one is called 'I Took My Wife From Behind And Made A Mess All Over That Carpet'." Again she commented: "How unusual," adding "you've got the job, but if anyone asks the names of your songs, please don't tell them. And do something about your clothes; you look terrible. Go and buy a tux for the party." The bum was happy about his new job and happy to buy a tuxedo but, as he had never bought one before, he wound up getting one that was three sizes too small. At the big party, the crowd was amazed at his performance. He bowed at the crowd back and forth and ripped out the whole rear end of his trousers. One lady stepped forward clapping and said, "Sir, you are a great piano player but do you know you have a hairy ass and your balls are hanging out?" With a smile, the bum replied, "Lady, know it? I wrote it."

✳✳✳✳

A tourist is sightseeing in a European city. She comes upon the tomb of Beethoven and begins reading the commemorative plaque, only to be distracted by a low scratching noise, as if something were rubbing against a piece of paper. She collars a passing native and asks what the scratching sound is. The local person replies: "Oh, that is Beethoven. He's decomposing."

****

How can you tell if a violin's out of tune? The bow is moving.

****

What do you get if you run over an army officer with a steam roller? A flat major.

****

What do you say to an army officer while your running him over with a steam roller? Be flat, major.

****

What do you say after you've run over an army officer with a steam roller? See, flat major.

****

A musical reviewer admitted he always praised the first show of a new theatrical season. "Who am I to stone the first cast?"

****

A Celtic harpist spends half her time tuning her harp, and the other half playing it out of tune.

****

Opera is when a guy gets stabbed in the back and, instead of bleeding, he sings.

****

What is another name for a bassoon? A farting bedpost.

****

"Haven't I seen your face before?" a judge demanded, looking down at the defendant. "You have, your Honour," the man answered hopefully, "I gave your son violin lessons last winter." "Ah, yes," recalled the judge. "Twenty years!"

****

How many sound men does it take to change a light bulb? One, two, three, testing, one, two, one, two.

****

Quaver: beginning violin class.

****

Crotchet: it's like knitting, but faster.

****

A cowboy and a biker are on Death Row, and are to be executed on the same day. The day comes, and they are brought to the gas chamber. The warden asks the cowboy if he has a last request, to which the cowboy replies: "Ah shore do, wardn. Ah'd be mighty grateful if'n yoo'd play 'Achy Breaky Heart' fur me bahfore ah hafta go." "Sure enough, cowboy, we can do that," says the warden. He turns to the biker, "And you, biker, what's your last request?" "That you kill me first."

****

What is the difference between a violin and a viola? The viola holds more beer.

What is the difference between a saxophone and a chainsaw? It's all in the grip.

★★★★

What is the difference between a bull and an orchestra? The bull has the horns in front and the arsehole in the back.

★★★★

While at a concert being performed by a very bad orchestra, George Bernard Shaw was asked what he'd like them to play next. "Dominoes," he replied.

★★★★

Person 1: "It must be terrible for an opera singer to realize that he can never sing again". Person 2: "Yes, but it's much more terrible if he doesn't realize it."

★★★★

Seems that the censors banned the transmission of a TV show that claimed to introduce young people to the worlds of jazz and classical music. Their reasoning? Too much sax and violins.

An accordion is a bagpipe with pleats.

★★★★

Disco is to music what Etch-A-Sketch is to art.

★★★★

This guy says to his wife, "Oh, baby. I can play you just like a violin."
His wife says, "But I'd rather have you play me like a harmonica."

★★★★

How do you get a guitar player to play softer? Give him a sheet of
music. How do you make him stop playing altogether? Put notes on it.

★★★★

How do you get five oboeists in tune? Shoot four of them.

★★★★

Semiconductors are part-time musicians.

★★★★

A musician dies of a heroin overdose, and finds himself in purgatory. There he meets an angel who is reading a large book with his name on the cover. The angel looks up at the newly-arrived spirit and says: "Hi, we've been expecting you." "Where am I?" asks the musician. "In purgatory," the angel answers. "I've been reading the book of your life, and your good deeds are evenly balanced by your bad deeds." "So, what's next?" "We've decided to let you pick where you are going,- heaven or hell. And, to help you make up your mind, we're going to give you a glimpse of each." So saying, the angel motions the musician over to a curtain labelled 'Heaven'. The angel parts the curtain, and before them is a bucolic scene of eternal spring with angelic choirs singing praises to God. The musician surveys the scene, and says, "Well, I could hang with that. But...what's hell look like?" In response, the angel motions the musician over to a curtain labelled 'Hell'. Parting the curtain reveals a smoke filled room with well-dressed people happily talking and dancing, while a quartet is playing a rather good version of *'Have You Met Miss Jones?'*. "Well, to tell you the truth," says the musician, "I've got nothing against heaven, but hell looks like a place that I could really dig." "No problem," answers the angel. With that, he pulls an unseen lever and the musician falls through a trap door. The musician lands with a large splash in a cauldron of boiling blood. There are screams of eternal agony in the distance. A horribly ugly demon begins poking the musician in the side with a large trident. "What's this?" cries the musician. "I've been tricked!" The demon answers, "Yeah, I know. But that thing up there sure is a top demo tape, eh?"

SPORT ON THE BOX

"I didn't see you in church last Sunday, Nigel. I hear you were out playing football instead." "That's not true, vicar. And I've got the fish to prove it."

****

If at first you don't succeed, skydiving is not your sport.

****

Hunters do it with a bang.

****

Remember the days when sex was safe and skydiving was dangerous?

****

A priest was walking along the cliffs at Dover when he came upon two locals pulling another man ashore on the end of a rope. "That's what I like to see," said the priest, "a man helping his fellow man." As he was walking away, one local remarked to the other: "Well, he doesn't know the first thing about shark-fishing."

"He's great on the court," a sportswriter said of a college basketball player in an interview with his coach, "but how's his scholastic work?" "Why, he makes straight As," replied the coach. "Wonderful!" said the sportswriter. "Yes," agreed the coach, "but his Bs are a little crooked."

****

In Africa, some of the native tribes have a custom of beating the ground with clubs and uttering spine-chilling cries. Anthropologists call this a form of primitive self-expression. In Britain we call it golf.

****

A minister is out playing a round of golf one day with three of his friends, who are also ministers, when on one of the par fives he reaches the edge of the green in three, leaving himself with about a 40 foot birdie putt. He lines the putt up so that he feels pretty comfortable with it and strikes what looks to be a perfect putt, headed straight for the hole. Just as the ball gets to the hole, it stops, hanging right on the rim of the hole. Being a preacher and a man of God, he looks up to the sky and says to God, "How about a little help?" Just as he says this, a moth flies onto the green, briefly buzzes around their heads and then decides to rest right on his ball, but the ball still doesn't move. So he says: "You didn't send a big enough moth." Just as he says this, the moth starts crawling around the ball, and eventually crawls to the hole side of the ball, causing the ball to drop straight into the hole. The minister simply looks up to the sky and says: "Amen!"

****

Man with unchecked parachute will leap to conclusion.

****

You know you've made the right decision to take up jogging if, on your first try at it, you have more jiggle than jog.

****

There's a fine line between fishing and standing on the shore looking like an idiot.

****

When another foursome is on the green, "Fore!" is not an excuse, "So what?" is not an apology and "Up yours!" is not an explanation.

****

Old hunters never die, they just stay loaded.

Golf is a game that needlessly prolongs the lives of some of our most useless citizens.

****

Tennis players have fuzzy balls.

****

Fishermen do it for reel.

****

Taffy gets his first golf lesson. His instructor tells him: "You see that little flagpole over there? Just hit the ball and try to get it as close to it as you can." So Taffy gives it a good whack and upon approaching the hole they see that he has ended up 5cm from the hole. "Very good," the instructor says, amazed. "Now, you have to hit it into the hole." "What!" exclaims Taffy. "Why didn't you say so in the first place?"

****

To catch the fish, it's not how you throw the bait, but how you wiggle your worm.

****

Golfers have it down to a tee.

****

After spending all day watching football, Harry fell asleep in front of the rugby and spent the whole night in the chair. In the morning, his wife woke him up. "Get up dear," she said, "it's twenty to seven." He awoke with a start and said, "To who?"

****

A man books into a new and fancy resort which advertises an all-inclusive, do-all-you-can kind of holiday. Looking through the hotel's book, he finds there are tennis courts on the premises, so he calls the desk to find out how to go about playing a set or two. "Just meet the pro at the tennis shop, he will lend you all that you need and will find you someone to play with." "How much is that going to cost me?" the man asks. "Nothing, this is on the room," answers a very polite clerk. So the man plays tennis all afternoon. The next day he decides to try horseback riding and again finds it doesn't cost him a penny more than the price of the room. After a week at the hotel he has done just about everything that's available except golf. On his last day, he decides to play a round so he goes to the clubhouse, gets what he needs and starts his game. At the end of his round the pro asks him how the game went. "Not so good," the man answers, "in fact I lost five balls." "Well," says the pro, "that will be £5000 sir." "What do you mean £5000, for five damn golf balls? You have to be kidding. I played an afternoon of tennis, went horse riding, scuba diving, deep-sea fishing and more, and was never charged a cent. Now that I have lost five balls you charge me £5000." "Well," says the pro, "you know, this hotel really gets you by the balls."

****

Why do mountain climbers rope themselves together? To prevent the sensible ones from going home.

****

What's the difference between a hockey game and all-in wrestling? In a hockey game, the fights are real.

****

All morning, the American businessman talks about golf in his office. The rest of the day, he discusses work on the golf course.

****

Did you hear about the moron who went elephant-hunting? He got a hernia carrying the decoys.

THE OLD CODGER AT THE BAR

A bloke gives his 85-year-old father a surprise visit from a whore as a birthday present. He answers the door, and she bubbles at him: "Hi, I'm here to give you super sex." He looks at her for a moment, and replies: "Um, thanks, I'll have the soup."

****

If you reach 90, you can help advance medical science. There isn't much we know about sex at that age. Rats don't live that long...

****

Two elderly men are sitting at the bar, watching the young girls go by. One says to the other: "You know, I'm still sexually interested in women. In fact, I always get excited when I see the young girls walking by. The real problem is that at this age, I don't see so well any more."

****

A couple in their late sixties decide to marry (their respective spouses having died), and move to Bournemouth. In preparation for this they talk through the sharing of household expenses and various other matters. Jane asks Harold what they should do about their present houses. "Well, we ought to each sell our home and then we can each fund half the purchase price of our new home." Jane agrees. Harold then asks Jane what she'd like to do about the grocery bills. She suggests: "Neither one of us eats very much, so maybe we ought to split that bill on a monthly basis." Harold agrees. Then what about the utility bill? Again, they decide to share. Then Jane asks Harold what he wants to do about sex, to which he replies: "Oh, infrequently." Jane looks at him and asks: "Is that one word or two?"

✱✱✱✱

What dominates the thoughts of men at different stages in their lives?

Age	Primary Concerns
0-3	Shitting and drooling
4-10	Shitting and drooling
11-15	Sex and beer
16-20	Sex and beer
20-40	Sex and beer
40-60	Sex and beer
60-80	Sex and beer
80-?	Shitting and drooling

✱✱✱✱

What dominates the thoughts of women at different stages in their lives

Age	Primary Concerns
0-3	Shitting and drooling
4-10	Dolls and shopping
11-15	Periods and shopping
16-20	Sex and shopping
20-40	Shopping and shopping
40-60	Getting old and wrinkly, and shopping
60-80	The price of coal and shopping
80-?	Whingeing and shopping

✱✱✱✱

An elderly man and his wife decided to separate. Before being allowed to do so legally, the Family Court insisted that they undergo some counselling from the marriage guidance mob, to see if their union could be saved. The counsellor did her best, but to no avail. The old folk were absolutely determined to go through with separation, leading to divorce. Finally, in some desperation, the counsellor said: "But you're 95 and your wife is 93. You've been married for 72 years. Why do you want to separate now?" The wife replied, "We haven't been able to stand each other for the last 46 years, but we thought we should wait until all the children died before we split up."

✱✱✱✱

An elderly man tells the doctor he is planning to marry a women aged 30 and asks if he has any suggestions. "Yes," says the doctor, "I would advise you to take in a lodger." A year later, at his eightieth birthday check-up, the doctor asks how everything is going. The man says: "Fine; my wife is pregnant." The doctor remarks, "so you took my advice and took in a lodger?" "Yes, I did," comes the reply, "and she's pregnant as well."

✳✳✳✳

An old man marries a girl barely out of her teens. Needless to say, she's pretty horny, so when they get into bed on the wedding night she asks him: "So are we going to have rampant sex tonight?" The man responds by raising his hand and outstretching his fingers. "What? Five times?" asks the eager girl. "No," he replies, "pick a finger."

✳✳✳✳

You're not from round 'ere, are you?

Jokes About Wales, Cornwall and Essex Girls

You're not from round 'ere, are you?

I heard they closed the zoo in Cardiff...the duck died.

****

Why are Essex girls' coffins Y-shaped? Because as soon as they are on their backs, their legs open.

****

How do you know when you're flying over Wales? You see toilet paper hanging on the clothes lines.

****

Following the assault of a young woman, the police rounded up the usual suspects for a line-up. Suddenly, the Welsh suspect stepped forward and screamed:"That's her!"

****

The only real problem holding women back is men.

****

A painting contractor was speaking with a woman about the job. In the first room she said she would like a pale blue. The contractor wrote this down and went to the window, opened it, and yelled out, "GREEN SIDE UP!" In the second room she told the painter she would like it painted in a soft yellow. He wrote this on his pad, walked to the window, opened it, and yelled, "GREEN SIDE UP!" The lady was somewhat curious but she said nothing. In the third room she said she would like it painted a warm rose colour. The painter wrote this down, walked to the window, opened it and yelled, "GREEN SIDE UP!" The lady then asked him, "Why do you keep yelling 'Green side up'?" "I'm sorry," came the reply. "but I have a crew of Essex girls laying turf across the street."

✳✳✳✳

What do you get when you offer an Essex girl a penny for her thoughts? Change.

✳✳✳✳

What do you see when you look into an Essex girl's eyes? The back of her head.

✳✳✳✳

What do you get when you cross an Essex girl and a lawyer? I don't know, there are some things even an Essex girl won't do.

Mr Smith: "Roger, where was yer son-in-law when y' first saw'n?"
Mr Jones: "Right smack in t' middle of my sights."

****

A Welshman goes to a whorehouse. The madam is out of women but, since the guy is Welsh, she thinks she can get away with a blow-up doll and he will never know the difference. Being a bit nervous because she has never tried this one before, the madam waits outside the door. The Welshman comes out in five minutes. "How was it?" says the madam. "I don't know," says the Welshman, "I bit her on the tit and she farted and flew out the window."

****

There was a Cornish girl who finally found a good job in the city. One night, shortly after arriving in the city, she was invited to a very exclusive party. She didn't know anyone, so she was trying to find someone to talk to when she saw an elegantly-dressed lady standing alone. She approached the lady and said, "Where'm you from?" The lady gave an indignant look and said, "Well! Where I am from, we DON'T end our sentences with a preposition. The young girl thought about it and replied, "Oh, well, where'm you from, slag?"

****

What about the Essex girl who gave birth to twins? Her husband is out looking for the other man.

✳✳✳✳

How does a Cornishman know when his girlfriend is having an orgasm? He doesn't care.

✳✳✳✳

Why can`t Essex girls water-ski? When they get their crotch wet they think they have to lie down.

✳✳✳✳

What do you call it when an Essex girl dyes her hair brunette? Artificial intelligence.

✳✳✳✳

Essex girl: "Excuse me, sir, what time is it?" Man: "It's 3pm." Essex girl: (with a puzzled look on her face) "You know, it's the weirdest thing, but I've been asking that question all day, and each time I get a different answer."

✳✳✳✳

Did you hear about the Welshman who studied for five days? He was scheduled to take a urine test.

****

How do you get a Welshman out of the bath tub? Throw in a bar of soap.

****

Did you hear about the Welsh helicopter crash? The pilot got cold, so he turned off the fan.

****

Did you hear about the Welsh girl who tried to trade her menstrual cycle in for a Honda?

****

Did you hear about the Welsh kamikaze pilot? He flew more than 48 successful missions.

****

Did you know that a Welsh firing squad stands in a circle?

How do you sink a Welsh battleship? Put it in water.

****

How do you stop a Welsh army on horseback? Turn off the carousel.

****

Why did the Essex girl want to become a veterinarian? Because she loved children.

****

A Welshman saw a priest walking down the street. Noticing his collar, he stopped him and said, "Excuse me, but why are you wearing your shirt backwards?" The priest laughed, "Because, my son, I am a Father." The Welshman scratched his head. "But I am a father too, and I don't wear my shirt backwards." Again the priest laughed. "But I am a father of thousands." To which the Welshman replied, "Well then you should wear your shorts backwards."

****

Why wasn't Christ born in Wales? Because they couldn't find three wise men and a virgin.

Why do Essex girls have vaginas? So guys will talk to them at parties.

****

What's the most popular pick-up line in Truro? "Nice tooth, m'dear."

****

Maggie's first pregnancy had produced triplets. With considerable pride, she was telling her Essex girlfriend how this happened once in every 200,000 times. The Essex girl's eyes widened: "How did you ever find time to do any housework?"

****

A 12-year-old boy comes up to the Welshman and says, "I was looking in your bedroom window last night and I saw your wife giving you a blow job. Ha ha!" The Welshman answers, "The joke's on you, Ivor. I wasn't even home last night."

****

Nappies and government ministers need to be changed frequently, and for much the same reason.

****

Three men are travelling in the Amazon; a German, an Englishman, and a Welshman, and they get captured by some Amazons. The head of the tribe says to the German, "What do you want on your back for your whipping?" The German responds, "I will take oil." So they put oil on his back, and a large Amazon whips him ten times. When he is finished the German has these huge welts on his back, and he can hardly move. The Amazons haul the German away, and say to the Welshman, "What do you want on your back?" "I will take nothing," says the Welshman, and he stands there straight and takes his ten lashings without a single flinch. "What will you take on your back?" the Amazons ask the Englishman. He responds, "I'll take the Welshman."

****

An Englishman is walking down the street when he sees a Welshman with a very long pole and a yardstick. He's standing the pole on its end and trying to reach the top of it with his yardstick. Seeing the Welshman's ignorance, the Englishman wrenches the pole out of his hand, lays it on the sidewalk, measures it with the yardstick, and says, "There, ten feet long." The Welshman grabs the yardstick and shouts, "You idiot! I don't care how long it is, I want to know how high it is."

****

They put one man on the moon. Why can't they put them all there?

Men call us birds; is that because of all the worms we pick up?

✱✱✱✱

Heard about the Welsh hockey team? They all drowned in Spring training.

✱✱✱✱

Why did the Essex girl take two hits of acid? She wanted to go on a round trip.

✱✱✱✱

Why did the Essex girl stare at orange juice for two hours? Because it said 'Concentrate'.

✱✱✱✱

How does an Essex girl spell farm? E-I-E-I-O.

✱✱✱✱

Why did the Essex girl snort Nutra-Sweet? She thought it was diet coke.

What does an Essex girl say after multiple orgasms? "Way to go, team!"

****

Who wears a dirty white robe and rides a sheep? Lawrence of Wales.

****

Why did the Essex girl put her finger over the nail when she was hammering? The noise gave her a headache.

****

What's delaying the Welsh space program? Development of a working match.

****

Why are Essex girls like pianos? When they aren't upright, they're grand.

****

How does an Essex girl part her hair? By doing the splits.

****

A Welshman is hired to paint the lines on the road. On the first day he paints ten miles, and his employers are amazed. But the second day he paints just five, and on only the third day, he paints only a mile of the road. Disappointed, his boss asks what the problem is. The Welshman replies, "Well sir, every day I have to walk farther and farther to get back to the paint bucket."

****

How do you get a one-armed Essex girl out of a tree? Wave to her.

****

How do you get a one-armed Welshman out of a tree? Wave to him.

****

In Cornwall in the good old days, men were 'real' men, women were 'real' women, and small furry animals were 'real' small furry animals. You knew where you stood. If you didn't, you planted a flag in the ground and claimed the place for King and Country, and everyone else knew where you stood. Nowadays, Cornishmen wear long hair and Cornishwomen wear trousers. People have sex with other people regardless of gender or species. Men are 'real' women, women are 'real' men, and small furry animals are real afraid.

✳✳✳✳

Boys will be boys but one day all girls will be women.

✳✳✳✳

What's an Essex girl's idea of safe sex? Locking the car door.

✳✳✳✳

Wales sent its top team of scientists to attend the international science convention, where all the countries of the world gathered to compare their scientific achievements and plans. The scientists listened to the United States describe how they were another step closer to a cure for cancer, how the Russians were preparing a space ship to go to Saturn and how Germany was inventing a car that runs on water. Soon, it was the Welsh scientists' turn to speak. "Well, we are preparing a space ship to fly to the sun." This, of course was met with much ridicule. They were asked how they planned to deal with the sun's extreme heat. "Simple; we're going at night."

Did you hear in the news that a 747 recently crashed in a cemetery in Wales? The Welsh officials have so far retrieved 2000 bodies.

****

Did you hear about the new automatic Welsh parachutes? They open on impact.

****

The May Day parade in Moscow is the largest, most important military parade of the year. For the 1993 parade, Yeltsin and Gorbachev invited Bill Clinton to come and watch it with them. The parade commenced with a battalion of tanks, followed by a division of infantry, followed by armoured personnel carriers and mobile artillery. They had mobile ballistic missile launchers, electronic jamming vehicles, and throughout the entire time the formations were overflown by squadrons of the most advanced interceptors, fighters,and long-range strategic bombers. Clinton was suitably impressed. Then he noticed that, way back at the end of the parade, there was a disorganized, messy bunch of men in rumpled suits tagging along behind the last artillery pieces. "Who are they?" he asked. "Ah," said Yeltsin, "those are our economists." "But I thought this parade was military..." said Clinton, confused. "Mr Clinton," said Gorbachev, "have you SEEN the damage those men can do?"

Have you seen the Welsh mine detector? He puts his fingers in his ears and starts stamping the ground with his foot.

✳✳✳✳

In Truro recently three armed men robbed a jeweller and decided to use his car for a getaway vehicle. Exiting the shop, they all piled into the car, only to discover that it had a manual gearstick, which none of the three knew how to operate...They were last seen fleeing on foot.

✳✳✳✳

Two Welsh hunters were out looking for pheasant when they came upon the local farmer's daughter, sitting naked on a fence, sunning herself. The first hunter asked, "Are you game?" She replied, "I sure am, baby." The second hunter shot her.

✳✳✳✳

What are the three biggest lies a Cornishman tells? 1) Yes, I do really have an O-level. 2) No, she's not my cousin. 3) Honest officer, I was only trying to help the sheep over the fence.

What do you call the layer of sweat between two Cornish folk having sex? Relative humidity.

****

Did you hear about the latest Welsh invention? It's a solar-powered flashlight.

****

The trouble with some women is that they get all excited about nothing and then marry him.

****

After the PLO and Israel shook hands and said that everything was fine, Clinton invited the Israeli Prime Minister back to the Oval Office. The Prime Minister looked at Clinton's desk and noticed that he had three phones, a black one, a red one, and a white one. The Prime Minister asked, "What is the red phone for?" Clinton said, "It's a direct line to Russia. Got to keep up with Yeltsin." Then the Prime Minister asked, "What's the white one for, then?" Clinton said, "That's a direct line to God. Did you know that it's a $5,000,000 a minute phone call to him?" The Prime Minister just nodded and went on with the tour. Weeks later, Clinton took a secret trip to Israel and, while he was there, toured the Prime Minister's office. He noticed that the Prime Minister had three phones just like his. He asked, "What's the red phone for?" The Prime minister replied, "It's a direct line to Russia." Clinton nodded and then asked, "What's the white one for?"

The Prime Minister replied, "It's a direct line to God." Clinton said, "How can a poor country like yours afford such an expensive phone call?" The Prime Minister said, "Oh, well, from here it's local rate..."

****

A young Essex woman is asked out on a date and accepts. The boy picks her up and they go to a nearby carnival in town. They ride a few rides, play a few games, and seem to be generally hitting it off well. During a sort of romantic lull, however, the boy says, "What do you want to do now?" "I want a weigh," she says. Well, okay, thinks the boy. They walk over to the fortune scales, and weigh her. They play a few more games and stop for food. "What do you want to do now?" asks the boy again. "I want a weigh," she says. "Hmmm, a little odd but I'll put up with it", thinks the boy. Again they get her weight and fortune. After yet another few games and an exquisite fireworks show, the boy repeats, "What do you want to do now?" "I want a weigh," she says. "Damn, thinks the boy,", she's just too weird for me. They get her weight and fortune, and the boy drives her home. As she walks into the house, her sister asks, "How'd your date go?" "Wousy," says the girl.

****

Two Welsh hunters were driving in the US, bear hunting. They came upon a fork in the road where a sign read "BEAR LEFT". They went home.

****

A Welshman wanted to learn how to sky-dive. He got an instructor and started lessons. The instructor told the Welshman to jump out of the plane and pull his rip cord. The instructor then explained that he himself would jump out right behind him so that they would go down together. The Welshman understood and was ready. The time came for the Welshman to jump and the instructor reminded the man that he would be right behind him. The Welshman jumped from the plane and, after being in the air for a few seconds, pulled the rip cord. The instructor followed by jumping from the plane but when he pulled his rip cord the parachute did not open. The instructor, frantically trying to get his parachute open, darted past the Welshman. The Welshman seeing this yelled as he undid the straps to his parachute, "So you wanna race, eh?"

****

Every man has it in his power to make one woman happy... by remaining a bachelor.

****

Why did the Welshman sell his water-skis? He couldn't find a lake with a hill in it.

****

Why did the Essex girl have blisters on her lips? From trying to blow out light bulbs.

****

What is the definition of gross ignorance? 144 Essex girls.

****

A Welshman, an Englishman, and a Frenchman are running away from the German soldiers when they come up to a forest and they decide to hide by each climbing a tree. When the Germans arrive, they go to the first tree where the English guy is, and shout, "We know you're up there; come down." The English guy, thinking fast, says, "Twit, twit, twit..." The Germans, thinking that it's a bird, move on to the next tree where the French guy is and once again shout, "We know you're up there; come down." The French guy, thinking fast, says, "Woo, woo, woo..." The Germans, thinking that it's an owl, move on to the next tree where the Welsh guy is and once again shout, "We know you're up there; come down." The Welsh guy thinks for a while and then says, "Moo, moo, moo..."

Why do Welsh police cars have stripes on the side? So the cops can find the door handles.

****

What's the difference between a good old boy and a Cornishman? The good old boy raises sheep. The Cornishman gets emotionally involved.

****

Mr Smith: "What'm yer son goin' t' be when he graduates, m'dear?"
Mr Jones: "An old man, I fancy."

****

Did you hear about the gay Welshman? He slept with women.

****

Why do blondes have more fun? Because they are easier to find in the dark.

****

What is the Essex girl's favourite battery? Everready.

What is 68 to an Essex girl? Where she goes down on you and you owe her one.

****

What's the difference between an Essex girl and an ice-cream cone? Ice cream cones don't lick back.

****

What's the difference between an Essex girl and a light bulb? The light bulb is smarter, but the Essex girl is easier to turn on.

****

What can save a dying Essex girl? Hair transplants.

What's the difference between an Essex girl and a brick? When you lay a brick it, doesn't follow you around for two weeks whining.

****

What's the first thing an Essex girl does in the morning? She introduces herself.

Did you hear about the Essex couple who were found frozen to death in their car at a drive-in cinema? They went to see 'Closed for the Winter'.

****

Did you hear about the Essex girl who robbed a bank? She tied up the safe and blew the guard.

****

Did you hear about the Essex girl with a Masters degree in psychology? She'll blow your mind, too.

****

Did you here about the Essex girl who shot an arrow into the air? She missed.

****

What did the really dumb Essex girl say when someone blew in her bra? "Thanks for the refill".

****

What is the difference between Essex girls and traffic signs? Some traffic signs say "Stop".

****

What do UFOs and smart Essex girls have in common? You keep hearing about them, but never see any.

****

How do you keep an Essex girl busy all day? Put her in a round room and tell her to sit in the corner.

****

What do you give the Essex girl who has everything? Penicillin.

****

How do you measure an Essex girl's intelligence? Stick a tyre-pressure gauge in her ear.

****

What do you call an Essex girl with a bag of sugar on her head? Sweet Fuck All...

What do you call an Essex girl golfer with an IQ of 125? A foursome.

****

How do you know an Essex girl has just lost her virginity? Her crayons are still sticky.

****

How do you get an Essex girl to marry you? Tell her she's pregnant.

****

What do you call an Essex girl's mother-in-law? An air bag.

****

How do you describe an Essex girl, surrounded by a bunch of drooling idiots? Flattered.

****

How do you confuse an Essex girl? You don't. They're born that way.

****

What do you call four Essex girls lying on the ground? An air mattress.

✳✳✳✳

What is the Essex girl doing when she holds her hands tightly over her ears? Trying to hold on to a thought.

✳✳✳✳

A Cornishman is visiting his cousin's farm, and the farmer shows him round the chicken sheds, the pig pens, the paddocks and so on. Finally he points to a tree about 30 feet away and tells the first guy: "Under that tree is where I first had sex." Then he points to another tree and says: "... and that's where her mother stood and watched us." The first guy gasps and asks: "What did she say?" His cousin grins, and replies: "Baaa."

✳✳✳✳

Why did the Welsh couple decide to have only four children? They'd read in the newspaper that one out of every five babies born in the world today is Chinese.

✳✳✳✳

A Welshman was walking down the street, carrying a brown paper bag. He ran into one of his friends, who asked, "Hey! What do you have in the bag?" The man told his friend that he had some fish in the bag. His friend said, "Well, I'll make you a bet. If I can guess how many fish you have in the bag, you'll have to give me one." The man says, "I'll tell you what. If you tell me how many fish I have in this bag, I'll give you both of them."

✱✱✱✱

What do you call an Essex girl between two brunettes? A mental block.

✱✱✱✱

This Welshman came home one day from work, hung up his coat, took off his hat and walked into his bedroom shouting, "I'm home, darling." What should he see but his best friend in bed with his wife. Infuriated, he rushed to the cupboard, pulled out his gun and put it to his head. His wife started laughing. "Don't laugh," he screamed, "you're next."

✱✱✱✱

A travelling salesman has an audience with the new Pope, David, and, not quite knowing what to say, tries to break the ice with a joke...

"Have you heard the one about the two Welsh priests, Holy Father?" "But I am Welsh, my son." There followed a pregnant pause while the salesman thought quickly..."That's okay, Holy Father, I'll tell it to you slowly."

****

Did you hear about the Cornishman who passed away and left his entire estate in trust for his widow? She can't touch it 'til she's 14...

****

Why are Essex girls like cornflakes? Because they're simple, easy and they taste good.

****

A Welshman was suffering from constipation, so his doctor prescribed suppositories. A week later the man complained to the doctor that they didn't produce the desired results. "Have you been taking them regularly?" the doctor asked. "What do you think I've been doing," the man said, "shoving them up my ass?"

****

A Welshman went to a carpenter and said: "Can you build me a box that is two inches high, two inches wide, and 50 feet long?" "Hmm," mused the carpenter, "it could be done, I suppose, but what would you want a box like that for?" "Well, you see," said the Welshman, "my neighbour moved away and forgot his garden hose."

✻✻✻✻

An Essex girl and a brunette were discussing their boyfriends. Brunette: "Last night I had three orgasms in a row." Essex girl: "That's nothing; last night I had over a hundred." Brunette: "My god! I had no idea he was that good." Essex girl. (looking shocked) "Oh, you mean with one guy."

✻✻✻✻

An Essex girl and her boyfriend were sharing a bath. The Essex girl said to her boyfriend: "Is it true that if you pull your finger out, I'll sink?"

✻✻✻✻

Where do Cornishmen meet girls? At family barbecues.

✻✻✻✻

Two Cornishmen were standing around on a sheep farm, during the coldest winter they'd had in years. Bill turned to Roger and confessed that he really couldn't wait until it was time to shear the flocks. The other nodded, rubbing his hands together in anticipation. "We'm be having a top time selling t' wool, and spending t' money on beer and women, eh?" "No, that bain't it," said Bill, "I'm just carn't wait t' see'm naked."

✳✳✳✳

An Englishman, a Frenchman and a Welshman are captured and thrown into prison. However, the guard is rather kind towards them, and says, "I am going to lock you away for five years, but I'll let you have anything you want now before I lock you away." The Englishman says: "I'll have five years' supply of beer." His wish is granted, and they lock him away with his beer. The Frenchman says: "I'll have five years' supply of brandy." His wish is granted, and they lock him away with his brandy. The Welshman says: "I'll have five years' supply of cigarettes." His wish is granted, and they lock him away with his cigarettes. Five years later the prisoners are released. First, they release the Englishman, who staggers out totally drunk. Then, they release the Frenchman, who also rolls out rather inebriated. Then, they release the Welshman, who comes out and says: "Has anyone got a light?"

✳✳✳✳

Theme Nights

Jokes About Guitarists, Students and Nuns

What should you do if you run over a guitar? Reverse.

✳✳✳✳

Mother Superior: "Sister Maria, if you were walking through town at night, and were accosted by a man with bad intentions, what would you do?" Sister Maria: "I would lift my habit, Mother Superior." Mother Superior (shocked): "And what would you do next?" Sister Maria "I would tell him to drop his trousers." Mother Superior: (even more shocked) "And what then?" Sister Maria: "I would run away. I can run much faster with my habit up than he can with his trousers down."

✳✳✳✳

What do you get when you throw a guitar and an accordion off the Empire State Building? Applause.

✳✳✳✳

Never let your schooling interfere with your education.

✳✳✳✳

One can pity the father with three kids at university. He tells his wife that they are getting poorer by degrees.

College: the fountains of knowledge where everyone goes to drink.

****

A nun and a priest were travelling across the desert and realized halfway across that the camel they were using for transportation was about to die. They set up a makeshift camp, hoping that someone would come to their rescue, but to no avail. Soon the camel died. After several days, they agreed that they were not going to be rescued. They prayed a lot (of course), and they discussed their predicament in great depth. Finally the priest said to the nun, "You know, Sister, I am about to die, and there's always been one thing I've wanted here on Earth – to see a woman naked. Would you mind taking off your clothes so I can look at you?" The nun thought about his request for several seconds and then agreed to take off her clothes. As she was doing so, she remarked, "Well, Father, now that I think about it, I've never seen a man naked, either. Would you mind taking off your clothes, too?" With a little hesitation, the priest also stripped. Suddenly the nun exclaimed, "Father! What is that little thing hanging between your legs?" The priest patiently answered, "That, my child, is a gift from God. If I put it in you, it creates a new life." "Well," responded the nun, "forget about me. Stick it in the camel."

****

It is Friday, and four nuns go to the priest at the local Catholic church to ask for the weekend off. They argue for a few minutes but finally the priest agrees to let them leave the convent for the weekend. "However," he says, "as soon as you get back on Monday morning I want you to confess to me what you have done over the weekend." The four nuns agree, and run off. Monday comes, and the four nuns return. The first nun goes to the priest and says: "Forgive me, Father, for I have sinned." The priest asks: "What did you do, Sister?" She replies: "I watched an X-rated movie." The priest looks up at heaven for a few seconds, then replies: "You are forgiven. Go and drink the holy water." The first nun leaves, and the fourth nun begins to chuckle quietly under her breath. The second nun then goes up to the priest and says: "Forgive me , Father, for I have sinned." The priest replies: "Okay, what happened?" She says: "I was driving my brother's car down the street in front of his house and I hit a neighbour's dog and killed it." The priest looks up to heaven for half a minute, then says: "You are forgiven. Go and drink the holy water." The second nun goes out. By this time, the fourth nun is laughing quite audibly. Then the third nun walks to the priest and says: "Forgive me, Father, for I have sinned." The priest asks: "Out with it. What did you do?" She says: "Last night, I ran naked up and down Main Street." The priest looks up at heaven for a full five minutes before responding: "God forgives you. Go and drink the holy water." She leaves. The fourth nun falls on the floor, laughing so hard tears run down her cheeks. The priest asks her: "Okay. What did you do that was so funny?" The fourth nun replies: "I pissed in the holy water..."

Guitar pickers: we tune because we care...

****

What's the best and fastest way to tune a guitar? With wire-cutters.

****

One day, a very attractive undergraduate visited the professor's office. She pulled the chair closer to the professor, smiled at him shyly, bumped his knee 'accidentally', and so on. Finally, the undergraduate said: "Professor, I really need to pass your course. It is extremely important to me. It is so important that I'll do anything you suggest." The professor, somewhat taken aback by this attention, replied: "Anything?" To which the undergraduate cooed: "Yes, anything you say." After some brief reflection, the professor asked: "What are you doing tomorrow afternoon at 3pm?" The student lied: "Oh, nothing at all, sir. I can be free then." The professor then advised: "Excellent! Professor Palmer is holding a help session for his students. Why don't you attend that."

****

No matter how much you tune it, it will still sound like a guitar!

****

Why don't guitar pickers like to go to the beach? Because cats keep trying to bury them.

****

Why don't guitar players get to take breaks between sets? It takes them too long to retune.

****

When professors want your opinion, they'll give it to you.

****

How can you tell if there's a guitar player at your door? They can't find the key, the knocking speeds up and they don't know when to come in.

****

When do guitar songs sound the best? When they're over.

****

What do you say to the guitar player wearing a three-piece suit? "Will the defendant please rise?"

How can you tell if the stage is level? If the guitar player drools out of both sides of his mouth.

****

There are two nuns in a bath. The first one says: "Where's the soap?" The second one replies: "Yes it does, doesn't it?"

****

Student: "What's your opinion on the paper I submitted last week?" Professor: "It's absolute drivel." Student: "I know, but let's hear it anyway."

****

While visiting a country school, the chairman of the Board of Education became provoked at the noise the unruly students were making in the next room. Angrily, he opened the door and grabbed one of the taller boys who seemed to be doing most of the talking. He dragged the boy into the next room and stood him in the corner. A few minutes later, a small boy stuck his head in the room and pleaded, "Please, sir, may we have our teacher back?"

****

Sister Catherine is asking all the Catholic school children in the fourth grade what they want to be when they grow up. Little Sheila says: "When I grow up, I want to be a prostitute!" Sister Catherine's eyes grow wide and she barks: "What in the name of God did you say?" "A prostitute," Sheila repeats. Sister Catherine breathes a sight of relief and says: "Thank God! I thought you said a Protestant."

****

There was a story around Oxford that the final exam on a maths degree always read: "Make up an appropriate final exam for this course and answer it. You will be graded on both parts." Then one year, a student answered as follows: "The exam question is: 'Make up an appropriate final exam for this course and answer it. You will be graded on both parts.' The answer is: 'Make up an appropriate final exam for this course and answer it. You will be graded on both parts.'" His reasoning was that since that was the best exam the professor could write, it certainly ought to be good enough for a student. He got an A. The professor specifically prohibited that answer from then on.

****

A professor is one who talks in someone else's sleep.

****

Why did the Boy Scout take up the guitar? They make good paddles.

✳✳✳✳

What is the definition of something suspicious? A nun doing press-ups in a cucumber field.

✳✳✳✳

There were these three catering students driving along an old country road one day when they saw a farm. So they pulled in, and knocked on the farmer's door. The farmer answered the door and the three students introduced themselves and said: "We were just passing by and saw your field of buttercups and were wondering if we could go and get a bucket full of butter" The old farmer scratched his head and said: "You boys ain't gonna get no butter from buttercups but you're more than welcome to try." About an hour later, the three came back, thanked the farme, and drove off with their bucket full of butter. The farmer once again scratched and shook his head, mumbled under his breath and went on about his business. About three months later, the same three students came up to the farm, knocked on the door, and asked the farmer if he remembered them. He chuckled and asked what he could do for them this time. One of them said: "We were just driving by and happened to see you now have a field of milkweed and we were wondering if we could go out and get a bucket of milk?" Once again, the old farmer chuckled, shook his head, scratched it and sarcastically said: "You boys go on out there and get your milk from my milkweeds." Once again, about an hour later, the three came back with their bucket overflowing with fresh milk and drove off. This time, the farmer was really confused, but just a little less sceptical. It was about three or four months later when the three agricultural students came back and again knocked on the farmer's door, this time saying that they were driving by and saw the field full of pussywillows. This time the farmer went with them.

✳✳✳✳

If you took all the students that fell asleep in class and laid them end to end, they'd be a lot more comfortable.

✳✳✳✳

Guitars are to music as Spam is to food...

✳✳✳✳

What's the difference between a skunk run over on the road and a guitar player run over on the road? You see skid marks in front of the skunk.

✳✳✳✳

Did you hear about the skeleton they just found in an old building at Roehampton Institute? It was the 1938 hide and seek champion.

****

At a convention of biological scientists, one researcher remarks to another: "Did you know that in our lab we have switched from mice to guitar players for our experiments?" "Really?" the other replies, "Why did you switch?" "Well, for several reasons. We found that guitar players are far more plentiful; the lab assistants don't get so attached to them; the animal rights activists leave us alone; and there are some things even a rat won't do...However, sometimes it is very hard to extrapolate our test results to human beings."

****

The seven dwarfs are in Rome and they go on a tour of the city. After a while they go to the Vatican and Grumpy gets to meet the Pope privately. Grumpy, for once, seems to have a lot to say; he keeps asking the pontiff questions about the church, and in particular, nuns. "Your Holiness, do you have any really short nuns?" "No, my son, all our nuns are at least 5 feet tall." "Are you sure? I mean, you wouldn't have any nuns that are, say, about my height? Maybe a little shorter?" "I'm afraid not. Why do you ask?" "No reason." Pause. "Positive? Nobody in a habit that's about two feet tall?" "I'm sure." "Okay." Grumpy looks dejected at this news, and the Pope wonders why. So he listens to the dwarves as they leave the building. "What'd he say? What'd he say?" chant the other six. Grumpy says: "He said they don't have any." And the other six start chanting: "Grumpy fucked a penguin! Grumpy fucked a penguin! Grumpy fucked a penguin!"

****

A catering student decides to raise chickens, so he goes to the pet shop and buys some baby chicks. He takes the chicks home, and plants them with their heads sticking up. He waters them, but they die. He goes back to the shop and tells the proprietor that he bought defective chicks, and gets another set. This time he plants them with their heads sticking down. He waters them, but they die. Finally he sends a letter to his old college, describing the problem and asking for advice. They send a letter back asking for a soil sample.

****

Why do they let guitar players play in pizza parlours? Because pizza is the only food that you can taste over the noise.

****

What's worse than a guitar player? Two guitar players. What's worse than two guitar players? Nothing.

What's the best thing to play on a guitar? A flame-thrower.

****

What is the definition of perfect pitch? Throwing a guitar into a toilet without hitting the seat.

****

Why do so many fishermen own guitars? They make great anchors!

****

Did you hear that they outlawed 'the wave' at Loughborough University? Two poor catering students drowned at a game last year.

****

I used to play guitar on TV but my Mum told me to get off before I broke it.

****

Guitar players never get out of line, just out of tune...

****

A philosophy professor stands at the front of the classroom with the following final exam question written on the blackboard: "How do you plan to make a living with a philosophy degree?"

****

How do you get a nun pregnant? Dress her up as an altar-boy.

****

What do you call a nun with a sex change operation? A trans-sister.

****

What do you call a nun who walks in her sleep? A roaming Catholic.

****

I recently had surgery on my hand, and asked the doctor if, after surgery, I would be able to play the guitar. He said, "I'm doing surgery on your hand, not giving you a lobotomy."

****

Guitar players play requests by multiple-choice, not fill-in-the-blank.

Guitar players spend half their lives tuning and the other half playing out of tune.

✳✳✳✳

How many catering students does it take to make chocolate chip cookies? Three: one to mix the batter and two to squeeze the rabbit.

✳✳✳✳

How many catering students does it take to eat a hedgehog? Three: one to do the eating, and two to watch for cars.

✳✳✳✳

A priest asks a nun if he can walk her back to the convent. She says, "Just this once." Upon arriving, he asks if he can kiss her. She replies, "Well, alright, as long as you don't get into the habit."

✳✳✳✳

Did you hear that they've isolated the gene for guitar playing? It's the first step to a cure!

✳✳✳✳

What is the definition of innocence? A nun working in a condom factory thinking she's making sleeping bags for mice.

✳✳✳✳

"If there are any idiots in the room, will they please stand up," said the sarcastic lecturer. After a long silence, one freshman rose to his feet. "Now then, mister, why do you consider yourself an idiot?" enquired the lecturer with a sneer. "Well, actually I don't," said the student, "but I hate to see you standing up there all by yourself."

✳✳✳✳

Ice is no longer available in the drinks at the cafeterias at Aston University. The student who knew the recipe graduated.

✳✳✳✳

Guitar player: "When I die, I want to leave the world a better place." Piano player: "Don't worry, you will."

✳✳✳✳

Two ex-catering students decide to have a reunion. One decides to visit the other one, living in a big town. The visiting student gets lost and calls his friend: "Hey buddy, I am coming over but I am lost and have no idea where I am." His friend replies: "It's okay, just look at the street intersection, there will be two signs, read them to me." The lost one looks over and then says: "Okay, okay, I see them, one says Walk, the other one says Do not walk." "Oh good, you are right down the street. I'll be over to pick you up."

✳✳✳✳

Why do ghouls and demons hang out together? Because demons are a ghoul's best friend!

✳✳✳✳

Listener: "Can you read music?" Guitar player: "Not enough to hurt my playing."

✳✳✳✳

How can you get a guitar player's eyes to sparkle? Shine a light in his ears...

✳✳✳✳

What's the difference between a guitar player and a puppy? If you ignore a puppy long enough it will stop whining...

What's the difference between a guitar player and a savings bond? A savings bond eventually matures and earns money.

****

What's the difference between a guitar and a lawnmower? Your wife gets upset when the neighbours borrow the lawnmower and don't return it.

****

How is lightning like a guitar player's fingers? Neither one strikes in the same place twice.

****

What is the difference between grapes and a guitar? You take off your shoes to stomp on grapes.

****

Striking teachers today rejected the government's latest pay offer saying that it was blatantly copied from a previous offer, contained too many erasures and misspellings and was handed in late.

****

What do you call a good musician at a guitar contest? A visitor.

****

What did the guitar player get on his IQ test? Spittle.

****

Three college friends, one each from the universities of Oxford, Cambridge, and Loughborough, decided to pool their funds and go to the Olympics in Barcelona. The airfare and hotel rates ate up most of their money so they didn't have enough to get into the stadium to see the events. So they stood around the gate watching all the other people get in and then noticed that some people didn't have to pay. Whenever an athlete passed the guard with his (or her) equipment, the guard would simply nod and let them through. So the three visitors quickly trotted off to a nearby hardware shop and came back to try to get in. The Oxford student walked up to the guard and gestured at the long pole he carried. "Pole vaulting," he said, and the guard waved him through. The Cambridge student, having rigged up a ball to a length of chain, approached the guard next and showed off his wares. "Hammer throwing," he said, and the guard shrugged and waved him through. The catering student from Loughborough came last, with a roll of chain-link on his shoulder. "Fencing."

****

It was a busy day for the electric chair. Three men were up for their death sentences. The first man was a political scientist from Oxford. He was strapped into the chair and asked if he had any final comments. He replied, "I had a promising career in politics until...I was framed, I tell you - framed!" His tirade was interrupted by the flick of the switch, but nothing happened. As was the custom at this particular prison, the Oxford man was taken from the chair and allowed to live after the failed execution attempt. The second man was a computer scientist from Cambridge. His final words were, "I had a promising career in computing, but I didn't think that tampering with the national air traffic control system would crash that many planes..." Again, the electrical switch was flipped and again nothing happened. The man was released from the chair and allowed to live. The third man was an electrical engineer, named Kev, from Roehampton Institute. Kev was strapped into the chair and asked if he had any final words. He says, "I had a promising career as an electrical engineer, but, wait a moment....if you cross that red wire over there with that blue wire, this thing will work."

✳✳✳✳

A professor was grading the essay finals he had just given his class and opened the exam book of a failing student to reveal blank pages and a £100 note. The only thing written in the book was "£100 = 100% – I get an A." A month later, the student approached the professor. "I don't understand," he said, "I failed the course.

Didn't you read my final?" The professor handed the student the exam book. The student opened it to reveal £50 and the phrase "£50 = 50% – you fail!"

****

How can you tell the difference between guitar songs? By their names.

****

The graduate with a science degree asks, "Why does it work?" The graduate with an engineering degree asks, "How does it work?" The graduate with a management degree asks, "How much will it cost?" The graduate with an arts degree asks, "Do you want fries with that?"

****

A student who changes the course of history is probably taking an exam.

****

How can you tell which person is the catering student on a drilling rig? He's the one throwing bread to the helicopters.

Did you hear about the catering student who was tap-dancing? He broke his ankle when he fell into the sink.

＊＊＊＊

What do guitar players and bottles of beer have in common? They're both empty from the neck up.

＊＊＊＊

Where do guitar players play best? In traffic.

＊＊＊＊

Why don't guitar players get any mail? Because they can't read notes.

＊＊＊＊

Why don't catering students eat barbecue beans? Because they keep falling through the holes in the grill.

＊＊＊＊

There is a costume party at a mental hospital. The theme of the party is war. The first person comes up on to the stage and says, "I'm an atomic bomb." He gets his applause and steps down. The second person comes up and says, "I'm a hydrogen bomb." Again, there's applause and he steps down. And then a naked little man comes up to the stage and says, "I'm dynamite." Everybody runs away hysterically. When one of them is asked why, he says, "Didn't you see how small his fuse was?"

****

You're lost in the desert and you see Bugs Bunny, a cactus and a good guitar player. Who do you ask for directions? You might as well try the cactus, the other two are figments of your imagination.

****

You're driving down the street and you see an accordion and a guitar – which one do you hit first? The accordion: business before pleasure.

****

Two nuns are walking down an alley at night. Two guys jump out and start raping them. The first nun looks to heaven and says, "Forgive them Father, for they know not what they're doing." The second nun looks up and says, "This one does."

****

Why do some people take an instant aversion to guitar players? It saves time.

****

Two Texas Longhorn students and a catering student were driving through the Texas countryside when their car broke down. Luckily, they were near a farmhouse. So they knocked on the door and asked the gruff old farmer if they could stay the night. The farmer agreed, but only on one bizarre condition. He told them to go out into his field, pick any fruit or vegetable they could find, then return to the farmhouse. Some time later, the two Longhorns found themselves dead and in line at the Pearly Gates. St Peter was there, listening to their tale. "Okay," said St Peter, "you went out and found some fruits and vegetables. How did you die?" "Well," continued one of the Longhorns, "my friend here returned first with a cherry. Then the farmer pointed his gun at him and commanded, 'Stick that cherry up your ass, and if you laugh I'll shoot you.'" "And?" prompted St Peter. "He laughed, and the farmer shot him." "Why did you laugh?" St Peter asked the second Longhorn. "It tickled," he said. "Then it was my turn," continued the first Longhorn. "I had also brought a cherry, and the farmer pointed his gun at me and told me the same thing. I laughed and he shot me." "And why did you laugh?" St Peter asked. "I saw the catering student coming up the walkway with a watermelon."

Why do bluegrass guitar pickers always die with their boots on? So they won't stub their toes when they kick the bucket.

****

Did you hear the one about the man who opened a dry-cleaning business next door to the convent? He knocked on the door and asked the Mother Superior if she had any dirty habits.

****

What kind of fun does a priest have? Nun.

****

What is the difference between a terrorist and a guitar player? Terrorists have sympathizers.

****

What's the difference between a guitar and a flute? Flutes don't burn!

****

Don't tell my mum I'm a guitar player. She thinks I'm a piano player in a whorehouse.

Down the Pub

Jokes for the Local

A woman arrives home after a shopping trip, and is horrified to find her husband in bed with a pretty, firm young woman. She is about to storm out of the house when her husband stops her by saying, "Honey, before you go, at least give me one chance to explain how on earth this happened!" The woman decides that she owes him this much at least, so stops to listen to his story. He begins, "Well, I was driving home in the pouring rain and I saw this poor thing at the bus stop, soaked. There's a bus strike on, so I offered her a lift and it turned out that she was really hungry. So I brought her home and gave her some of last night's leftovers. I noticed her clothes were shabby so I offered her that jumper you wore once and didn't like and those trousers that don't fit you any more. I noticed her shoes were full of holes, so I gave her a pair of your shoes that you never liked, too. Anyway, so just as she was about to leave she asked me, 'And is there anything else that your wife doesn't use any more?' So here we are!"

****

There's a bar where all the regulars are really into body-building. The owner is a body-builder and he only employs body-builders as bar staff. The walls are covered in body-builder photos and they are always having body-builder competitions. On the wall behind the bar is a sign that says, "Win 1,000: Beat The Bartender." Written below it are the rules to the competition: "The bartenders are so strong that, after any one of them has squeezed a lemon with his bare hands, nobody can ever squeeze anything else out of it: anyone who can will win the prize." The space around the bar is filled with photos of people who have tried to win the competition but failed. One day a skinny little man walks into the bar and announces that he'd like to try for the prize. It is a Saturday night, the bar is packed and everybody starts to laugh. The guy's head is about the size of the bartender's hand and nobody believes he has a chance. The bartender picks up a lemon and starts to squeeze it. The juice gushes out quickly, but after a few seconds it stops as the man squeezes everything out: juice, pips, pith and even squashed rind. The bartender then hands the lemon to the tiny old man. The man puts his hand around the wizened, almost unrecognizable lemon and starts to squeeze. To the astonishment of everyone present, juice begins to drip from the fruit and before long seven, eight, nine, and then ten full drops have been squeezed! Everyone starts to cheer and the bartender coughs up the money. "That's amazing – really amazing," says the bartender. "Are you a secret body-builder? Are you a martial arts expert? How did you do it?" "Easy enough," says the man, "I work for the Inland Revenue."

✳✳✳✳

A man gets on a plane and is surprised to be seated next to a parrot. He doesn't really say anything, but thinks it a bit odd. When the stewardess comes around to see if anyone wants drinks, she asks the man. He says he'd like a cup of coffee, and as he says this the parrot squawks, "And get me a whisky on the rocks, bitch!" The stewardess is visibly shaken and walks off. She comes back a few minutes later and hands the parrot his whisky, but she has forgotten the man's coffee. The man points this out and asks again. As he does so, the parrot squawks, "And bring me another whisky on the rocks, you slut!" The stewardess goes off again and comes back – again with the parrot's drink, but with no coffee for the man. The man is a bit sick of this so he decides to use the parrot's approach. So he barks, "That's twice I've asked you for coffee, you useless cow, what the hell do I have to do to get a friggin' drink around here?" The next thing the man knows he's been picked up by two huge stewards and thrown out of the plane. He has the parrot next to him and, as they both start their plunge to earth, the bird turns to him and says, "Phew-ee, for someone who can't fly, you sure are one gobby bastard!"

✱✱✱✱

A man walks into a bar. He has a monkey with him. The man orders a drink, and while he drinks it the monkey just runs wild around the whole bar, annoying everyone, including the man. While the man is drinking, the monkey runs up to the pool table, climbs up a cue, grabs the cueball, sticks it in his mouth and swallows it. The barkeeper walks up to the man and says, "Did you see what your bloody monkey just did?" "No, what did the little prick do this time?" replies the man. "He just swallowed the cueball from my pool table, that's what he just did," says the barkeeper, angrily. "Well, hopefully it'll kill the little bastard, because I'm effing sick of him and his little tricks," says the man. He then finishes his drink and leaves. A couple of weeks later the same man enters the bar with the same monkey. He orders the same drink and the monkey runs wild around the whole bar, in the same manner as the previous time. While the man is drinking, the monkey finds some peanuts on a tray on the bar. He picks one up, sticks it up his arse, takes it out again and eats it. The barkeeper finds this disgusting, so he walks up to the man again. "Did you see what your bloody monkey just did?" "No, what did the little prick do this time?" sighs the man. "He just stuck a peanut up his arse, took it out and ate it," says the barkeeper. "Well, what do you expect?" asks the monkey's owner. "Ever since he ate that sodding cueball he has to measure everything first!"

****

A guy walks into a pub and asks for ten tequila shots. "Sorry, mate," the bartender says, "but that's too much for one go." The guy says, "I just found out that my brother is a homosexual and I'm finding it really hard to deal with," so the bartender says that's OK and that he can have his ten shots of tequila. The next day the very same man walks into the same pub and asks for 20 tequila shots. "Sorry, mate," the bartender says, "but that's too much for one go." The guy says, "I just found out that my son is a homosexual and I'm finding it really hard to deal with," so the bartender says that's OK and that he can have his 20 shots of tequila. The next day the very same man walks into the same pub and asks for 30 tequila shots. The bartender, who's had enough, says to him, "What the hell's the matter – doesn't anyone in your house like pussy?" "Oh, yes," the guy replies, "my wife!"

****

A man walks into a bar. He has a frog attached to his forehead. He says to the barman, "I'll have a gin and tonic, please." The barman pours him the drink – all the while looking at the frog – and gives it to the man. "I'm sorry to be so curious, sir, but I was wondering how on earth you ended up with that thing on you?" he asks. Quick as a flash the frog replies, "I don't know; it started out as a wart on my bum five years ago!"

****

An old boy sits down in his local and asks the barman, an old friend, for a drink. The old boy is wearing a big, old-fashioned stovepipe hat, a black jacket and waistcoat, and a false, square beard. The barman serves him a drink and says, "You off to a party tonight, then?" "Yup," says the man, "I've come as my love life." "What are you going on about?" asks the barman. "You look like Abraham Lincoln." "Indeed I do," says the man, "my last four scores were seven years ago!"

****

Two little old ladies are sitting outside their nursing home having a smoke because it's a no-smoking establishment. It begins to rain and one of them pulls out a condom, cuts the end off and puts it over her cigarette, keeping it nice and dry. The other lady asks her what that thing is. "It's a condom," the little old lady replies. "And where do you get them from?" her friend asks. "Any chemist will sell them to you," the lady replies. The next day, the woman's friend goes off to her local chemist and walks up to the counter. "I'd like some condoms, please, young man," she says to the man behind the counter. "Yes, ma'am," he says, giving her a funny look. "Would you like any particular brand?" "Not really," the little old lady replies, "as long as they'll fit a Camel!"

****

It was the last day of nursery school and all the children had bought presents for their teacher, whom they'd never see again. Because it was the last day, the teacher decided to make a game of guessing what the presents were. First of all the sweetshop owner's daughter comes up with a box. It is quite heavy so the teacher shakes it and says, "Is this full of sweets?" "Yes, miss, it is," replies the little girl. Then the flowershop owner's son comes up with a box. It is very light, so the teacher shakes it and says, "Are these flowers?" "Yes, miss, they are," replies the little boy. Then the wine merchant's son comes up with a box. It is very heavy, so the teacher shakes it a little and notices that it is leaking a bit. She touches a drop of the liquid with her finger and tastes it. "Is this full of wine?" she says. "No, miss," comes the reply. So the teacher tries another drop and then says, "Is this full of champagne?" "No, miss," comes the reply. "In that case I give up," says the teacher, "What's in the box?" "A puppy," the boy says.

****

A guy walks into a bar and orders a double whisky – straight. As he begins to drink he reaches into his wallet and pulls out a photograph. He takes a quick peek at it and then puts it back quickly in his wallet. He then finishes his whisky, calls the barman over and orders another. He begins to drink it and, as he does so, he reaches into his wallet and pulls out the photograph again, looks at it and then puts it quickly away. He continues doing this for about an hour. Eventually the barman asks him, "Hey, mate, what's with the photo? I'm not worried by the amount you're drinking, I'd just really like to have a look at the picture – what on earth is it?" The man replies, "It's a photograph of my wife. When she starts to look good, I know it's time to go home!"

****

A man walks into a bar with a really trendy new shirt on. The bartender is a woman and she says, "Hey, nice shirt. Really suits you. Where d'you get it?" "Oh, René Kent," comes the reply and the woman is impressed. Shortly afterwards, a man walks into the bar with a really trendy new pair of trousers on. The bartender says, "Hey, nice trousers. Really suit you. Where d'you get them?" "Oh, René Kent," comes the reply and the woman is impressed. Then another man walks into the bar with a really trend, new pair of shoes on. The bartender says, "Hey, nice shoes. Really suit you. Where d'you get them?" "Oh, René Kent," comes the reply and the woman is impressed. After a while the door to the bar suddenly bursts open and a man dressed only in his underpants runs in. "Who the hell do you think you are?" asks the bartender. "I'm René Kent!" comes the strained reply.

****

Two men are drinking together in the bar on the top floor of the Empire State Building. The first one says to the second, "You know what? I bet you a hundred bucks I can jump out of that window and not hurt myself." "Bullshit – you're on," says the second man and the first man walks over to the window, opens it and jumps out. Two seconds later – whoosh! – and he is thrown back in. The second guy admits that this is incredible but thinks it must be a fluke, so he offers double or nothing if the first guy can somehow do it again. The first guy takes him up on the bet and walks over to the window, opens it and jumps out again. Two seconds later – whoosh! – and he is thrown back in again. The second guy is amazed again, but now he figures that there must be one of those freak gusts of wind that you get around tall buildings. So he says to the first guy, "How about this, then: double or quits again, but this time I jump out of the window?" "You're on," says the first guy and the second guy walks up to the window, opens it and jumps out. Five seconds later – whoosh! splat! – he is squashed flat and dead on the sidewalk, 70 floors below. The barman pours another drink and says to the remaining man, "You can be a real wanker when you've been drinking, Superman!"

✱✱✱✱

Four men are sitting in a bar when a guy comes up to them and offers them a bet. He reckons that he can place a pint glass on the bar, 25 feet away, stand behind their table and piss right into – and fill – the pint glass. The men all confer and decide that there's no way this guy can do it. They quickly stump up the £100 that he's offering. The man walks to the bar, places an empty pint glass on it and returns to where the men are. He stands there, drops his trousers and begins to piss. It goes everywhere apart from the pint glass – he doesn't even get close to it and even pisses on the men with whom he's made the bet. They can't help but laugh at his piss-poor effort. When the guy has finished, he hands over the £100. One of the men turns and asks him, "What the hell made you think you could fill that glass all the way over there?" "I never thought I could," said the guy, "but I bet the bartender £500 that I could piss all over you blokes and you'd just laugh about it!"

****

A drunken bum has collapsed on the corner of the street. A policeman comes up to him and asks him what he's up to. "Well," the bum says, "apparently the world rotates on a 24-hour cycle, so I'm waiting for my house to come by. I don't think it'll be long, though, because I saw my neighbour not so long ago!"

****

A man walks into a bar and sits down for a beer. Now, this guy likes his beer, so when he sees a sign behind the bar that claims, "A lifetime's free beer for he or she who can pass the test," he starts thinking this could be his lucky day. When the owner of the bar comes in, the man says to him, "So what's this about some test, then?" The owner says, "Well, I'll tell you this much: many have tried and many have failed my test and to this day none has passed! It consists of three parts. The first part is simple: just drink one whole gallon of pure jalapeño-laden tequila in one go, without shuddering or uttering a noise. The second part is a little more difficult: there's a vicious croc outside – a pet of mine – and he's got a sore tooth. You have to wrestle him unconscious and get that tooth out using only your bare hands! The third part is tough, too: there's a woman upstairs who hasn't had an orgasm in her 70 years on this earth, and you have to make her come! Complete the three and you will drink free beer in this bar to the end of your days!" Now the man thinks that maybe it's going to be too tall an order, and he settles down for a decent evening's drinking. After a couple of hours the beer brain takes over and he starts to think, "You know, I reckon I could chin that 'Kila, take out that 'croc and I could do that bird – hell, yes!" So he shouts for the owner to come out and watch him pass the test: "Gizza go on that tequila, why don'tcha?" The owner puts the gallon jar of tequila on the bar and the man picks it up. He drains the whole huge bottle without saying a word and the tears stream from his eyes. Then he walks outside and for the next 20 minutes the sound of beating, ripping and screaming come from the backyard. Then, the door is kicked open and the man is standing there with his shirt ripped to shreds, covered in mud and sweat and panting for breath. And he says, "Now, where the hell's that woman with the bad tooth?"

****

There's a regular-drinking guy whose local is called Sally's Legs after an old song. One Friday he knocks off work early, planning to spend the entire evening there getting steadily drunk. Unfortunately he doesn't count on the bar not opening until after work time, so he is forced to sit and wait for the staff to show up. As he is parked outside, a suspicious policeman walks up to his window and raps on it. "Yes, officer?" he says, "what can I do for you?" "What do you think you're doing hanging around here at this time of day?" says the policeman. "Well, sir," says the man, "I'm just waiting for Sally's Legs to open so I can be the first in to get a drink!"

✳✳✳✳

A drunken bum has too much to drink one night in his local. He can hardly stand up, but he knows that he absolutely has to take a piss. He staggers over to the toilets, getting his cock out as he does so. He crashes through the door, penis in hand, only to bump into two women because he's stumbled into the ladies instead. One of the women screams and shouts, "This is for ladies, my good man!" and the bum replies, as he fumbles to put away his thing, "So is this, lady!"

✳✳✳✳

Once upon a time there was a very keen policeman who liked to hang around outside bars and nab people as they left to drive home with too much alcohol inside them. One night he's waiting outside his regular haunt and he sees someone come staggering out. The guy walks up to first one car and tries his key in the lock, then the next and then the next. None of them opens for him, and it isn't until he gets to the fifth car in the car park that he gets in and, after five minutes' fumbling, starts the engine. He backs the car up, narrowly missing most of the others in the car park, and he wheelspins across the road and away. The keen policeman follows him quickly with his lights already flashing and his siren screaming. He pulls the guy over only just round the corner from the bar and takes it easy as he warns him and gives him the breathalyzer test. To the by-now-smug cop's surprise, the guy does not seem to have a drop of alcohol in his system. "What's that all about, then?" asks the amazed young policeman, to which the man replies, "I'm tonight's designated decoy, officer!"

****

A man is sitting in a rough bar drinking. He orders a fresh pint, but is suddenly overcome with the urge to go to the toilet. He doesn't trust anyone in the crummy bar, but he has to go, so he scribbles on a cigarette paper, "I spat in this: don't drink it!" and he gums the paper to the side of his pint glass. He goes off to the toilet and comes back a couple of minutes later to find another cigarette paper stuck to his glass. On it is written, "So did we!"

****

A little boy and his younger brother were bored one day so decided to do interesting, grown-up stuff like swearing. The older boy says to his brother, "I know: next time we're downstairs with mum, I'll say 'Hell' and you can say 'Ass' – how's about that?" The younger boy nods his agreement and they troop off downstairs to have their breakfast. As they walk into the kitchen their mother says to the older child, "And what would you like for your breakfast, dear?" to which he replies, "Well, hell, mum, I'd like some cornflakes, please." Upon hearing such profanity, the mother whacks the child really hard around the back of the head. The boy starts crying and runs off upstairs. The mother turns to the younger boy and looks him square in the face. "And what would you like for your breakfast, young man?" she says. "I don't really know, mum," he starts to say, "but you can bet your ass it won't be cornflakes!"

****

A farmer is in court fighting for a large insurance claim following a serious road accident he didn't cause. He is being questioned by the insurance company's lawyer and is being given a hard time because of his conflicting statements. The lawyer asks, "So, Farmer Brown; you are trying to claim substantial damages from the person you claim caused the accident, yet I have a sworn statement from the police officer who was present at the scene claiming that when asked how you were feeling, immediately following the accident, you said, and I quote, 'I'm fine, officer; in fact, I've never felt better in my life!'" There is a gasp around the courtroom. "Now, is this or is this not true, Farmer Brown?" continues the brief. "Well, yes, but…" the farmer starts, but he is interrupted by the barrister: "Just a simple yes or no answer will suffice, Farmer Brown." "Yes," says Farmer Brown. After a while, it was the turn of the lawyer for the farmer's insurance to question him. "So, Farmer Brown, tell us the exact circumstances surrounding your statement of good health that my learned friend just made you discuss," the barrister says to the farmer. "Well, sir, as I was trying to say," Farmer Brown explains, "I had just had this horrific accident and I was lying in the middle of the road injured. My horse had been injured, too, and so had my dog. So, after a little while a policeman comes up to the horse, sees it struggling for life and shoots it. Then he walks over to my dog, hears it howling and shoots it. Then he walks over to me, bleeding on the ground, and says, 'How are you, sir?' Now what the hell would you have said in those circumstances?"

****

It's a beautiful day in County Kerry and people all over the county are sitting outside the pubs enjoying stout by the pint. In a cosy pub one man turns to his friend and says, "You see that man over there?" His friend nods. "Have you noticed that he's the spitting image of me? It's bloody uncanny, that's what it is, to be sure. I'm going to go over there and ask him a few questions: after all, 'tis not every day that you get to meet someone who could be your exact double, now is it?" And off he goes to see the man he is talking about. He taps him on the shoulder and says, "Excuse me, I couldn't help noticing from over there that you look almost exactly the same as me. I was thinking what an incredible coincidence that was!" "Me too, me too," replies the man, "I noticed you earlier and I was just about to come over and talk when I saw you coming over anyway. 'Tis an incredible thing to be sure. So whereabouts are you from?" he asks. "Well, I'm from Galway, originally," says the first man. "No, that's incredible!" says the second, "Me too! It's just unbelievable. What street did you live in?" "Why, I lived in Moher Street for 20 years, so I did," comes the reply from the first man. "No! I can't believe it – I did, too," says the second. "And what number in that street was it?" he asks. "Why, I lived in number 20." "Unbelievable," comes the reply, "that's the number I lived in. And what were your parents' names?" "Ruari and Siobhan," comes the reply. "This really is uncanny," the first man says, "those are the exact names of my parents, too!" At this point, the two men continue talking the new bar staff turn up for their shift. The new guy asks, "Anything happening?" and the guy about to go replies, "No, not really; just the Rix twins drunk again!"

****

A man walks into a bar. It is totally empty apart from the barman, who walks over to serve him. The man buys his beer and sits down in a corner. He then decides he'd like a chaser, so he walks up to the bar again. The barman has just gone out back for a second, but the guy hears a little squeaky voice say, "Nice shirt, mate." He looks around and he can't see anyone anywhere. He turns around to go and sit down and hears a similar voice say, "Great arse." He spins around quickly but he can't see anyone and the barman is definitely still out back. The man is a bit put-out so he decides to go and buy some smokes. As he approaches the cigarette machine he hears the most dreadful swearing, aimed at him. "You miserable wanker piece of crap; you suck, you dumbarse twat!" The insults seem to be pouring from the machine, so he retreats and goes back to the bar. The barman is back by this time, so the man asks him, "Look, pal; what's going on with the funny voices in this place?" The barman looks at him and says, "Of course, well, you must mean the complimentary peanuts; and I'm sorry, but the cigarette machine is out of order!"

****

A trampy-looking man walks into a bar with a small dog under his arm. He walks straight up to the bar and puts the dog on it. The barman tells him that animals aren't allowed in the bar and that he'll have to leave. The man says that this dog is special, that it can talk and that if anyone wants to bet him $500 he'll take them on. The bartender laughs, but decides to indulge the old guy anyway and takes him up on the bet. So the guy turns to the dog and says slowly, "Now, Jock; what do we call the thing on top of this bar that keeps the rain off our heads when the weather's bad and the sun off our heads when the weather's good?" The dog shakes his head and then barks, "ROOF!" The barman looks at the man and bursts out laughing. "I'm not paying for that crap – you must be joking!" So the man says, "OK, OK, I'll show you again," and he turns to the dog and says slowly, "Jock, who was the greatest baseball player of all time?" The dog shakes his head and then barks, "RUTH!" The bartender hops over the bar, picks up the dog and the man and throws them both out. As they both lie on the sidewalk the dog looks up at the man and says sheepishly, "Should I have answered DiMaggio?"

✳✳✳✳

Had it off yet?

Jokes for the
Healing Process

A man is suffering from premature ejaculation, so he decides to see a doctor about it. The doctor says there is nothing physically wrong with the man, but that he has a mental block. The doctor suggests that to cure the problem the man should try to shock himself when he feels that he is about to ejaculate. The doctor suggests using a starting pistol: the man should fire it when he feels the need, and that this should help prevent the problem. The man thanks the doctor and runs off to the sports shop to get himself a starting pistol. He rushes home to his wife, whom he finds naked on the bed, all ready for him. Things go well, and they find themselves in the 69 position. Moments later, the man feels the urge to ejaculate, so pulls the trigger.

The next day the man finds himself back at the doctor's surgery. The doctor asks, "So, how did it go? Any improvements?" "Not really," begins the man, "When I fired the pistol, my wife crapped on my face and bit three inches off my penis, and my neighbour jumped naked out of the cupboard with his hands in the air!"

✳✳✳✳

At a conference, four surgeons are discussing operating on people from different professions. The first surgeon says, "My favourite are accountants. I love to open up accountants: when you do, everything is numbered." The second surgeon says, "Not bad, but you should try electricians. I love to open up electricians: when you do, everything is colour-coded." The third surgeon says, "Not bad, but you should try filing clerks. I love to open up filing clerks: when you do, everything is in alphabetical order." The fourth surgeon says, "Not bad, not bad, but you're all wrong. The easiest to operate on are lawyers. I love to open up lawyers: when you do, there are no guts, no heart, no spine, and the head and arse are completely interchangeable!"

****

A man goes to his doctor complaining that he cannot get his wife pregnant. The doctor is a little surprised because the man is 75. Not wishing to stand in his way, however, the doctor asks the man to provide him with a sperm sample and gives him a jar to place it in. Two days later the old man walks back into the surgery and gives the doctor the empty jar back. "What's that all about?" asks the doctor and the man begins his explanation. "Well, first of all, doc I tried with my left hand. That didn't work, so I tried with my right hand. That didn't work either, so I asked my wife to help. She's younger than me and she tried first with her left hand and then her right, but there was still no joy. Then she tried with her mouth – even between her teeth – but still nothing. As a last resort we called the neighbour over from next door. The woman tried, with both hands and then with the mouth, too, but it just really wouldn't work." The doctor was a bit shocked by this and asked, "Even your neighbour?" 'Yes, doc," said the man. "We tried and tried and tried, but no matter what we did, none of us could get the lid off that bloody jar!"

****

A really beautiful woman makes the mistake one day of going to see an unscrupulous gynaecologist. He is badly behaved at the best of times, but when he sets eyes on this fantastic-looking creature he can hardly hold himself back. He tells her to undress immediately and proceeds to examine her without even asking what her problem is. He begins by stroking her thigh. As he does so, he says, "Do you know what I'm doing?" and the woman replies, "Yes, doctor; you are checking the area around my pubic region for any abrasions or abnormalities in case my problems stem from there." "That's very good," says the doctor, who then begins to stroke her breasts. "And do you know what I'm doing now?" he asks. "Yes, doctor; you are checking me for any odd lumps or abnormalities in my mammary region." "That's very good," says the doctor, who then takes out his "pork thermometer" and proceeds to rub it on the woman's pussy. "And do you know what I'm doing now?" he asks. "Yes, doctor," the woman replies. "You are contracting herpes, which is the reason I came in here today!"

****

A man and a woman meet up at a party. They get on well and it is lust at first sight, so they go back to the woman's house to make the beast with two backs. They are getting it on and the man takes off his shirt and then the woman's shirt. He then gets up and washes his hands. A few minutes later he removes his trousers and her skirt. He then gets up and washes his hands. A few minutes later he removes his underwear and then her underwear. He then gets up and washes his hands. After this the woman gives him a strange look and says, "You must be a dentist." "Why, that's right," he says. "How on earth did you know?" "Easy," she says. "You wash your hands after every procedure, and the only people who do that are dentists." So they carry on, and they end up having sex. Afterwards, when the dentist has washed his hands, they are talking. The woman says, "You must be a really good dentist." The man replies, "Why, yes; I am, as it happens. I was top in my class at dental academy and I have won prizes around the world for my dentistry. How do you know?" The woman says, "Because I didn't feel a thing!"

✳✳✳✳

A husband and wife are talking one night at dinner and the wife announces that she's thinking of having her breasts enlarged with plastic surgery. The husband says, "You don't need to pay some quack to make your tits bigger, honey: I know how you can do it for pretty much nothing!" "Oh, really?" says the wife, "and how would that be then?" "Just rub toilet paper in between your tits twice a day," says the husband. "Oh, really?" says the wife, "and how on earth does that work, then?" "I don't know," says the husband, "but it sure did the trick for your arse!"

✳✳✳✳

A man goes to hospital for a circumcision operation and he wakes up in the morning surrounded by hospital staff. He wonders what the hell is going on and then he feels an enormous piece of padding between his legs. The head surgeon says to him, "Look here, sir; we're all really, really sorry, but I'm afraid we made a mistake and got a bit carried away with the chopping. We've ended up giving you a complete sex change operation." The man screams and shouts and cries his eyes out. "Oh, my God," he says eventually. "There's so much I'll never be able to do again. I will never, ever be able to experience an erection." The surgeon strokes him on the head and says, "Of course you will, of course you will. It just won't be yours, that's all!"

****

A man and a woman could not have children and spent a long time working out why this was. Eventually it turned out that it was the man's problem, so they decided to get the woman artificially inseminated. They booked an appointment at the clinic, but at the last minute the husband was called away on urgent business, so the wife had to go alone. She walked into the clinic and was shown to her room for insemination. After a couple of minutes a doctor walked in and told her to remove her clothes from the bottom half of her body and to lie back on the bed with her feet in the stirrups. The woman complied. After she had done this, the doctor dropped his trousers and pants and began to walk towards her. "Er, doctor, what on earth are you doing?" she asked, a little worried. "What's the problem?" said the doctor. "Don't you want to get pregnant?" "Well, yes, doctor, I do…" began the wife. "Well, just lie back and think of England," said the doctor, "because we're out of the bottled variety and you'll have to take what's on tap!"

****

A man goes to the doctor with a strange problem. "Doctor, whenever I break wind there is no smell at all. It's really strange, and no matter what I eat, I get the same result – no smell whatsoever!" The doctor has a cursory investigation and then asks the man if he can possibly break wind there and then. The man drops his trousers and pants and farts extremely loudly. The doctor sniffs at the air a couple of times and immediately says, "Oh yes, this is a common one. I know exactly what the problem is," and he walks out of the room. He comes straight back with a six-foot pole with a large brass hook on the end. "Jesus Christ, doctor; what the hell are you going to do with that pole?" asks the man. "I'm going to open the bloody window," says the doctor, "You've got a blocked nose!"

****

"Doctor, I'm not feeling so well," says the patient. "Would it be possible to run some tests?" "Sure thing," says the doctor. "Stop by the surgery some time today and ask the nurse. Bring a urine sample, too. We'll talk about the results over the phone." The patient does as instructed and waits for the results. One day passes: nothing. The following day he gets a phone call from his doctor who says: "Well, I have good news and bad news." "What is the good news?" the patient asks. "You have 24 hours left to live." "WHAT? What's the bad news, then?" "I forgot to call you yesterday."

****

348

A psychiatrist and a proctologist became good friends and agreed to share offices to cut down on expenses. To economize even further, they had just one sign printed:

Dr John Wayland, Psychiatrist

Dr Stan Smith, Proctologist

SPECIALIZING IN ODDS AND ENDS

****

A man has been suffering from a tenacious cold for the past week. He goes to his doctor, who prescribes him some tablets. A week later, the same guy comes back, every bit as ill as before. Frowning, the doctor prescribes him a stronger version of the drugs and sends him home. It doesn't work, though, and the man comes back a week later just as miserable as before. The medicine obviously doesn't work and the doctor reckons it is a case of 'intractable cold of an unknown nature'. "All right," says the doctor. "What I want you to do is to open your bedroom window tonight and spend an hour naked in front of it." "What?" exclaims the patient. "I'll catch pneumonia!" "Pneumonia is fine," the doctor replies. "I can treat pneumonia."

****

A nurse walks into a ward to see patients early in the morning. "Well, nurse, it seems to me you got up from the wrong side of the bed this morning," says one patient. "Why do you say that?" "You're wearing the surgeon's slippers."

****

After years of battling with himself, John finally went to a psychiatrist. "Doc," he said, "I've got trouble. Every time I get into bed, I think there's somebody under it. If I get under the bed, I think there's somebody on top of it. I *know* there's no one in my bed or under my bed, but it doesn't matter, I have to check. You have to help me, it's been going on for years and I am going mad." "It's all in your head. Just put yourself in my hands for two years," said the shrink. "Come to me three times a week, and I'll cure your fears." "How much do you charge?" asked John, suspiciously. " 50 per visit." " 50, three times a week, for two years?" chokes John. "No way!" and he storms off. Six months later the doctor meets John on the street. "Why didn't you ever come to see me again?" asked the psychiatrist. " 50 a visit? A bartender cured me for the price of a beer." "Is that so?" says the doctor scornfully, "How?" "He told me to cut the legs off the bed!"

✳✳✳✳

A lady wanted bigger breasts, so she went to her doctor to refer her to a plastic surgeon. "I can do that," said her doctor, "but I would like you to try a simple exercise before surgery or drugs." He stood up to demonstrate, holding his arms straight out to the side, rotating them counter-clockwise, and singing, "Ashes to ashes, dust to dust, if I do this enough, I'll have a big bust." "Do that as often as you can and come back in a week." One week later, she's back at the doctor, and tells him that it didn't work. "How often have you done the exercise?" the doctor asks her. "Three to four times a day," she says. "Bah! Not nearly half enough!" the doctor scoffs. "Do it at least 30 to 40 times a day and come back in a week." She tries this, performing the exercise whenever she can, which means that she does it on her local Tesco parking lot, before getting into her car. "Ashes to ashes, dust to dust, if I do this enough, I'll have a big bust." The driver of the car parked next to hers turns around, looks at her with round eyes and asks: "Do you see Dr. Johnson?" "Well, yes, as a matter of fact. How did you know?" she queries. The man faces her, places both hands on his hips, moves his hips in a circular motion, and says, "Hickory dickory dock..."

****

A young lady entered the doctor's office carrying an infant. "Doctor," she explained, "the baby seems to be ailing. Instead of gaining weight, he lost three ounces this week." The doctor examined the child and then started to squeeze the lady's breasts. Too stunned to react, she lets him unbutton her blouse, deftly removing the bra and stroking her right nipple, emitting a thoughtful "Mmmm..." "Young lady," he announced, "No wonder the baby is losing weight, you haven't got any milk!" "Of course not!" she shrieked. "It's not my child; it's my sister's!"

****

After the baby was born, the panicked Japanese father went to see the obstetrician. "Doctor," he said, "I'm a little upset. You see, my baby daughter has red hair. She can't possibly be mine." "Don't worry," the doctor said genially. "Even though you and your wife both have black hair, one of your ancestors might have contributed red hair to the gene pool." "This is impossible," the man insisted. "We're pure Oriental. There have never been redheads in any of our families." "Well," said the doctor, "let me ask you this. How often do you have sex?" The man seemed ashamed. "I've been working very hard for the past year. We only made love once or twice a month." "There you have it!" the doctor said confidently. "It's just rust."

✳✳✳✳

Three patients in a mental institution prepare for an examination given by the head psychiatrist. If the patients pass the exam, they will be free to leave the hospital and go back to a normal life. However, if they fail, the institution will detain them for another five years. The doctor takes the three patients to the top of a diving board looking over an empty swimming pool, and asks the first patient to jump. The first patient jumps headfirst into the pool and breaks both arms. The second patient, who has just witnessed what has happened, jumps enthusiastically into the empty pool and breaks both legs. The third patient looks over the side and backs off from the diving board. "Congratulations! You're a free man. Just tell me: why didn't you jump?" asked the doctor. "Well, doc, I can't swim!"

✳✳✳✳

A man, looking like a mechanic in stained overalls, comes into the reception of the posh local surgery, full of mothers and their children, well-to-do professionals and retired people looking at him with disdain. He approaches the receptionist and says, in a voice that is altogether too loud for this sort of place: "There's something wrong with my dick." "We don't use this kind of language here," says the nurse reprovingly. "Please try again and be more polite this time: say you have a problem with your ear or something." The man seems about to explode but, with visible effort, decides just to let it go. He takes a deep breath and says: "There is a problem with my ear." "Is there, my dear?" the receptionist says smugly. "What kind of problem?" The man gives her an evil grin and says: "I can't piss out of it."

✳✳✳✳

Bill has a problem and goes to the doctor. He has trouble getting an erection. The doctor examines him fully and explains to him that he's got a problem with the muscles around the base of his penis. They are very damaged and there is currently no known treatment. The doctor does offer a solution, however, and that is a new experimental cure which involves grafting muscles from a baby elephant's trunk onto the base of his penis. Bill is a bit worried by this, but he figures it's better to try and fail rather than never to have sex again, so he agrees to try it out. Months later, Bill is fully recovered from the operation and finds that everything is functioning normally. He takes his girlfriend out for a candlelit dinner with the hope of a romantic encounter later. About halfway through the meal, Bill starts to feel uncomfortable around his groin and the feeling gets worse and worse as the meal continues. Eventually Bill can bear it no longer and unzips his fly to release the pressure. As soon as he does this, his penis springs out, bounces to the top of the table, grabs a bread roll and returns to his underpants. His girlfriend squeals with shock – and possibly delight. "Bill – that was amazing! Can you do it again?" Bill replies, "Probably, darling, but I don't think I've got room up my arse for another bread roll!"

****

It took Bob a little while to accept the fact that his penis seemed to grow. Of course he was delighted, as was his wife, but it soon grew to an impressive 20 inches and Bob decided it was time to go and see a doctor. After an initial examination, the physician explained to the couple that, though rare, Bob's condition could be cured through corrective surgery. "We just have to operate – a simple thing, really – and all will be fine again." "And how long will Bob be on crutches?" the wife asked anxiously. "Crutches? Why would he need crutches?" the surprised doctor asked. "Well," said the wife suspiciously, "You are planning to lengthen Bob's legs, aren't you?"

****

The doctor entered the waiting room. "I have some good news for you, Mrs Douglas." "Pardon me," she interrupted coldly, "but it's Miss." The doctor corrected himself and said, "I have some bad news for you, Miss Douglas."

****

A woman went to her doctor for a follow-up visit after the doctor had prescribed testosterone (a male hormone) to her. She was a little worried about some of the side-effects she was experiencing. "Doctor, the hormones you've been giving me have really helped. I feel much better, but I'm wondering if you got the dosage right. I've started growing hair in places that I've never grown hair before." The doctor reassured her. "A little hair growth is a perfectly normal side-effect of testosterone. Just where has this hair appeared?" "On my balls."

****

A woman went to the surgery. She was seen by one of the new doctors, but after about four minutes in the examination room she burst out, screaming as she ran down the hall. An older doctor stopped and asked her what the problem was, and she explained, obviously in shock. The older doctor marched back to the first and demanded, "What's the matter with you? Mrs Johnston is 67 years old: she has four grown children and seven grandchildren, and you told her she was pregnant?" The new doctor smiled smugly as he continued to write on his clipboard. "Cured her hiccups, though, didn't I?"

****

A man goes to the doctor with a terrible problem with bad breath. "I've tried everything, doctor," he says, nearly in tears. "I changed toothpaste ten times, tried mints, mouthwash – you name it. I can't get rid of this terrible odour." The doctor nods and asks the guy to get undressed. After a thorough examination, he allows him to put his clothes back on. "You seem to have a rash around your anus. We will have to treat this first. In the meantime, try not to chew your fingernails."

****

A man walks into the office of an eminent psychiatrist and sits down to explain his problem. "Yes, well, you see, I've got this problem," the man says. "I keep hallucinating that I'm a dog. A large, white, hairy Dulux dog. It's crazy. I don't know what to do!" "Ah, a common canine complex," said the doctor soothingly. "It's all right: we can cure this together if we work hard and concentrate. Come over here, lie down on the couch and tell me more about it." "Oh no, doctor," the man says, horrified, "I'm not allowed on the furniture."

****

A few days before his proctological exam, a one-eyed man accidentally swallowed his glass eye. He was worried for a while and kind of expected to see it pop up at some point, but there were no ill effects, it didn't re-appear and so he forgot about it. The day for the appointment arrived and he was lying on his belly, after having changed into a surgical gown behind a screen. The doctor approached, lifted the gown up and came face to face with the glass eye stuck in his patient's anus staring right back at him. "You know," he says in a gentle, reproving tone, "you should learn to trust me better than that."

****

A busy doctor in an ER department is rushing down the corridor when he is stopped by a nurse who needs him to sign a patient's chart. The doctor reaches behind his ear puts the pen in his mouth in concentration while reading the form, before spitting out in horror. "Arghhh," he cries, realizing he's been sucking on the wrong end of a thermometer. "some arsehole's got my pen again!"

****

A young woman was going to marry one of those elderly, wealthy eccentrics who want a virgin bride. Since she wasn't, she went to a doctor to reconstruct her hymen. The doctor told her that would cost around 500 to do it surgically, but that there was another way that would cost only 50 and could be done straight away in his office. The woman agreed to try the cheap way, paid the money and lay down on the consultation bed, feet in the stirrups. The doctor worked on her for several minutes, then congratulated her on her forthcoming marriage and showed her the door. After the honeymoon, the woman came back to the doctor and told him that it was perfect: the pain, the blood, everything was there. "How did you do it?" she asked. "Very simple," he replied. "I tied your pubic hair together."

****

A man comes to a doctor and, twitching his fingers and stuttering, finally manages to say, "Doctor, I have a... er... sexual performance problem. Can you help me?" "Oh, that's not a problem for us men any more!" announces the proud physician with a broad wink. "This new pill just came out – a new wonder drug called Miagra. That does the trick! You take a few of these and it's the end of your problems!" So the doctor gives the man a prescription for a packet of Miagra and sends him on his merry way. A couple of months later, the doctor runs into his patient on the street. "Doctor, doctor!" exclaims the man excitedly, "I've got to thank you! This drug is a miracle! It's wonderful!" "Well, I'm glad to hear that," says the physician, rather pleased with himself. "And what does your wife think about it?" "Wife?" the guy said with a silly grin on his face, "I haven't been home yet!"

✱✱✱✱

An attractive young woman goes for her annual check-up and is asked by the new doctor to get undressed, for he must take her temperature rectally to be sure. She agrees, but a few minutes later says indignantly, "Doctor, that's not my rectum!" "Madam," says the doctor, "that's not my thermometer."

✱✱✱✱

The only treatment to save a patient is a brain transplant. His family is gathered in the doctor's office, taking in the bad news. "Er, doctor, how much is this going to cost?" "Well, it's about £600,000 for a male brain and £200,000 for a female brain," the specialist answers. The men in the room all sit up and start chuckling, a superior expression appearing on their faces. The youngest daughter casts her eyes towards the ceiling and asks the doctor: "And why is a female brain cheaper?" "Oh, it's standard practice, Miss," he replies. "The brain has to be marked down because it's used."

✳✳✳✳

A guy walks into the doctor's office and says, "D-d-d-doct-tor-r-r, I've b-been st-t-tuttering f-for y-y-years and I-I-I-I'm t-t-tired of it. C-c-can y-y-you he-he-help me?" The doctor examines him swiftly and says, "Well I think I know what the problem is." The guy says, "W-w-well, w-w-what is it, d-doc?" The doctor says, "Well, it's your penis, you see. it's about a foot long and all the downward pressure is putting a strain on your vocal cords." The guy says, "I d-d-d-didn't kn-n-n-n-now it c-c-c-could c-c-cause a p-p-p-p... p-p-p-p-p... p-p-problem. W-w-what c-c-can we d-do?" The doctor advises, "Well, I can cut it off and transplant a shorter one. The pressure will disappear and so will your stutter." The guy thinks for a minute then says, "D-d-do it!" He has the operation and, three weeks later, he returns to see the doctor and says, "Doc, you solved the problem and I don't stutter anymore, but I've only had sex once in the past three weeks. My wife doesn't like it any more. She liked it with my long one. I don't care if I have to stutter: I want you to put my long one back on." The doctor says, "N-n-n-no. A d-d-d-deal's a d-d-d-deal!!!"

✳✳✳✳

A rather embarrassed man goes to see his doctor and tells him: "Well, I have this problem, you see: I can't get it up for my wife anymore, if you see what I mean." "It's quite all right," the doctor says. "Get undressed and we'll see what the problem is." He does so, but can find nothing wrong with the patient. "Come back tomorrow," he advises. "Bring your wife with you. I'd like to examine her, too." The anxious patient turns up the following day with his wife, as promised. The doctor has a quick look at the woman, then asks her to take her clothes off. "Mmm... I see... Now turn around please. Mmmm... Can you crouch down for me? That's it. Gooooood, now get on all fours on the carpet. Yes, this way... Mmmm... It's OK, you can put your clothes back on." While the wife is getting dressed, the doctor takes the husband aside and tells him: "You're perfectly healthy. Don't worry. Your wife didn't give me an erection either."

****

After a long time procrastinating, a man finally agrees to see a doctor about a lump on his belly, but only if his grown-up son goes with him. On the appointed day, they receive the terrible news that he is suffering from cancer and that he doesn't have long to live. They are both shocked and the son decides to take his dad to his local for a pick-me-up. In the pub they find all his father's friends and his dad tells them in hushed tones that he is going to die of AIDS. The son is rather surprised and, when they find a table to sit at for a chat, he asks his dad: "Tell me; why did you tell your friends you're dying of AIDS? You don't have AIDS." "I know," the father replies, "but I don't want them screwing your mother after I'm gone!"

****

It is the ophthalmologist's 40th birthday and, in the middle of the party, he is blindfolded and taken by the hand to a table in the centre of the dining room. His loving wife takes the blindfold off with a flourish and he finds himself in front of a huge cake with 40 eyes made of marzipan around it. The specialist stares at the cake and then erupts in laughter. He laughs so much that a couple of his friends have to pick him up from the floor. After a few minutes, wiping a tear of mirth from his eye, he says: "I'm sorry: this is a great cake. It's just that I suddenly thought about my colleague Terry, who's a gynaecologist. It's his 50th birthday tomorrow."

****

A new clinic, with several different specialists, opened in a trendy part of the city. Wanting to be different and creative with the design, the administration decided that each doctor's office door would, in some way, be representative of his practice. So, when construction was complete…the eye doctor's door had a peep-hole, the orthopaedist's door had a broken hinge, the psychiatrist's door was painted all kinds of crazy colours. As for the gynaecologist's door, it was left open… just a crack.

****

A man staggers into hospital with two black eyes and a golf club tightly wrapped round his throat. The doctor on duty asks him what happened. "Well, Doc, it was like this," the man says. "I was out for a quiet round of golf with the missus and she shanked her ball something terrible. It landed in a field full of cows, so we both went to look for it. I was having a good look round but couldn't find it. Anyway, I noticed a white thing in the arse of one of the cows so I walked over, lifted up its tail and there was my wife's golf ball, rammed right up there. That's when I made my only mistake." "And what was that, then?" asked the doc. "Well, I turned to get my wife's attention, lifted the cow's tail and shouted, 'Hey! This looks like yours!'"

✱✱✱✱

A doctor is having an affair with his young, enthusiastic, if a bit dumb, nurse. The nurse gets pregnant and the doctor, of course, doesn't want his wife to know. So he says to his mistress: "You go and lie low somewhere, say Italy, for a while, until the baby is due. When the baby is born, just send me a postcard with 'spaghetti' written on it and I'll know. By this time, I'll have spoken to my wife." "Why 'spaghetti'?" she asks. "Because you'll be in Italy, that's why," the doctor says, just on this side of panicking. Not finding anything logical to reply to that, the girl agrees and flies off to Italy. After nine months, the doctor receives a call from his wife, who tells him she has just received the strangest postcard. "Don't worry, honey," the doctor says. "I'm coming home and I'll explain everything." Back home, he picks up the postcard, wondering what he is going to say to his wife, reads it, stares at it for a second or two and then topples over and dies of a massive heart attack. Stunned, her wife re-reads the mysterious postcard through tears of grief. It says: "Spaghetti, spaghetti, spaghetti,

spaghetti, three with sausage and meatballs, one with mussels."

****

A famous heart surgeon is having a friendly charity barbecue when he is approached by a loudmouth. "Hey, Doc," the guy says, "I'm the best mechanic in town. I can take an engine apart, take the valves out, clean them, tune them and after I put everything back together the baby will purr like a newborn kitten. We're basically doing the same job, so how come you get more money than me, hey?" "Try to do that with the engine running," the heart surgeon says softly.

****

A 92-year-old man went to the doctor to get a physical check-up. A few days later, the doctor saw the man walking down the street with a gorgeous young lady on his arm. A couple of days later, when the old man had an appointment with the doctor again, the doctor said, "You're really doing great, aren't you? You seem chirpy enough!" The man replied, "Just doing what you said, doctor: 'Get a hot mama and be cheerful,' and it works wonders." Horrified, the doctor said: "I didn't say that! I said, 'You've got a heart murmur. Be careful!'"

****

A man goes to see a doctor and tells him he hasn't been feeling very well lately. The doctor examines him for a few minutes and then takes three jars of big coloured pills from a medicine cabinet. "Here is your treatment: you are going to take this green pill in the morning, with a big glass of water, then the yellow pill after lunch, with a big glass of water and finally this red pill, again with a big glass of water. As you can see, these pills are pretty big, you might actually need two glasses of water at night." The patient stares at the huge pills, horrified. "Jeez, doc; that's a lot of pills…Er…what exactly is my problem?" "You're not drinking enough water," the doctor replied.

✳✳✳✳

A young man enters the doctor's office complaining of being run-down. "Well, what can I say?" says the doctor. "Book a few days off and rest – take a vacation, even: spend the weekend at home and sleep." "I can't do that, doctor," the young man replies, shaking his head. "I work in the stock market; it's a very profitable line of work and I'll lose a lot of money if I take time off." "In that case, change your lifestyle, don't go clubbing and so on: cut down on sex, for instance." "What? I'm a young man, I'm in my prime, and you want me to give up sex?" "Well, you could get married," the doctor mused. "That way you could taper off gradually."

✳✳✳✳

One afternoon, two new doctors from India were having an animated discussion in a corridor of an American hospital. "I say it's spelled 'W-H-O-O-M'," said the first Indian doctor. "No, you're mistaken: it is spelled 'W-H-O-M-B'," said the other Indian doctor. A haughty American nurse passing by said smugly, "Excuse me: you are both wrong. It is spelled 'W-O-M-B'." "Thank you, nurse," said one of the doctors, rather coldly, "but we prefer to settle this argument ourselves. Besides, I don't think you're in a position to describe the sound of an elephant passing wind under water, are you?"

****

Two friends were deaf-mutes and had grown up together, attending the same schools and everything. After university they had lost touch but one day, ten years later, they met up again in the street, quite by chance. They got around to talking via sign language and they chatted for ages. It turned out that one of them was no longer mute but had learned to talk. The other guy was amazed and was also really curious to know exactly how his friend had learned to talk after all this time. The guy who could now talk explained to his friend that he'd visited an extraordinary doctor who had performed revolutionary new surgery on him, but that it was rather expensive. He gave his friend the doctor's address and bade him good day. The deaf-mute hopped straight into a cab and shot over to the address. He was given an interview with the doctor straight away, and the doctor explained that he would have to come in every day for 26 days and that the course would cost him exactly one million euro. The man thought this very expensive but agreed, having seen the result on his friend earlier that day. He paid the money and begged the doctor to start on him right away. The doctor agreed and asked the man to strip naked and to lie on the examination table. The doctor walked over to the cupboard in the room and took out a broom handle with a doorknob on the end and a huge jar of Vaseline. The doctor dipped the doorknob in Vaseline and, taking a running leap, proceeded to shove the whole lot up the deaf-mute's arse. "Aaaaaaaaaaaaaah!" screamed the deaf-mute. "Very good," replied the doctor, "and tomorrow we'll work on 'B'."

****

A dentist is treating a Buddhist monk for a nasty cavity and is quite surprised to hear the patient say 'No' to painkillers. "But why?" the dentist asks. "It is just an anaesthetic." "I want to transcend dental medication," the monk replies.

****

"My husband and I have been trying anal sex recently," the woman says, somewhat red-cheeked, to her doctor. "I mean, is this OK?" "Do you enjoy it?" the doctor asks. "As a matter of fact, we do," she replies "Does it hurt you?" "No, it's fine," she replies. "Well, I don't see why you shouldn't carry on, as long as you're careful not to get pregnant." "Pregnant?" the woman says, astonished. "I can get pregnant this way?" "Well, of course: where do you think lawyers come from?" the doctor replies.

****

A woman had just given birth to her first baby. She was tired and haggard, but she noticed that the baby was nowhere to be seen. "Where's my baby?" she asks. "I want to see my baby." The doctor, apologizing, says: "Er, well, you see, mmm… I know it will come as a shock, but there's a problem with your baby: she has no arms…" The mother is stunned. "Wh… What..? No arms?" Then she wails: "I don't care: she's my baby – I want to see my baby! I hurt all this time to get her: I want to see her!" "Er…" says the doctor, eyes downcast, "you see, she has no legs either…" The mother is speechless for a few seconds, then erupts in tears and wails: "I want to see my baby!" The doctor relents and nods to the nurse outside, who brings in a cot. The blonde mother peers inside and the smile dies on her face. Inside the cot is a big ear. "Is… is this my baby?" she whispers. "Speak louder," says the doctor, "she's deaf."

✳✳✳✳

A woman has twins and, because she can't take care of them properly, gives them up for adoption. One of them goes to a family in Egypt and is named Ahmal. The other goes to a family in Spain; they name him Juan. Years later, Juan sends a picture of himself to his birth mother. Upon receiving the picture, she goes to see her doctor and says: "I feel so bad! I want to see my children again! Look, Juan sent me a picture!" She hands the picture over to the doctor. "I want a picture of his brother, too!" she wails. Her doctor answers: "Come on, they're twins! If you've seen Juan, you've seen Ahmal."

✳✳✳✳

Deep into an international flight, a guy finds himself desperate to go to the toilet. It is busy for ten, then 20, then 30 minutes. He calls the stewardess and asks if he cannot just use the ladies' toilet, just this once. She says that that will be fine, but that he mustn't use any of the buttons that he'll see on the wall. The man says that's fine and he promises not to press any of the buttons. So he goes to the bathroom and does his business, but all the time he's looking at these four buttons on the wall next to the toilet. He gets really curious and says to himself that nothing could be that bad, and that he'll just try the first button. So he presses it. There is a noise, and suddenly a warm, gentle, soothing jet of warm water sprays from the toilet, cleaning his arse. "This is fantastic," thinks the man. "I must try the second button." So he presses the second button. There is a noise and warm air comes flowing up from the toilet, drying his arse. "This really is fantastic," he thinks to himself, "I've got to try the third button." So, he presses the third button. There is a noise and some gentle, soothing powder is deposited on his arse. "Unbelievable," he says to himself. "I really have to try the last button," which has the initials "ATR" stamped upon it. So he presses the fourth button and the next thing he knows he is waking up in a hospital bed, surrounded by doctors and covered in bandages. There is blood all over the place and he is hooked up to a drip. "What the hell happened to me?" he asks the nearest doctor. "You pressed the ATR button, didn't you?" says the doctor. "Well, yes," says the man, "but I never knew what it meant!" The doctor replies, "Automatic Tampon Removal!"

✳✳✳✳

A woman takes her 16-year-old daughter Chrissy to the doctor. "So, Mrs Jones, what's the problem?" he asks genially. The mother says,

"Well, it's Chrissy. She keeps getting these cravings, she's putting on weight and is sick most mornings." Sighing inwardly and guessing what he's going to find, the doctor nonetheless gives Chrissy an examination. Then he turns to the daughter and says, "Well, I don't know how to tell you this but, Chrissy, you're pregnant – about four months would be my guess." The mother says, "What? Pregnant?! She can't be: she's never, ever been left alone with a man! Have you, Chrissy?" Her daughter says, in tears, "No, mother! I've never even kissed a man!" The doctor slowly walks over to the window and just stares out for five minutes. Puzzled, the mother finally asks, "Is there something wrong out there, doctor?" The doctor replies, as if coming out of a reverie, "No, not really; it's just that the last time something like this happened, a star appeared in the east and three wise men came over the hill. I'll be damned if I'm going to miss it this time!"

✱✱✱✱

A doctor and his wife are sitting in front of the TV one evening and the good doctor is relaxing by throwing peanuts in the air and catching them in his mouth and eating them. It goes on for a while until the end of the program, when a comment his wife makes distracts him and the peanut lands in his ear. He tries to shake it out, to no avail. Trying to take it out with his little finger, he just manages to get the damn thing even deeper. "Come on," says his worried wife. "Let's go to the hospital and get this out." The doctor agrees, sighs heavily and puts his coat on, just as their daughter comes back from the cinema with her boyfriend. He explains what has happened while his wife is looking for the car keys. On hearing the story, the boyfriend comes forward and says he can help. He asks the good doctor to sit down again, unceremoniously sticks two fingers up his nose and tells him to blow as hard as he can. Sure enough, the peanut pops out of the doctor's ear and goes "Ping!" against the mirror on the mantelpiece. As the daughter and her boyfriend go through to the kitchen to get drinks, the doctor and his wife sit down to discuss their luck. "So," the wife says, "What do you think he'll become after he finishes school? A GP or a surgeon?" "Well," replies the doctor, rubbing his nose, "by the smell of his fingers, I think he's likely to be our son-in-law."

✳✳✳✳

A friendly young doctor from a college town treated a lot of college-age girls. One day, one of them came in for a routine check-up. She took off her T-shirt to reveal a big, but faint, "H" shape on her chest. How curious, he thought, so asked her how she got it. "Oh that," she giggled. "That's Harvey, my boyfriend. He was so proud of getting into Harvard that he never takes his Harvard T-shirt off, even when we're in bed." The next day, another college girl came in for her check-up. She took off her T-shirt, and there was a big, but faint, "Y" shape on her chest. How curious, the doctor thought again, so asked her how she got it. "Oh that," she giggled, "that's Youssef, my boyfriend. He was so proud of getting into Yale that he never takes his Yale T-shirt off, even when we're in bed." The next day, a third college girl comes in for her check-up. She takes off her T-shirt, and there is a big but faint "M" on her chest. "Don't tell me – you have a boyfriend at Michigan," the doctor quips. "No, but I have a girlfriend at Wisconsin!" the girl replies.

****

The Smiths were having marital problems, so they went to see an eminent sex therapist. After a couple of hours of tests he agreed to help them. The solution to their problem was for them to buy a pound of grapes and a dozen doughnuts on the way home. When they got back they were to sit opposite each other, totally naked, and Mr Smith should roll the grapes across the floor and eat the ones that ended up in Mrs Smith, while she should throw the doughnuts at him, and eat the ones that stayed on him. A couple of weeks later, the Joneses came to see the same sex therapist. "Our friends the Smiths recommended you highly," they said. After a couple of hours of tests, the therapist informed the Joneses that there was nothing he could do for them. "But you helped the Smiths, didn't you? What about us?" they said. After hours of begging, the therapist said that there was only one thing they could do and it wasn't guaranteed to work. "On your way back home, stop off and buy a pound of oranges and a packet of Polos…"

****

Fun things to do with an ambulance:

Drive too fast over speed bumps.
Stop with the siren on at a petrol station to fill it up.
Get involved in an accident.
Stop several times to ask for directions.
Drive by a McDonald's to ask if they want to buy fresh meat.

Shoot at the dogs which always chase the ambulance.
Replace the siren with the music of an ice-cream van.
If there's not enough work, drive over people yourself.
Fill the air tanks with liquids.
Ask your boss for the new Lamborghini Diablo ambulance.
Put a twirling disco light in the back.
Drive around the graveyard.
Paint "Satan loves you" on the side.
Throw bloody lamb chops out of the back door.
Keep circling the same block with your head out of the window and your tongue hanging out.
Drive to a morgue and ask if they've got any live ones they want you to take.

****

How many psychiatrists does it take to change a light bulb? Only one, but the light bulb has to want to change.

****

What does it mean when the doctor says you have six months to live? You have five months to pay.

****

In the Army Now

Jokes for the Regiment

The General arrived at his office on a Sunday morning and discovered that none of his private aides was there. Grimly, he remembered it had been one aide's birthday party the previous evening and he had no doubt as to what condition they were in. At around ten o'clock, five aides arrived, unshaved and dressed in rather piteous attire. They salute as smartly as they can and brace themselves for the General's grilling. "I presume you were at Smith's birthday party last night, weren't you?" "Sir, yes, Sir," one aide answered. "And you couldn't get up early enough this morning to get to the office because you were too drunk!" thundered the General. "Er, no, Sir," the aide said timidly, looking at his friends. "So what is your excuse, young man?" the General wondered, sitting down, with a dangerous, vicious smile on his lips. "I can explain. You see, we did run a little late, I admit. We ran to the bus but we missed it; we hailed a cab but it broke down; we found a farm and bought eight horses but they dropped dead; we ran ten miles, and now we're here. It's just a logistical problem, really, General, Sir!" The General eyed him suspiciously, but as he hadn't heard such a good one for a long time, he let the men go. An hour later, the last aide showed up, in the same dishevelled state. "Sorry, Sir," he said. "I ran late; tried to catch a bus but missed it; I hailed a cab but…" "Let me guess," the General interrupted. "The cab broke down, so you bought a horse in a farm but it died on you, so you ran for ten miles. Do you really think I'm going to swallow this?" "Er, no, Sir; you see, there were so many dead horses on the way that it took forever to go around them."

✶✶✶✶

A famous Admiral and an equally famous General were fishing together in a boat when all of a sudden a squall came up. They both fell in the water and spent some time spluttering, struggling helplessly and swallowing quite a quantity of water, until the Admiral floundered his way back to the boat and pulled himself painfully in. Then he fished out the General. Catching his breath, he puffed: "Please don't say a word about this to anyone. If the Navy found out I can't swim, I'd be disgraced." "Don't worry," the General said ruefully. "Your secret is quite safe. I myself would hate to have my men find out I can't walk on water."

✳✳✳✳

A guy comes to the military enlistment office. "What would you like to be?" the Officer asks him. "A pilot," he answers. "Good choice, son." The Officer enrols the guy and sends him to study flying. Unfortunately, he doesn't have what it takes to be a pilot and fails his exams. He is sent back to the military enlistment office again. "Sorry, but you can't be a pilot any more: I'm sure you can see that. Select something else." The guy thinks for a few seconds and speaks: "I want to be in the Air Defence." "First a pilot, then air defence? Why AD?" "If I can't fly, nobody will fly!" the guy answers pugnaciously.

✳✳✳✳

A Corporal announces: "The platoon has been assigned to unload 'luminum…" "Er, aluminium, not 'luminum, Sir," corrects a trooper.

"The platoon is going to unload 'luminum," repeats the Corporal, "and the intellectual here is going to load shit."

✳✳✳✳

The Captain calls for the Sergeant. "I have some bad news for Private Johnson," he tells him. "His mum died last night. I'd like you to break the news to him gently, you know: he's a good guy. Tell him to come and see me." The Sergeant nods, salutes and departs for the morning roll-call. "Listen up," he says in front of the men. "The company has been assigned cleaning duties in the south yard. Douglas, you are needed at the depot and Smith, at the Mess By the way, Johnson, your mother died yesterday: report to the Captain." Later that day, the Captain says to the Sergeant: "Sarge, that was a pretty harsh way to break the news to Johnson. Next time, be a bit more tactful when things like this happen, you know?" The Sergeant nods and says that he will. A few days later the captain receives the sad news that Private Allen's mum died of a heart attack during the night. He sends for the Sergeant and tells him to inform Allen – tactfully – of the tragedy and to send the unfortunate soldier to him. The Sergeant nods, salutes and departs. At the roll-call, when all the men are lined up, he pauses for a minute, then says: "Right, listen up! All of you who have a mother, two steps forward! Not so fast, Allen!"

✳✳✳✳

A General to a Major: "Do you have a couple of smart Captains?" "Yes, I do." "Send them to me. I need to move my furniture around."

A soldier, not noted as being very bright, was sitting at the table, looking at a mug upside-down. A Sergeant came to sit next to him with his lunch and the soldier told him: "I can't drink from this mug. It has no opening." The Sergeant examined the mug and says: "You're right. And besides, it has no bottom either."

✳✳✳✳

It was a dark, stormy night. The young soldier was on his first assignment – guard duty. The General stepped out, taking his dog, a healthy-looking, very strong German Shepherd, for a walk. The nervous young soldier snapped to attention, made a perfect salute and shouted: "Sir, good evening, Sir!" The General, out for some relaxation, returned the salute and said, "Good evening, soldier: nice night, isn't it?" Well it wasn't a nice night, as it was raining and the soldier had only the standard coat on while the General had a waterproof overcoat and a pair of gloves, but the Private wasn't going to disagree with the General, so he replied, "Sir, yes, Sir!" The General continued, "You know, there's something about a stormy night that I find soothing: it's really relaxing. Don't you agree?" The soldier didn't really agree, but then the soldier was just a soldier, and responded, "Sir, yes, Sir!" The General, pointing at the dog, said: "This is a German Shepherd, the best type of dog to train. Very intelligent, very sensitive and very faithful." The private glanced at the dog, saluted yet again and said: "Sir, yes, Sir!" The General continued, "I got this dog for my wife." The soldier simply said: "Sir, good trade, Sir!"

✳✳✳✳

Four people were travelling in the same carriage on a French train. There was an old, distinguished lady wearing a fur coat and a haughty expression; what was probably her granddaughter, a stunning 20-year-old of *Playboy* calibre; a highly decorated General; and a soldier fresh from boot camp. They spend the time chatting about trivial things, and then entered a very long tunnel. While in the tunnel, the sound of a kiss was distinctly heard, followed by the unmistakable sound of a hand slapping a cheek. Silence followed, as all were lost in their respective thoughts: The old lady was thinking: "Isn't it wonderful that, in this day and age, there are still young people ready to defend young women's honour!" The young woman was thinking: "How strange that he would want to kiss the old hag beside me, when I am available!" The General was thinking whilst rubbing his stinging cheek: "I am outraged that any woman could think I would try to sneak a kiss in the dark." The soldier had a big grin on his face and was thinking: "Isn't it great that someone can kiss the back of their own hand, then smack a General in the face and get away with it?"

****

One October, during a dark and stormy night, the following radio conversation took place off the eastern coast of Canada:

Americans: Please divert your course 15 degrees to the north to avoid a collision. Over.

Canadians: Recommend you divert *your* course 15 degrees to the south to avoid a collision. Over.

Americans: This is the Captain of a US Navy ship. I say again, divert *your* course. Over.

Canadians: No. I say again, you divert *your* course. Over.

Americans: This is the aircraft carrier *USS Lincoln*, the second largest ship in the United States' Atlantic fleet. We are accompanied by three destroyers, three cruisers and numerous support vessels. I demand that you change your course 15 degrees north. That's zero-one-five degrees north or countermeasures will be undertaken to ensure the safety of this ship. Over.

Canadians: This is Rock Point Lighthouse, Newfoundland. Your call.

✱✱✱✱

A General visits the infirmary to check on his men. He goes to the first soldier, lying in his bed and asks: "What's your problem, soldier?" "Chronic syphilis, Sir." "I see…And what treatment are you getting?" "Five minutes with the wire brush and Dettol each day, Sir." "As it should be! And what's your ambition?" "To get back to the front, Sir." "Good man," says the General, and he goes to the next bed. "What about you? What's your problem, soldier?" "Chronic piles, Sir." "Nasty, that… what treatment are you getting?" "Five minutes with the wire brush and Dettol each day, Sir." "What an efficient infirmary this is! And what's your ambition, soldier?" "To get back to the front, Sir." "Good man," says the General, and he goes to the next bed. "What's your problem, soldier?" "Chronic gum disease, Sir." "Unusual… And what treatment are you getting?" "Five minutes with the wire brush and Dettol each day, Sir." "This is really a top infirmary! And what is your ambition, soldier?" "To be treated before the other two, Sir!"

✱✱✱✱

Officer: "Soldier, do you have change for a tenner?" Soldier: "Yeah, sure, buddy." Officer: "That's no way to address an Officer! Now let's try it again. Soldier, do you have change for a tenner?" Soldier: "Sir, no, Sir!"

****

A soldier serving in Hong Kong got quite upset when his girlfriend wrote to him, breaking off their engagement and asking for her photograph back. Out of spite, the soldier went out and collected all the unwanted photographs of women that he could find from his friends, bundled them all together and sent them back with a note saying, "Regret cannot remember which one is you. Please keep your photo and return the others."

****

A mum catches her son on the doorstep, a backpack on his shoulder. "Fred, where are you off to now?" she asks. "I'm going to join the Army," the son replies. "But you can't! You're my little baby!" "That's all right. I'm going to join the infantry."

****

Two military policemen were chasing a fleeing draftee from the base. The draftee ran into the courtyard of a convent where a nun was seated on a bench beneath a tree quietly reading a book. "Quick, sister; please hide me! I don't want to be drafted and the MPs are chasing me!" he said to her. "OK. Hide under my skirt." The two policemen finally entered the convent and asked the nun if she had seen anyone. "I am sorry, officers, I didn't," she replied. After they left, she told the young boy that the coast was clear. "Thank you, sister!" the boy said, very relieved. Then he felt he'd better give her some kind of compliment as a way to show his appreciation of her sacrifice. "Say," he started, "you have a nice set of legs for a nun!" "Don't get any ideas," the nun growled. "If you reach up a little farther you'll find a set of balls – I'm not going to be drafted either!"

****

In the canteen: "Pass me the chocolate pudding, would you?" "No way, José!" "And why not?" "It's against regulations to help another soldier to dessert!"

****

An F-16 was flying escort with a B-52 and the pilot was generally making a nuisance of himself by flying rolls and other silly show-off manoeuvres around the lumbering old bomber. Fed up with the smaller plane's antics, the pilot of the B-52 announced on the radio to the F-16: "Anything you can do, I can do better." Not to be outdone, the fighter pilot announced that he would rise to the challenge. "OK, then. Try this." The B-52, however, continued its flight, straight and level, apparently not having changed anything. Perplexed, the fighter pilot asked, "So? What did you do?" The B-52 pilot replied, "We just shut down two engines."

****

During camouflage training in a forest, a soldier is disguised as a tree. Suddenly, just as the visiting General approaches his spot, he starts shouting, lurches forward and jumps up and down a few times while spinning frantically on the spot. "You idiot!" the Officer in charge barks, quite angry at having his otherwise uneventful training disrupted right in front of the General. "Don't you know that by jumping and yelling the way you did, you could have endangered the lives of the entire company?" "Yes, Sir," the soldier answered apologetically, brushing away a branch from his brow. "But, if I may say so, I did stand still when a flock of pigeons used me for target practice and shat on my head. And I never moved a muscle when a large dog peed on my lower branches. But when two squirrels ran up the leg of my fatigues and I heard the larger of the two say, 'Let's eat one now and save the other until winter,' I couldn't take any more."

****

A Marine reconnaissance platoon was on patrol when the Corporal noticed a lone Special Forces soldier standing on a hilltop. As an exercise, the Corporal told two of his men to go and take out that man. They promptly ran as fast as they could toward the soldier, who disappeared over the other side of the hill. For the next few minutes, bloody screams were heard and dust flew in the air. Then, as quickly as it had started, the noise stopped and the Special Forces soldier reappeared on the hilltop. He brushed off his uniform, straightened his beret, crossed his arms and stood there looking at the Marines. The

Corporal, rather pissed off, called for a squad to go and get that arrogant soldier. They promptly ran as fast as they could towards him, and once again he disappeared over the other side of the hill just before the squad reached him. For the next few minutes there were bloody screams and dust flew in the air. Then, as quickly as it had started, the noise stopped and the Special Forces soldier came up on the hilltop. He brushed off his uniform, straightened his beret, crossed his arms and stood there looking at the Marines. This was simply too much for the Corporal. He ordered the rest of his platoon to attack the bloody Special Forces soldier, pretty sure that the supremacy in numbers would ensure victory for his patrol. They all ran up the hill screaming war cries and followed the lone soldier over to the other side of the hill. For many minutes, there were bloody screams and dust flew in the air. It continued and continued. Finally, one lone Marine crawled back to the top of the hill and towards the Corporal, all bloody and feeble, his uniform torn, cuts bleeding all over his body. The Corporal gathered the beaten-up soldier in his arms and heard him say: "Run, Corporal, it's a trick. There are two of them!"

★★★★

A soldier is telling his friends that his sister just enlisted, disguising herself as a bloke. "Wait a minute: she'll have to get changed and shower with the other blokes, won't she?" one of his friends points out. "So what?" "Well, won't they find out?" "Probably," replies the soldier with a wink, "but who'll tell?"

****

Two young men join the Army and are soon put on street patrol in a city with a military curfew. They are given instructions to shoot anybody who's on the streets after six o'clock. So one day, they're out at twenty to six when one of them spots a man walking on the other side of the street. He lines up the man in his sights and shoots the man dead. The other soldier is shocked. "What are you doing? It's not six yet!" "I know what I'm doing," replies his companion. "I know where he lives and he wouldn't have made it!"

****

Four friends in the Army were doing very well indeed – so well that they decided to have a little party before the final exams. Off they went to the local whorehouse and had a wonderful time. When they woke up the following day though, they realized that they had missed the examination by a few hours. Gutted, they went to see their teacher: "Sir, we did have a little pre-exam party yesterday, but nothing much really; only this morning, er, the car blew a tyre. That's why we were late…" one of the friends lied glibly. "Is that so?" asked the teacher. "That's unlucky indeed, especially since your results have been outstanding up until now…" After deliberation with his colleagues, the teacher agreed to let them take the exam in the afternoon. "The problem is that we can't get someone to keep an eye on you while you're sitting the exam, so you'll have to use four separate rooms," they were told. Not believing their luck and amazed that their lie had actually worked, they agreed to the conditions and each entered their own examination room. The first question counted for five points and was ever so easy. Elated, sure of passing the exam, they turned the page on their exam paper to discover that the next question, counting for 95 points, said: "Which tyre?"

****

A private who was going to be court-martialled asked the lawyer representing him for advice on what to wear. "Wear your shabbiest uniform. Let them think you are sorry and repentant," the lawyer replied. Then he asked a friend the same question, but got the opposite advice. "Don't let them intimidate you. Wear your best uniform, with all the decorations and awards you got." Confused, the man went to his chaplain, told him of the conflicting advice and requested some resolution of the dilemma. "Let me tell you a story," replied the chaplain. "A woman, about to be married, asked her mother what to wear on her wedding night. 'Wear a heavy, long, flannel nightgown that goes right up to your neck.' But when she asked her best friend, she got conflicting advice. 'Wear your most sexy negligee, with a V-neck right down to your navel.'" The private protested: "What does all this have to do with me getting court-martialled?" The priest replied, "No matter what you wear, you are going to get screwed."

****

A young naval student was being grilled by an old sea captain: "What would you do if a sudden storm sprang up on the starboard bow?"

"Throw out an anchor, Sir," the student replied. "What would you do if another storm sprang up after?" "Throw out another anchor, Sir." "And if another terrific storm sprang up forward, what would you do then?" asked the Captain. "Throw out another anchor, Sir." "Hold on," said the Captain, holding up his hand. "Where are you getting all these anchors from?" "From the same place you're getting your storms, sir."

****

A Private was brought up before the unit commanding officer for a minor offence. "Here's your choice, Private," the CO said "One month's restriction or 20 days' pay." "All right, Sir," said the bright soldier, "I'll take the money."

****

The physical training instructor was drilling a platoon of soldiers. "I want every man to lie on his back, put his legs in the air and move them as though he were riding a bicycle," he explained. "Now begin!" After a few minutes, one of the men stopped. "Why did you stop, Smith?" demanded the officer. "I'm freewheeling for a while," said Smith.

****

A young man, freshly promoted to the rank of Second Lieutenant, takes possession of his new office. He lovingly arranges a set of plaques and medals in prominent view on his desk, puts up a full-length mirror, spends some time looking in it and wonders whether his shoulder buttons need another polish. Then a young soldier comes in. Wishing to pass for a hotshot, the Second Lieutenant picks up the phone, waves the soldier to stand at attention and wait. He then starts throwing in the names of a few Generals, hints at a golfing date, whispers the name of, and describes, the amorous behaviour of a fictitious young lady and various other rubbish. This comedy lasts for ten minutes, after which he hangs up and turns his attention to the soldier. "Can I help you, soldier?" "Yes, Sir. I'm here to activate your phone line."

****

An Army brat was boasting about his father to a Navy brat. "My dad is an engineer. He can do everything. Do you know the Alps?" "Yes," said the Infantry brat. "My dad built them." Then the naval kid spoke: "And do you know the Dead Sea?" "Yes." "Well," said the naval kid, "it was my dad who killed it!"

****

During a training exercise, a commanding officer's jeep got stuck in mud. The CO, seeing some men lounging around nearby, asked them to help him get unstuck. "Sorry, Sir," said one of the loafers, "but we've been classified dead and the umpire said we couldn't contribute in any way." The CO turned to his driver and said, "Go and drag a couple of those dead bodies over here and throw them under the wheels to give us some traction."

****

A soldier arrives in a small town a bit late: in fact, just after a whole infantry platoon. He cannot find a free hotel room until a manager takes pity on his tired state and tells him: "Well, I may have something. There is this guy who comes here every time his company stops by and he always sleeps in the same room. He's snoring so much we have to put him apart from the other tenants, but there's a spare bed in his room." "That's fine: I'll take it," says the soldier, relieved. "But what about the snoring? Let me tell you, this man snores very loudly!" "I'll deal with the snoring, trust me." The manager leads the soldier to the room. Indeed, the guy's snores can be heard two corridors away. The soldier thanks the manager and enters the room. The following morning, he goes to pay the bill. "So, did you have a good night's sleep after all?" the manager sneers. "Never better: you run a very good hotel," the soldier replies. "How did you manage to sleep through the snoring?" the manager asks, baffled. "The guy didn't snore!" "How come?" "It's quite simple," the soldier explained. "Just before going to bed I woke him up, kissed him on the cheek and said, 'Goodnight, beautiful.' He spent the whole night awake watching me."

****

A British pilot gets shot down behind enemy lines. He wakes up in a German hospital, his uniform gone, with a funny feeling in his left leg. A German doctor comes to his bed and says: "I am a doctor before I am a German, and I will treat you with the respect to which any patient is entitled. I must tell you, however, that it is quite possible we'll have to amputate your left leg." The pilot is shocked, but manages to say: "Thank you for your kindness, doctor, and for agreeing to treat me, although I am an enemy." He pauses, then says: "Do you think it would be possible to send my leg back to my family in England?" The doctor is a bit surprised by this request, but he agrees. Unfortunately, a month later, the second leg has to go, too, and again the pilot asks him to send it to England. The doctor agrees. Another month goes by and he is forced to admit to himself that the pilot's right arm will soon have to come off. He breaks the news very gently to him and is not surprised to hear that the pilot would like his arm to be shipped home with the rest of his bits. The doctor complies, but, when it comes to the time for the right arm to come off, he is accompanied to the unfortunate pilot's bedside by two German security officers. "So this is the pilot who gets his arms and legs sent to England," one of them says. "Tell me... you're not trying to escape, are you?"

✳✳✳✳

After a briefing on land-mines, the Captain asked for questions. An intrepid solder raised his hand and asked: "If we do happen to step on a mine, Sir, what do we do?" "Normal procedure, soldier, is to jump 200 feet in the air and scatter oneself over a wide area."

✳✳✳✳

Why did King Kong join the Army? He wanted to know about gorilla warfare.

****

Things to do to have the military psychiatric nurses worry over your case:

Jam tiny marshmallows up your nose and try to sneeze them out
   while on parade.
Use one credit card to pay off another credit card bill, then say
   you are under stress from the military life.
When one of your roommates says, "Have a nice day!" tell them
   you have other plans and remind them you are in the Army
   to die.
During your next roll-call, sneeze and then loudly suck the
   phlegm back down your throat.
Find out what a frog in a gun barrel really looks like.
Make a list of things you have done in your life and a list of the
   people you have ever met, then pin them on the wall and
   shoot them repeatedly.
Dance naked in front of the flagpole on the Winter Solstice.
Put your uniform on backwards, then go to breakfast as if
   nothing was wrong.
Thumb through *Gun Monthly*, making little cooing noises.
Drive your tank in reverse.
On parade, drop a rabbit on the ground and stop to admire its
   fluffy coat for 15 minutes, dragging the other conscripts
   around you.

****

The five most dangerous things you can hear in the Army:

1. A Private saying, "I learned this in Basic…"
2. A Sergeant saying, "Trust me, Sir…"
3. A Second Lieutenant saying, "Based upon my experience…"
4. A Captain saying, "I was just thinking…"
5. A Warrant Officer chuckling, "Watch this shit…"

Hard &
Soft(ware)

Jokes for
Computers

A computer programmer was out walking one day when a frog called out to him and said: "If you kiss me, I'll turn into a beautiful princess." Delighted with his find, he bent over, picked up the frog and put it in his pocket. The frog spoke up again and said: "If you kiss me and turn me back into a beautiful princess, I will stay with you for one week." The computer programmer took the frog out of his pocket, smiled at it and returned it again. The frog then cried out: "If you kiss me and turn me back into a princess, I'll stay with you for one week and do *anything* you want." Again the computer programmer took the frog out, smiled at it and put it back into his pocket. Finally, the frog asked: "What's the matter with you? I've told you I'm a beautiful princess, that I'll stay with you for a week and do anything you want. Why won't you kiss me?" The computer programmer said: "Look, I'm a computer programmer. I don't have time for a woman in my life: but a talking frog – now *that's* cool."

✳✳✳✳

Three software engineers were in the toilet, standing at the urinals. The first engineer finished and walked over to wash his hands. He then proceeded to dry them very carefully, using paper towel after paper towel and ensuring that his hands were completely dry. Turning to the other two engineers, he explained, "At Hughie Pickering, we are trained to be extremely thorough." He then began to check the fit of his suit. The second engineer finished his task at the urinal and, in his turn, proceeded to wash his hands. He used a single paper towel and made sure that he dried his hands using every available portion of it. He turned and said, "At Adomo, not only are we trained to be extremely thorough, but also extremely efficient." He then started grooming his hair in the mirror. The third engineer, rather peeved, finished his business and walked straight for the door, shouting over his shoulder: "At Affel, we don't pee on our hands."

****

Macronought today announced the release of JoeBloogs Operating System™, especially targeted at British thirtysomething yobboes, yuppies and club-goers. The operating system, commercialized with the motto "An OS for the mates", doesn't have a spreadsheet, a database program or even a word processor, but it can keep track of the football season, lists the best pubs between Inverness and Dover and can even order curry and beer at the click of a mouse.

****

The new aggressive office jargon:

Blamestorming – Sitting around in a group discussing why a deadline was missed or a project failed and who was responsible.
Body Nazis – Hardcore exercise and weightlifting fanatics who look down on anyone who doesn't work out obsessively.
Chainsaw Consultant – An outside expert brought in to reduce the employee headcount, leaving the top brass with clean hands.
Cube Farm – An office filled with cubicles.
Ego Surfing – Scanning the Net, databases, print media and so on, looking for references to one's own name.

Elvis Year – The peak year of something's popularity: *Survivor*'s Elvis Year was 1993.

404 – Someone who is clueless, from the World Wide Web error message "404 Not Found", meaning the requested document couldn't be located: "Don't bother asking him, he's 404."

Mouse Potato – The on-line generation's answer to the couch potato.

Ohnosecond – That minuscule fraction of time in which you realize you've just made a big mistake.

Prairie Dogging – Something loud happens in a cube farm, as people's heads pop up over the walls to see what's going on.

SITCOM – Stands for Single Income, Two Children, Oppressive Mortgage.

Stress Puppy – A person who thrives on being stressed-out and whiny.

Tourists – Those who take training classes just to take a vacation from their jobs – "We had three serious students in the class; the rest were tourists."

Uninstalled – Euphemism for being fired.

Xerox Subsidy – Euphemism for swiping free photocopies from a workplace.

✶✶✶✶

Why are computers like women?

Nobody, however long they work with one, understands their internal
logic.

Even your smallest mistakes are immediately, permanently committed
to memory for future reference.

The native language used to communicate with other computers is
incomprehensible to everyone else.

The message "Bad command or file name" is about as informative as,
"If you don't know why I'm mad at you, then I'm certainly not
going to tell you."

As soon as you make a commitment to one, you find yourself
spending half your pay cheque on accessories for it.

****

Software magnate Jim Portal has finally died and Satan greets him.
"Welcome, Mr Portal, we've been waiting for you," he purrs. "You've
been a naughty boy, flooding the world with version after version of
software that didn't work and not permitting any other software to
exist. You are now in Hell and this will be your home for all eternity."
Satan eyes Jim Portal and resumes his welcome speech: "But you're
lucky, because I am in a good mood today and I will present to you
three Hells for you to choose to be locked up in." Satan takes Jim to a
huge lake of fire in which millions of poor souls are tormented and
tortured. He then takes him to a massive amphitheatre where
thousands of people are chased about and devoured by starving,
nightmarish creatures. Finally, he takes Jim to a tiny room in which, to

Jim's delight, there is a PC and, next to it, a cup of coffee. Without hesitation, Jim says: "I'll take this option." "Fine," says Satan, locking up Jim in the room. Outside, his second-in-command is waiting for him to process the next unfortunate soul. "So he chose this room, master, as you predicted," the aide says. "But I don't understand. You gave him quite a nice room, and with a PC, too…" "Ah, but you see, this is no ordinary PC," Satan sniggers. "The Control, Alt and Delete keys are missing and it's running Windows 95!"

✳✳✳✳

Your computer is lying to you.

It says: "Press Any Key."
It means: "Press any key you like, but I'm not moving."

It says: "Fatal Error. Please contact technical support quoting error no. 1A4-2546512430E."
It means: "… where you will be kept on hold for ten minutes, only to be told some crap that will hide the fact they can't understand a word I say either."

It says: "Installing program to C:\…"
It means: "…. and I'll also be writing 200 megabytes of files into various directories and you'll NEVER find them."

It says: "Please insert disk 11."
It means: "Because I know darn well there are only ten disks."

It says: "Please Wait…"
It means: "… Indefinitely."

It says: "Directory does not exist…"
It means: "… any more. Whoops."

It says: "The application caused an error. Choose Ignore or Close."
It means: "… Makes no difference to me, you're still not getting your work back."

✳✳✳✳

The Ultimate Computer had finally been built and, after making sure that the intensive indoor tests all proved 100 per cent positive, the Ultimate Computer was presented to the CEO. The engineer stepped forward to give his prepared demo. "This," he said, "is the Ultimate Computer. It will give an intelligent answer to any question you may care to ask it." The CEO, amused, asked: "Where is my father?" After an infinitesimal pause, the super computer answer comes through the laser printer: "Your father is fishing off the coast of Florida." The COE's face falls. "Actually, my father is dead. He died five years ago," he says, in a tone suggesting he is not amused any more. The engineer gulps and mutters: "You should re-phrase the question – make it more precise. That might produce a correct answer this time." The CEO frowns and says: "All right. Where is my mother's husband?" There is a small pause again and the printer spits out the answer to the second question: "Your mother's husband is dead. However, your father is still fishing off the coast of Florida."

✳✳✳✳

New PC software error messages:

Smash forehead on keyboard to continue.

File not found. Should I fake it? (Y/N)

Runtime Error 6D at 417A:32CF: Incompetent User.

Enter any 11-digit prime number to continue.

Press any key to continue or any other key to quit.

Press any key except... no, *no, no, not that one*!

Press Ctrl-Alt-Del now for IQ test.

Close your eyes and press Escape three times.

Bad command or file name! Go stand in the corner.

This will end your current session. Do you want to play another game?

CONGRESS.SYS Corrupted: Re-boot Washington DC. (Y/N)?

Windows message: "Error saving file! Format drive now? (Y/Y)"

BREAKFAST.SYS halted... Cereal port not responding.

✳✳✳✳

The librarian noticed a young man sitting in front of a computer, staring at the screen, his arms across his chest. After 15 minutes, he realized that the young man hadn't changed his position and was still there, doing nothing, staring blankly at the screen. Puzzled, he went to him and asked: "May I help you?" "It's about time!" he answered, "I pressed the Help button over 20 minutes ago!"

✳✳✳✳

A woman had been married three times and protested that she was still a virgin. Somebody asked her how that could be possible. "Well," she said. "The first time I married an octogenarian and he died before we could consummate the marriage. The second time I married a naval officer and war broke out on our wedding day. The third time I married a PC operating system programmer and he just sat on the edge of the bed and kept telling me how good it was going to be."

✳✳✳✳

Information age proverbs:

Home is where you hang your @.
The e-mail of the species is more deadly than the mail.
A journey of a thousand sites begins with a single click.
You can't teach a new mouse old clicks.
Great groups from little icons grow.
Speak softly and carry a cellular phone.
C:\ is the root of all directories.
Don't put all your hypes in one home page.
Pentium wise; pen and paper foolish.
The modem is the message.

Too many clicks spoil the browse.

The geek shall inherit the earth.

A chat has nine lives.

Don't byte off more than you can view.

Fax is stranger than fiction.

****

A man walks into a Silicon Valley pet store looking to buy a monkey. The owner points towards three identical-looking monkeys in politically-correct, animal-friendly, natural mini-habitats. "The one on the left costs $500," says the owner. "Why so much?" asks the customer. "Because it can program in C," answers the owner. The customer inquires about the next monkey and is told, "That one costs $1,500, because it knows Visual C and Object-Relational technology." The startled man then asks about the third monkey. "That one costs $3,000," answers the store owner. "$3,000!!" exclaims the man. "What can that one do?" The owner replies, "To be honest, I've never seen it do a single thing, but it calls itself a consultant."

****

Dad was happily typing away on his computer and didn't notice his six-year-old daughter sneaking up behind him. Then she turned and ran into the kitchen, squealing to the rest of the family, "I know Daddy's password! I know Daddy's password!" "What is it?" her sister asked eagerly. Proudly she replied, "Asterisk, asterisk, asterisk, asterisk, asterisk!"

****

Alternative Windows slogans:

Double your drive space: Delete Windows!
Windows and DOS: A turtle and its shell.
A computer without Windows is like a fish without a bicycle.
Bang on the left side of your computer to restart Windows.
I still miss Windows, but my aim's getting better.
I'll never forget the first time I ran Windows, but I'm trying.
Out of disk space. Delete Windows? [Y]es, [H]ell Yes!
Windows 3.1: The best solitaire game you can buy.
Windows NT: Insert wallet into Drive A: and press any key to empty.

****

Tech Support: "Tell me, in the bottom left-hand side of the screen, can you see the 'OK' button displayed?" Caller: "Wow. How can you see my screen from there?"

****

Two programmers were walking across their company's campus when one of their colleagues appeared on a brand-new bicycle. "Where did you get such a great bike?" asks the first programmer. 'Well, I was walking along yesterday minding my own business when a beautiful woman rode up on this bike. She threw the bike to the ground, took off all her clothes and said, 'Take what you want.'" The second IT guy nodded approvingly. "Good choice; the clothes probably wouldn't have fitted."

✳✳✳✳

Programming today is a race between software engineers striving to build bigger and better idiot-proof programs, and the Universe trying to produce bigger and better idiots. So far, the Universe is winning.

✳✳✳✳

Errors are human, but if you really want to screw things up, you need a computer.

✳✳✳✳

Beware of computer programmers who carry screwdrivers.

✳✳✳✳

The perfect computer has been developed. You just feed in your problems and they never come out again.

✳✳✳✳

A computer once beat me at chess, but it was no match for me at kick-boxing.

✳✳✳✳

Alpha. Software undergoes alpha testing as a first step in getting user feedback. Alpha is Latin for "Doesn't work".

Beta. Software undergoes beta testing shortly before it's released. Beta is Latin for "Still doesn't work".

****

A few definitions of computer terms:

Bit: The increment by which programmers slowly go mad.

Branch instruction: Advice from a district office.

Chaining: Method of attaching programmers to desks until output speeds up.

Character density: The number of very weird people in the office, divided by the floorspace.

Checkpoint: Where a programmer draws his salary from.

Computer: A device designed to speed up and automate errors.

Constant: A type of pressure felt by programmers.

Core storage: A receptacle for the centre section of apples.

Debugging: Removing the needles from the haystack.

Default directory: Black hole. Default directory is where all files that you need disappear to.

DSE: Dedicated Solitaire Engine (any PC computer).

Error: Someone else's non-satisfaction with your computer output.

External storage: Wastebasket.

D-word: Four-letter words used by programmers in a state of confusion.

File: A document that has been saved with an unidentifiable name. It helps to think of a file as something stored in a filing cabinet – except that when you try to remove the file, the cabinet gives you an electric shock and tells you the file format is unknown.

Garbage: Highly aromatic computer output.

Hardware: The parts of a computer which can be kicked.

Help: The feature that assists in generating more questions. When the Help feature is used correctly, users are able to navigate through a series of Help screens and end up where they started from without learning anything.

High-speed printer: Wife writing cheques

Input: Food, whisky, beer, Nurofen.

Input/Output: Information is input from the keyboard as intelligible data and output to the printer as unrecognizable junk.

Internal sort: The stomach, liver and kidneys keep changing positions.

Keyboard: An instrument used for entering errors into a system.

Language: A system of organizing and defining error messages.

Loop: *See* loop.

Low-order position: The programmers' place in the chain of command.

Machine-independent program: A program which will not run on any machine.

Macro: The last half of an expression: for example "Holy Macro".

Mathematical model: 46-26-38.

Mathematical check: The remuneration received by a mathematical model.

Memory dump: Immediate amnesia after a glimpse of a normal life.

Microcomputer: One millionth of a computer.

Microsecond: The amount of time required for a program to hang.

Null string: The result of a four-hour database search.

Off-line: Failure to pass a sobriety test.

On-line: Full of alcohol, but not drunk.

Output: Four-letter words.

Overflow: The result of drinking too much alcohol.

Parameter: The absolute limit before the secretary yells for help.

Printer: A printer consists of three main parts: the case, the jammed paper tray and the blinking red light.

Program library: An organized collection of obsolete programs.

Reference manual: Object that raises the monitor to eye level. Also used to compensate for that short table leg.

Users: Collective term for those who stare vacantly at a monitor. Users are divided into three types: novice, intermediate and expert.

✱✱✱✱

Sex Manual for Tech Nerds

1. Be user-friendly.
2. Take bytes.
3. Fondle joystick.
4. Spread sheet.
5. Fix surge protector.
6. Activate hardware.
7. Insert disk... all the way.
8. Do it until megabytes.
9. Back it up.
10. Eject floppy.

****

Tech Support: "What does the screen say now?" Caller: "It says, 'Hit ENTER when ready'." Tech Support: "Well?" Caller: "How do I know when it's ready?"

****

One of Jim Portal's marketing assistants approached an applicant in a market research panel and said, "Excuse me. If a company made a version of a PC OS which only crashed once a year, would you buy it?" The customer's eyes glistened and he seemed to be making the sign of the cross: "Oh, yes!" The marketing assistant carried on: "… and if they made a version which crashed every five minutes?" The customer glared at him and said, "And what kind of customer do you think I am?" "We've already established that," the guy said. "We're just haggling over the frequency."

****

Windows versions:

Windows 1.0: Good joke, eh?

Windows 2.0: Still funny, isn't it?

Windows 286: Yeah, we're still kidding.

Windows 386: It's wearing thin, so we'll publish something you can actually use real soon.

Windows 3.0: It's finally worth buying!

Windows 3.1: It's finally worth using!

Windows 95: Going boldly where Mac has been for years.

Windows 98: More usable! Less stable!

Windows 98SE: More stable! Less usable!

Windows ME: Less usable *and* less stable!

NT 1.0: Give me more hardware! *Now*!

NT 2.0: Dammit, I said *More hardware*! *Now*!

NT 3.0: Which part of *more hardware* do you not understand?

NT 3.5: With enough hardware, I'd work. Honest.

NT 4.0: Does less than Win98 with twice the hardware at half the speed.

Windows 2K: Works almost as well as Windows 98! Honest!

Windows XP: It just works. Sometimes.

✷✷✷✷

If software companies made toasters:

Every time you bought a fresh loaf of bread, you would have to buy a toaster, or at least renew your licence for it.

Toaster 98 would weigh 15,000 pounds (hence requiring a steel-reinforced worktop), draw enough electricity to power Birmingham, take up 95 per cent of the space in your kitchen and would claim to be the first toaster which lets you control how light or dark you want your toast to be.

This toaster would secretly interrogate your other appliances to find out who made them and send the details back to the parent company.

It would have a protection device that will not let you toast bread.

It will give you advice you don't need, such as: "Don't put your hand in the boiling water, only pasta," and would monitor your behaviour in the kitchen to record your bread-related habits to serve you better.

If your toaster ever caught you running with scissors, the parent company will sue you.

It would have a reset button, the only place worn out on an otherwise shiny toaster.

Everyone would hate toasters, but nonetheless would buy them since most of the good bread only works with their toasters.

✱✱✱✱

One of the main host computers of a very busy internal network went down, bringing down with it half the intranet of the building which depended on it. The network in-house engineer soon gave up and told his boss to call for a specialist. The specialist arrived, had a talk with the engineer, then took one look at the computer and nodded thoughtfully. He then opened his briefcase, produced a small rubber hammer and, his ear stuck to the computer case, hit a spot softly, after which the system made a kind of "Wooosh" noise and restarted straight away. Two days later the office manager received a bill from the consultant for $2,000. Immediately he called the engineer's agency and exclaimed, "Two thousand dollars for fixing that computer? You were only here five minutes! I want the bill itemized!" The next day the new bill arrived. It read, "Tapping computer with hammer: $1. Knowing where to tap: $1,999."

****

A young man comes into the computer store: "I'm looking for a mystery adventure game with lots of graphics: you know – something really challenging." "Well," replied the clerk, "have you tried Windows XP?"

****

Viruses are the bane of modern technology. Here is a list of dangerous new viruses you *don't* want to see spreading:

AIRLINE VIRUS
You're in London, but your data is in Inverness.

TONY BLAIR VIRUS

It doubles the files on your hard drive while stating it is decreasing the number of files; increases the cost of your computer; taxes its CPU to maximum capacity and then uses Quicken to access your bank accounts and deplete your balances.

BILL GATES VIRUS

This dominant strain searches for desirable features in all other viruses via the Internet. It then either engulfs the competing viruses or removes their access to computers until they die out.

DIET VIRUS

Allows your hard drive to lose weight by eliminating the FAT table.

DISNEY VIRUS

Everything in the computer goes goofy.

ELVIS VIRUS

Your computer gets fat, slow and lazy and then self-destructs, only to resurface at shopping malls and service stations across rural America.

FREUDIAN VIRUS

Your computer becomes obsessed with its own motherboard, or it becomes very jealous of the size of your friend's hard disk.

LORENA BOBBITT VIRUS

It turns your hard disk into a 3.5-inch floppy.

MISSING VIRUS

Virus '98 is promised for initial Beta release by the second quarter of this year, but recent court actions by the Federal government have cast doubt on the parent company's ability to incorporate this virus into the main OS in a seamless manner.

POLITICALLY CORRECT VIRUS

Never calls itself a virus, but instead refers to itself as an electronic micro-organism.

SPICE GIRL VIRUS

Has no real function, but makes a pretty desktop.

STAR TREK VIRUS

Invades your system in places where no virus has gone before.

TEENAGER VIRUS

Your PC stops every few seconds to ask for money.

X-FILES VIRUS

All your icons start shape-shifting.

TOBACCO INDUSTRY VIRUS

It contends that there is no reliable scientific evidence that viruses can harm your computer or that it targets adolescent computer users.

A collection of 'Ass' emoticons

(_E=mc2_) A smart ass.

(_$_) Money coming out of his ass.

(_!_) A regular "nice" ass.

(__!__) A large ass.

(!) A tight ass.

(_._) A flat ass.

(_^_) A bubbly ass.

(_*_) A sore ass.

(_!__) A lop-sided ass.

{_'_} A squishy ass.

(_o_) An ass that's been around.

(_O_) And more…

(_x_) Kiss my ass.

(_X_) Get off my ass.

(_zzz_) A tired ass.

(_o^o_) A wise ass.

(_13_) An unlucky ass.

****

Sure signs that your co-worker is a hacker :

You told him off once and your next phone bill was for £20,000.

He's won the Reader's Digest sweepstakes three years running.

When asked for his phone number, he gives it in hex.

Seems strangely calm whenever the office LAN goes down.

Somehow manages to get Sky Sports on his PC at work.

Mumbled, "Oh, puh-leeez" 95 times during the movie *The Net*.

Massive £40,000 contribution to the ritual Christmas booze trip to Calais made in one-cent increments.

His video dating profile lists "public-key decryption" among turn-ons.

When his computer starts up, you hear, "Good morning, Mr President."

You hear him murmur, "Let's see you use that credit card now, bitch!"

✱✱✱✱

How many Internet mail list subscribers does it take to effect the changing of a light bulb?

1331 – one to change the light bulb and to post to the mail list that the light bulb has been changed.

14 – to share similar experiences of changing light bulbs and how the light bulb could have been changed differently.

7 – to caution about the dangers of changing light bulbs.

27 – to point out spelling/grammar errors in posts about changing light bulbs.

53 – to flame the spell-checkers.

156 – to write to the list administrator complaining about the light bulb discussion and its inappropriateness to this mail list.

41 – to correct spelling in the spelling/grammar flames.

109 – to post that this list is not about light bulbs and to please take this email exchange to alt.lite.bulb.

203 – to demand that cross-posting to alt.grammar, alt.spelling and alt.punctuation about changing light bulbs be stopped.

111 – to defend the posting to this list saying that we all use light bulbs and therefore the posts **are** relevant to this mail list.

306 – to debate which method of changing light bulbs is superior, where to buy the best light bulbs, what brands of light bulb work best for this technique and what brands are faulty.

 27 – to post URLs where one can see examples of different light bulbs.

 14 – to post that the URLs were posted incorrectly, and to post corrected URLs.

  3 – to post about links they found from the URLs that are relevant to this list which makes light bulbs relevant to this list.

 33 – to concatenate all posts to date, then quote them including all headers and footers, and then add "Me Too".

 12 – to post to the list that they are unsubscribing because they cannot handle the light bulb controversy.

 19 – to quote the "Me Too's" to say, "Me Three."

  4 – to suggest that posters request the light bulb FAQ.

  1 – to propose new alt.change.lite.bulb newsgroup.

 47 – to say this is just what alt.physic.cold_fusion was meant for: leave it here.

143 – votes for alt.lite.bulb.

****

A trucker is driving a trailer loaded with computer equipment on the highway near Silicon Valley when he decides to stop for a bite to eat.

He slows down and pulls over at a roadside café which has a sign outside saying: "Non-computer geeks only. If you *are* a computer geek, enter at your own risk." Finding this a bit strange, the trucker goes in and sits at the bar, where a suspicious barman looks him up and down and says: "You're sure you're not a computer geek?" "Hell no. I'm a truck driver." The barman leans over the bar and sniffs him unceremoniously. "You smell like one," the barman accuses. "Well, my trailer's full of computer equipment, that would be why," the trucker replies quickly, starting to feel a tad freaked out. The barman stares at him in the eye for a few seconds and then apparently decides the trucker is telling the truth and serves him lunch. While the trucker is having his lunch, a guy wearing an Apple hat, a calculator-wristwatch and carrying a laptop enters the bar, obviously preoccupied with some difficult programming problem. The barman silently picks up a shotgun from behind the bar, walks around and coldly shoots the geek down. While a couple of waitresses are grumpily disposing of the body, the barman explains that these things happen all the time round these parts. "Oh yeah," he says to the trucker. "Disposing of computer geeks is a state law here. There's just too many of them in Silicon Valley: we need to control the population, you know?" Puzzled, the trucker pays for his food and heads off. Unfortunately, his lunch makes him drowsy and soon he finds himself with his trailer in the ditch, doors open, computer gear on the tarmac. There are a lot of people wearing suits and glasses hurriedly grabbing computers, monitors and keyboards. Remembering the barman's words, he reaches for his shotgun and starts shooting computer geeks, too. He's starting to have fun when a patrol car stops and a couple of policemen restrain him. "What's the matter?" the trucker asks. "I thought it was a state law to get rid of computer geeks." "Oh, it is," one of the policemen says, "but you're not allowed to bait them."

****

What does a baby computer call his father?
Data.

****

What is a computer's first sign of old age?
Loss of memory.

****

What happened when the computer fell on the floor?
It slipped a disk.

****

How many Microsoft engineers does it take to screw in a light bulb?
None. They just redefine the status of darkness.

****

How do you tell an experienced hacker from a novice?
The latter thinks there are 1,000 bytes in a kilobyte, while the former
is sure there are 1,024 metres in a kilometre.

****

Why do computer scientists make such lousy lovers?
Because they always want to do the job faster than before. And when
they do, they say the performance has improved.

****

WARNING: There is a new virus called Viagra! It turns your 3.5-inch
floppy into a hard drive!

****

How many Pentium designers does it take to screw in a light bulb?
Approximately 1,999,042,740,172.23554177896 – but that's close
enough for non-technical people.

****

One on One

14

Jokes in a
Line or Two

What did the sign on the door of the brothel say?
Beat it – we're closed.

Why were glow-in-the-dark condoms invented?
To enable gay people to play *Star Wars*.

Why is air a lot like sex?
Because it's no big deal until you aren't getting any.

Why did the snowman drop his trousers?
He heard the snowblower coming.

What's another name for pickled bread?
Dill-dough.

What do you do with 365 used condoms?
Melt them down, make a car tyre and call it a "Goodyear".

Why is sex just like KFC?
You start with breast, work your way down the thigh, and all you're
ever left with is a greasy box to put your bone in!

What do you call a lesbian dinosaur?
Lickalottapus.

****

Chat-up lines to make her laugh:

I'll cook you dinner if you cook me breakfast.

Can I have your phone number? I don't seem to be able to find my own.

You must be jelly, because jam doesn't shake like that.

I definitely go down on the first date: how about you?

If you think you might regret this in the morning, we can always sleep until the afternoon.

Do you have a mirror in your pocket? Because I could see myself in your underwear.

I'm a necrophiliac – how good are you at playing dead?

Do you know why you should masturbate with these two fingers? Because they're mine.

I hope you know CPR, because you take my breath away!

Excuse me: do you want to screw, or should I apologize?

Do you want to go out for a coffee and sex? What, you don't like coffee?

Look at you: all those curves and me with no brakes.

Let's go back to my place and get something straight between us.

Have you ever tried those prickly condoms?

Can I tickle your belly from the inside?

Do you know what winks and fucks like a beast? [Then wink, you dozy sod!]

Are you free tonight, or is it going to cost me?

Inheriting eighty million Euro doesn't mean a lot when you have a weak heart like me.

If you were a car, I'd buff you up and ride you all over town.

There are 265 bones in the human body. How would you like another one?

Oh, I'm sorry, I thought that was a Braille name-tag.

If you cut your arms off, you'd look just like Venus de Milo.

I'd really love to screw your brains out, but it looks like someone beat me to it.

I'm a birdwatcher and you seem to have some of the characteristics of the Big-Breasted Bed Thrasher... I'd like to do more research.

Why don't you sit on my lap and let us see what pops up?

If I could re-arrange the alphabet, I'd put U and I together.

I may not be Fred Flintstone, but I bet I can make your bed rock.

Excuse me, is that dress felt? Would you like it to be?

I wish you were a Postman Pat van outside Tesco's, because then I could ride you all day for a quid.

I like every bone in your body, especially mine.

I'm pretty sure I could fall madly in bed with you.

Nice shoes. Wanna fuck?

If I gave you sexy underwear, would there be anything in it for me?

Excuse me, ma'am, do you go down on strangers? No? Well, allow me to introduce myself.

If you've lost your virginity, can I have the box it came in?

Do you sleep on your stomach? Do you mind if I do?

Let's go to my place and do all the things I'll tell everyone we did anyway.

Screw me if I'm wrong, but do you want to kiss me?

If your left leg was Christmas and your right leg was New Year, could I spend some time between the holidays?

Forget that. Playing doctor is for kids. I prefer to play gynaecologist.

Is that a Tic-Tac in your trousers or are you just pleased to see me?

Nice dress – can I talk you out of it?

Is it hot in here or is it just you?

You must be from the Carribean, because Jamaican me crazy.

Want to play 'Down at the Fair'? That's where you sit on my face and I try to guess your weight.

You may not be the best-looking girl here, but beauty is only a light switch away.

Do you know the difference between a hamburger and a blowjob? You don't? Wanna do lunch?

Hey baby, do you want to see something really swell?

Do you believe in love at first sight, or should I walk past again?

The word of the day is 'legs'. Let's go back to my place and spread the word.

Screw me if I'm wrong, but is your name Sirenija?

Do you wash your underwear with Windex? Because I can really see myself in it.

I was just thinking that your outfit would look great in a crumpled heap on my bedroom floor tomorrow morning.

You know what would look really good on you? Me.

Do you like short love affairs? I hate them. I've got all weekend.

That shirt is very becoming on you, but if I were on you, I'd be coming, too.

You've got the whitest teeth I've ever come across.

✳✳✳✳

What was the smartest thing that ever came out of a woman's mouth?
Einstein's dick.

What do you call a lesbian from Canada?
A Klondyke!

How is a woman like a laxative?
They both irritate the shit out of you.

What do a woman and a computer have in common?
Both can take a 3.5-inch floppy.

What's worse than a male chauvinist pig?
A woman that won't do what she's told.

Why do women rub their eyes when they wake up?
Because they don't have balls to scratch.

What do you call a virgin lying on a waterbed?
A cherry float.

What do you call a lesbian from India?
Minjeeta.

What's hairy on the outside, wet and slimy on the inside, begins with a 'C' and ends in 'T'?
A coconut.

Why did God give men penises?
So they'd have at least one way to shut a woman up.

Why do women paratroopers always wear tampons?
So they don't whistle as they make their way down.

✳✳✳✳

What's the difference between a woman with PMT and a pit bull?
Lipstick.

Why do most women pay more attention to their appearance than improving their minds?
Because most men are stupid, but not many are blind.

Why do women like to have sex in the dark?
They can't stand seeing a man have a good time.

What term describes a woman paralyzed from the waist down?
Married.

Why do men die before their wives?
They want to.

What does a 75-year-old woman have between her breasts that a 25-year-old doesn't?
Her navel.

What's a wife?
An attachment you screw on the bed to get the housework done.

What happened to the guy who figured out what it was with women?
He died laughing before he could tell anybody.

Why are hangovers better than women?
Hangovers will go away eventually.

Why do women have tits?
So men will talk to them.

What do the small bumps around a woman's nipples represent?
Braille for "Suck here".

✸✸✸✸

What's the difference between your wife and your job?
After five years your job will still suck.

Why did God make Man first?
He didn't want a woman looking over his shoulder.

Why don't women need to wear watches?
There's a clock on the stove!

What's six inches long, two inches wide and drives women wild?
Cash.

What do a woman and a washing machine have in common?
They both drip when they're fucked!

Why did the woman cross the road?
Who cares? How did she get out of the kitchen?

How many women does it take to change a light bulb?
Who cares? Let her cook in the dark!

What is the difference between a woman and a washing machine?
You can bung your load in a washing machine and it won't call you a
week later.

If your wife keeps coming out of the kitchen to nag you, what have
you done wrong?
Made her chain too long.

What's the difference between a pregnant woman and a light bulb?
You can unscrew a light bulb.

Why can't you trust women?
How can you trust something that bleeds for five days and doesn't die?

Why do women have periods?
They deserve them.

****

What's the difference between your pay cheque and your penis?
You don't have to beg your wife to make her blow your salary!

What's the difference between your wife and a wheelie bin?
You only need to take a wheelie bin out once a week.

Why are women's feet small?
So they can stand closer to the sink.

How do you make your girlfriend scream out loud while you're having sex?
Phone her to let her know what she's missing!

What's the ultimate in sexual rejection?
Your hand falls asleep while you're masturbating!

Have you heard about the new super-sensitive condoms?
They hang around and talk to the woman after you've rolled over, farted and fallen asleep.

Who's the world's greatest athlete?
The man who gets gold and silver medals in the masturbation contest.

Why didn't the man report his stolen credit card?
The thief was spending less than his wife.

Why haven't we sent a woman to the moon?
It doesn't need cleaning.

What did the banana say to the vibrator?
What are you shaking for? It's me she's going to eat!

Why do men pay more for car insurance? Women don't get blowjobs
while they're driving.

✳✳✳✳

What do bungee-jumping and prostitutes have in common?
They both cost too much for an afternoon, and if the rubber breaks, you're fucked!

How do you know if you have a high sperm count?
If the girl has to chew before she swallows.

How do you make two kilos of fat look good?
Stick a nipple on top.

Why are Wonderbras so called?
When a woman takes one off, you wonder where her tits went!

Your dog is barking to be let in the back door and your wife is barking to be let in the front door. Which do you let in first?
The dog – once he's in, at least he shuts up!

What's the definition of a 'yankee'?
It's like a 'quickie', but you do it alone!

What do you call two lesbians in a canoe?
Fur traders.

How do you know when your wife is dead?
Your sex life remains the same but your dirty clothes basket overflows.

Did you hear about the new lesbian leather shoes?
They're called Dikes, have an extra-long tongue and you can get them off with only one finger!

Why do women cease menstruating when they begin the menopause?
They need all the blood for their varicose veins!

How do you turn a fox into an elephant?
Marry it.

What tells you you are getting old?
When your dreams stay dry and your farts get wet!

****

What's better than roses on your piano?
Tulips on your organ.

What did Cinderella do when she got to the ball?
She choked!

What do you do if your dishwasher stops working?
Shout at her.

What do parsley and pubic hair have in common?
You push them both aside and keep on eating!

What do a toilet seat and a pussy have in common?
They both feel good, but you wonder who was there before you.

Do you know what the *Oxford English Dictionary* definition of a menstrual period is?
A bloody waste of fucking time.

Why don't witches wear panties when flying on their broomsticks?
Better traction.

Why do women pierce their belly-buttons?
Gives them somewhere to hang air freshener.

How did Pinocchio discover he was made of wood?
His hand caught alight!

What's the difference between pussy and apple pie?
You can eat mom's apple pie!

What is the difference between a clever midget and a venereal disease?
One's a cunning runt...

✳✳✳✳

What do tightrope-walking and a blowjob from your granny have in common?
You don't look down.

What do women and police cars have in common?
They both make a lot of noise to let you know they're coming.

What is better than a cold Bud?
A warm bush.

What's the difference between a lawyer and a prostitute?
A prostitute will stop screwing with you when you're dead!

Why do women have two per cent more brainpower than cows?
So that when you pull their tits they won't shit on the floor.

What do a virgin and a balloon have in common?
One prick and it's all over.

Why can a prostitutes make more money than a drug dealer?
Because she can wash and re-sell her crack.

What do you do if your girlfriend starts smoking?
Slow down and lubricate.

What's the difference between a woman and a fridge? A fridge doesn't make a squelching noise when you pull your meat out!

What do women and linoleum floors have in common?
You lay them right the first time and you can walk all over them for 20 years!

What is it when a man talks dirty to a woman?
Sexual harassment.

What is it when a woman talks dirty to a man?
Two euro a minute.

✱✱✱✱

What is the definition of making love?
Something a woman does while a man fucks her.

What's the difference between a whore and a bitch?
Whores sleep with everyone at the party and bitches sleep with
everyone at the party apart from you.

What does the sperm clinic say to donors when they leave?
Thanks for coming.

What's the definition of macho?
Jogging home from your own vasectomy.

How do you have sex with a fat bird?
Roll her in flour and screw the wet bit.

What do a gynaecologist and a pizza man have in common?
They can both smell it, but they can't eat it.

How many men does it take to open a beer bottle?
What the hell? It should be open when she brings it to you!

Why is the space between a woman's breasts and hips called a waist?
Because there's enough room for another pair of tits in there.

What do a fat bird and a moped have in common?
They're both great fun to ride until your mates catch you.

How many newspapers can a woman hold between her legs?
One *Post*, two *Globes* and as many *Times* as you can.

What's the difference between pink and purple?
Grip!

✱✱✱✱

What do you call a lesbian with fat fingers?
Well-hung.

Where do homosexuals park?
In the rear.

Why do women have two holes so close together?
If you miss the pink you can go for the brown!

What do you call haemorrhoids on a homosexual?
Speed bumps.

What's the difference between a sumo wrestler and a feminist?
A sumo wrestler has a feminine side.

What's the smallest hotel known to man?
A pussy – leave the bags outside.

What do you do in case of fall-out?
Put it back in and take shorter strokes!

What do you call three lesbians in bed together?
Menage à twat.

What's the difference between a man buying a lottery ticket and a man arguing with his wife?
The man buying the ticket at least has a one in 16 million chance of winning!

How can you tell a hardcore lesbian bar?
Even the pool table has no balls.

What's the difference between a bandleader and a gynaecologist?
A gynaecologist sucks his fingers…

How can you spot the head nurse?
She's got dirty knees!

****

What's the late-night difference between a bachelor and a married man?
A bachelor comes home, sees what's in the refrigerator and goes to bed. A married man comes home, sees what's in the bed and goes to the refrigerator.

Why do brides always wear white?
Aren't all kitchen appliances that colour?

How do you confuse a female archaeologist?
You give her a used tampon and ask her what period it's from.

How do you tell when an auto mechanic has just had sex?
One of his fingers is clean.

Why do women wear black underwear?
Mourning – for the stiff they buried the night before.

✳✳✳✳

Have you heard about the new mint-flavored birth control pill for women that they take immediately before sex?
They're called Pre-dickamints.

What's the difference between parsley and pussy?
Nobody eats parsley.

What's the difference between mad cow disease and PMS?
Nothing.

What is the difference between an ice hockey game and a school reunion?
At a hockey game you see fast pucks…

How can you tell when your girlfriend wants you?
You put your hand down her underwear and it feels like you're feeding a horse.

Why are women like tyres?
You can always find a spare.

✱✱✱✱

What's good about having a homeless girlfriend?
You can drop her off wherever you want!

Why did God give women arms?
Do you know how long it would take to lick a bathroom clean?

What do homosexuals and ambulances have in common?
They both load from the back and go whoo-whoo!

What's the difference between a hangover and a woman?
A hangover will go away eventually.

What do being in the military and getting a blowjob have in common?
The closer you get to discharge, the better it gets.

What's the definition of eternity?
The time between when you cum and she leaves.

Did you hear about the new gay sitcom?
It's called *Leave It, It's Beaver.*

Why is a laundrette a bad place to pick up chicks?
If she can't afford a washing machine, she'll never be able to support you.

Did you hear there's a new PC word for lesbian?
Vagitarian.

What's the difference between sin and shame?
It's a sin to put it in, but it's a shame to pull it out.

Did you know that 70 per cent of the gay population were born that way?
The other 30 per cent were sucked into it.

✳✳✳✳

How does a man show he's planning for the future?
He buys two cases of beer instead of one.

Why do doctors slap babies' arses as soon as they're born?
To knock the penises off the clever ones.

How many men does it take to tile a bathroom?
Two – if you slice them thinly enough.

What's the difference between a cream cracker and a lesbian?
One's a snack cracker...

What has eight arms and an IQ of 60?
Four guys watching a football match.

Why do men have holes in their penises?
So their brains can get some oxygen occasionally.

What does it mean when a man is in your bed gasping for breath and calling your name?
You didn't hold the pillow down long enough.

Why do female black widow spiders kill their partners after mating?
To stop the snoring before it starts.

Why do only ten per cent of men make it to Heaven?
Because if they all got there, it would be Hell.

What do husbands and lawnmowers have in common?
They're hard to start in the morning, they belch out noxious odours
and half the time they don't even work.

What does it take for a man to plan a candlelit dinner?
A power failure.

✳✳✳✳

Things never to say to an excited, naked man:

I've smoked fatter joints than that.

Wow – and your feet are so big!

Why don't we skip right to the cigarette?

Is that an optical illusion?

Does it come with an air pump?

It's OK: we'll work around it!

Maybe it looks better in natural light.

Maybe if we water it, it'll grow.

But it still works, right?

How sweet: you brought incense.

Can I be honest with you?

Why, oh, why is God punishing me?

Oh no… a flash headache! (giggle and point)

Can I paint a 'smiley face' on it?

Why don't we just cuddle?

Only if you get me real drunk first.

This explains your car.

You know, they have surgery to fix that.

Ahhhh, isn't it cute!

Are you cold?

It looks so unused.

It's a good thing you have so many other talents.

Make it dance!

At least this won't take long.

I suppose this makes me the 'early bird'.

What *is* that?

Will it squeak if I squeeze it?

I never saw one like that before.

So this is why you're supposed to judge people on personality.

****

Why is psychoanalysis quicker for men than for women?
When it's time for regression, men are already there.

What do theme parks and Viagra have in common?
They both make you wait hours for a two-minute ride.

How do men sort their dirty clothes?
'Dirty' and 'dirty-but-wearable'.

What did the elephant say to the naked man?
How do you breathe through something that small?

Why don't men give their penises female names?
Because they don't want a woman running their life.

What's the difference between a man and ET?
ET phoned home.

What do Santa's female reindeer do on Christmas Eve while the male reindeer pull his sleigh and deliver presents?
They head into town to blow a few bucks.

Why don't little girls fart?
Because they don't get arseholes until they're married.

What do a Rubik's cube and a penis have in common?
They both get harder the longer you play with them.

How do you ruin a man's ego?
By asking, "Is it in yet?"

✱✱✱✱

Why does it take one million sperm to fertilize one egg?
None of them bother to stop for directions.

Why is it so difficult to find men who are sensitive, caring and good-looking?
They already have boyfriends.

What's the difference between a singles' bar and a circus?
Clowns don't talk at the circus.

Why do men find it difficult to make eye contact?
Tits don't have eyes.

Why can't women read maps?
Because only the male mind can comprehend the concept of an inch equalling a mile.

What do a clitoris, an anniversary and a toilet have in common?
Men will always miss them.

What do you get if you cross a rooster with peanut butter?
A cock that sticks to the roof of your mouth.

Why does a bride smile when she walks down the aisle?
She knows she's given her last blowjob.

Why do women prefer elderly gynaecologists?
Shaky hands!

What's the difference between a new husband and a new dog?
The dog is still excited to see you a year later.

Why don't women blink during foreplay?
They don't have enough time.

Why does a man eating oysters improve a woman's sex life?
Because if he'll eat one of those, he'll eat anything!

✳✳✳✳

Which two words clear out a men's changing room quickest?
Nice cock!

Why do penises have a hole in the end?
So men can be open-minded.

What did Adam say to Eve?
"Stand back: I'm not sure how big this thing gets!"

What's the difference between "Oh!" and "Aaah!"?
About two inches.

How many honest, intelligent, caring, sensitive men in the world does
it take to do the dishes?
Both of them.

Why is sleeping with a man like a soap opera?
Just when it's getting interesting, it's all over until next time.

What's the sex speed limit?
68, because at 69 you have to turn around.

What must be the lightest thing known to man?
A penis – even a thought can raise it!

What is the difference between a golf ball and a G-spot?
Men will spend hours searching for a golf ball.

How do you know when it's Barbie's period?
You can't find any of your Tic-Tacs!

Why do schools in Kentucky only have driving education classes two days a week?
Because they need their cars for sex education classes for the other three days!

What do you call a guy who never farts in public?
A private tutor.

****

What's the last thing 'Tickle Me Elmo' receives before he leaves the factory?
Two test tickles.

What's the difference between a girl snowman and a boy snowman?
Snowballs.

What's the only animal with an arsehole in the middle of its back?
A police horse.

What do bulls do to stay warm on cold days?
Go into the barn and slip into a nice warm Jersey.

Did you hear about the Morning After Pill for men?
It changes your blood type!

What has one hundred balls and screws old ladies?
Bingo.

Why do bunny rabbits have soft sex?
Because they have cotton balls!

How do you describe a '69' in Chinese?
Twocanchew!

What happens when you kiss a canary?
You get chirpes and it can't be tweeted because it's a canarial disease.

Why did God create alcohol?
So ugly people would get to have sex.

How do you make four old ladies swear?
Get a fifth old lady to shout "Bingo!"

What's the difference between oral and anal sex?
Oral sex makes your day; anal sex makes your hole weak.

****

How do you eat a frog?
You put one leg over each ear.

What has two grey legs and two brown legs?
An elephant with diarrhoea.

Did you know they just discovered a new use for sheep in Wales?
Making wool!

What does the female part of a snail say during sex?
Faster, faster, faster!

What happened to the Pope as he went to Mount Olive?
Popeye nearly killed him!

What is 'egghead'?
What Mrs Dumpty gives to Humpty.

Why did the Avon Lady walk funny?
Her lipstick.

What is the noisiest thing in the world?
Skeletons bonking on a tin roof.

How do you find a blind man in a nudist colony?
Keep looking – it's not hard.

What's another name for an adolescent rabbit?
A pubic hare.

What did the cannibal do after he dumped his girlfriend?
Wiped his arse.

How do you tell if you have acne?
Blind people can read your face.

✱✱✱✱

Why did the lumber truck stop?
To let the lumber jack off.

What do Eskimos get if they sit on ice for too long?
Polaroids.

What's green, slimy and smells like Miss Piggy?
Kermit the Frog's finger.

What's the difference between a toad and a horny toad?
One goes "Gribbit"; the other goes "Grabbit".

What do you call an Amish man with his hand up a horse's arse?
A mechanic.

What do you call a nun with a sex change operation?
A tran-sister.

What's sticky, white and falls from the sky?
The Lord's second cumming!

What did the woman say to the swimming instructor?
"Will I really drown if you take your finger out?"

What do you call a Welsh farmer with a sheep under each arm?
A pimp.

What's brown and sits on a piano stool?
Beethoven's First Movement.

What is the square root of 69?
Ate something.

Why did the woman get thrown out of the riding stable?
She wanted to mount the horse her way.

✻✻✻✻

What do you find in a clean nose?
Fingerprints!

What's the worst bit about a lung transplant?
The first time you cough, it's not your phlegm!

What's bad about being a test tube baby?
You know for sure that your dad was a wanker.

How do you know when a male porn star is in your petrol station?
Just before the petrol tank's full, he pulls out the hose and sprays petrol
all over the car.

Why did the rag doll get thrown out of the toy box?
She kept sitting on Pinocchio's face and shouting, "Lie to me, lie to me!"

What do you call a vegetarian with diarrhoea?
A salad shooter.

What's the difference between a Spice Girls video and a porno?
The porno has better music!

What's the biggest crime committed by transvestites?
Male fraud.

What do you get when you cross a male chicken with a flea?
An itchy cock.

What's grey, sits by a bed and takes the piss?
A dialysis machine.

Did you about the two gay men who argued in the bar?
They went outside to exchange blows.

Did you hear the one about the blind circumciser?
He got the sack.

✳✳✳✳

Why are eggs frustrated?
They only get laid once, eaten once, and you have to boil them if you want to eat them hard!

Why do walruses go to Tupperware parties?
They hope to find a tight seal.

What's the difference between love and herpes?
Love is not forever.

Why did the washing machine laugh?
Because it was taking the piss out of the knickers!

What did the lesbian frogs say to each other?
We do taste like chicken!

What do the letters 'DNA' stand for?
National Dyslexics' Association.

Your family is so poor that when I went over to visit you at your house I stepped on a cigarette butt and your momma said, "Who turned off the heating?"

What would happen if the Founding Fathers had killed cats instead of turkeys?
Americans would be eating pussy every Thanksgiving.

Why did the man put his money in the freezer?
He wanted some cold, hard cash!

What's brown and sticky?
A stick!

How do you know that carrots are good for your eyesight?
Have you ever seen a rabbit wearing glasses?

What do you call a surgeon with eight arms?
A doctopus!

Why do men prefer to take showers rather than baths?
Pissing in a bath is revolting!

✳✳✳✳

What do you call kids born in whorehouses?
Brothel sprouts.

Did you know that Cher is re-forming the Spice Girls?
She'll be Old Spice.

Why did the one-handed man cross the road?
To get to the second-hand shop.

How do you know when your cat's finished cleaning itself?
He smokes a cigarette.

What's the definition of trust?
Two cannibals giving each other a blowjob.

What's the difference between a tampon and a cowboy hat?
Cowboy hats are for arseholes.

Did you hear about the streaker who was thinking of retirement?
He decided to stick it out for one more year!

Which meat is cheapest in the USA?
Deer balls – you'll find them under a buck.

Did you hear the one about the constipated mathematician?
He worked it out with a pencil.

Why don't skeletons fight each other?
None of them has the guts!

What did the alien say when he landed in the garden?
"Take me to your weeder!"

****

More Tea Vicar?

15

Not for the Faint-hearted

A native American Indian went to his father one day because his school was doing a project on how people get their names and where names come from. He first asked, "Father, why was it that you named my first sister Buffalo Grazing?" The chief looked at his son and said, "On the morning after the birth of your first sister, I walked out of the hot, sweaty teepee and I looked around the plains. I saw great beauty around me, and I saw the fields where the graceful buffalo graze peacefully. I hoped that she would know peace like these fine animals, and decided to name her Buffalo Grazing." "That's great," said the son, "and why did you name my other sister Full Moon Shining?" "Well,' said the chief, "on the evening of the birth of your other sister, I walked out of the hot, sweaty teepee and looked around me. It was still dark and the only light came from the moon above. I thought of the light of life that had just been breathed into the little one and decided to name her Full Moon Shining." "That's great, dad," said the boy. And the father looked at him once more, and asked, "But why do you ask, Two Dogs Humping?"

✳✳✳✳

A husband and wife went to see a poncey European art movie at their local cinema. It was pretty strong stuff and involved a lot of graphic sex – all in the name of art, of course, nothing porno about it. The husband thought it was great, but the wife was a bit disturbed by the content, particularly by a scene of people masturbating which left nothing to the imagination. As the couple were having a drink afterwards, the wife said to her husband, "You know dear, I find it very difficult to deal with masturbation in the movies," to which the husband replied, "Oh, sorry love, I'll stop doing it then!"

✳✳✳✳

Marty was doing some river fishing. A big one bit, and when he fished it out he had a big surprise: it was a goldfish. "Oi, fisherman," said the fish, "if you set me free I'll give you whatever you want. I'm a magic fish and I'll grant you three wishes." "Sounds good to me," thought Marty, "I've got it made now." "OK, then," said Marty. "My first wish is to have a truck full of money." "At your command," said the goldfish. A top-of-the-range truck filled to the brim with cash appeared on the road next to the river; the key appeared in Marty's hand. "My second wish is to have a different top model to sleep with every night of every year." "At your command," said the goldfish, and a diary appeared in Marty's hand with a full schedule of women filled in. "My third wish is for my cock to touch the floor," said Marty. "At your command," said the goldfish, and he cut Marty's legs off.

✳✳✳✳

A boy's mother is pregnant, so she has to go off to hospital. The night before she goes, the boy chances upon her in the bathroom and sees hair between her legs. He asks, "What's that, Mummy?" and she tells him, "It's my washcloth, dear." A couple of weeks later the mother is back from hospital, but she had to have her pubic hair shaved during the birth. The boy chances in on her again and notices that her hair has gone. He asks, "What happened to your washcloth, Mummy?" and his mother replies, "I lost it dear." A couple of days later the boy is running through the house shouting "Mummy, I found your washcloth," so his mother stops him and says, "What do you mean, dear?" "I found your washcloth, Mummy," the boy says again. The mother finds this pretty odd, but decides to go along with it so she asks him, "And where did you find it, dear?" So the boy says, "The maid has it now, and she's washing Daddy's face with it!"

✳✳✳✳

Trailertrash Cletus was enjoying his normal Saturday afternoon activities (watching TV and drinking beer) when his wife came storming into the trailer. "Cletus, some man's been real rude to me and I want you to go and kick his ass!" she screamed. "Why, sure thing, Maylene," said Cletus, "you jus' tell me what he done did to you." "Well," said Maylene, "I was at the supermarket and I dropped something. When I bent over to pick it up this man looked up my dress." Cletus started stamping his feet. "And then, when I got back up, he said, 'I'd like to fill you up with beer and drink the lot from down there!'" Cletus sat down straight away. Maylene asked, "Ain't you goin' do nothin', Cletus?" Cletus said, "You must be kidding, Maylene – I ain't gonna mess with someone who can drink that much beer!"

✳✳✳✳

Two village idiots are discussing safe sex: "So, matey, how do you protect yourself from AIDS?" says the first. "I wear a condom constantly," says the second. "Don't you ever take it off?" says the first. "Of course: when I go to the bathroom and when I have sex!" says the second.

****

"So, Cletus; how did your first day of upper school go?" said Cletus' father. "It was great, Daddy," said Cletus. "Teacher asked each one of us to count to one hundred. Some of the kids couldn't get past the number 30, but I counted all the way to one hundred without making a single mistake. It was great." "That's great, son," said the father, "it's because you're from Arkansas." The next day the father asked, "So how was school today, Cletus?" Cletus said, "It was fine: we had to say the alphabet in class today, Daddy. Some of the kids couldn't get past the letter Q, but I got all the way from A to Z without any mistakes. It was great." 'That's great, son," said the father, "it's because you're from Arkansas." After the third day, Cletus came back with a worried look on his face. "What's the matter, son? No good news from school today?" asked Daddy. "Well, Daddy," said Cletus, "we had PE today, and after the lesson, in the shower, I noticed that I had the biggest weewee of anyone in the class. It must have been ten times longer and hairier than anyone else's. Is it because I'm from Arkansas?" "Not quite, son," said Daddy. "It's because you're 18 years old!'

****

Little Billy was famous for his rectal prowess, but it was starting to disrupt classes, so the teacher called him back after school to discuss the problem with him. She began by asking him why he kept breaking wind all the time when he knew it offended many people. "Well, miss, it's because I'm the best and I'm really proud of myself. I want to share my gift with the world." "So, in that case," said his teacher, "if I can do it better than you, will you stop doing it in the classroom?" Little Billy said he surely would, mainly because he didn't think she would be able to do it better than him. So the teacher set up the test: she placed two pieces of paper covered in chalk dust on the floor, the idea being to blow as much dust as possible from the paper. Little Billy steps forward first, drops his trousers and pants and crouches down over the paper. He rips out his best effort and it clears most of the chalk dust from the page. At the teacher's turn, she hitches up her skirt, drops her knickers and squats over her piece of paper. She lets fly a huge blast that completely clears the chalk dust and also blows the paper across the room. Little Billy is impressed and asks the teacher if she can repeat what she's just done. She is flattered, so agrees to do it just one more time. As she crouches down, Little Billy takes a quick peek up her skirt. "Hey, that's not fair," he begins. "No wonder you won, miss: yours is double-barrelled!"

✳✳✳✳

One upon a time a long way away there was a kingdom with a king who had a daughter. He wanted her to marry a brave man who would desire her and make her happy. So he devised a test: if any man could swim across his huge lake of crocodiles they could have the choice of a castle, untold riches or his daughter's hand in marriage. People gathered from miles around and many volunteered to try. "I can do it," a man cried, jumped into the water and was instantly swallowed up by the crocodiles. "I can do better than that," said another, who jumped in and was instantly swallowed up by the crocodiles. Next, there was a loud splash and a man began to swim. He made it all the way and was greeted by the king. "Would you like the castle, the cash or the fair princess, brave sir?" he asked. "None of them," the man replied, "I want the dirbag who pushed me in in the first place!"

✶✶✶✶

A priest thinks his sermons need modernizing a bit, so he decides to preach on windsurfing instead of the usual fire and brimstone, or condemnation of sex. He tells his wife, who thinks it's a great idea, despite the priest's inexperience with the subject matter, but is sorry she won't be able to hear his new-style sermon because she has a sick friend to see. On his way to church the priest has second thoughts. "I don't know a thing about windsurfing and I can't relate it to anything," he said to himself. "I'll just stick to what I know," and proceeded to preach his usual sermon on the sinfulness of sex. After the service, and before the priest gets home, one of the lay readers walks past the priest's house. The priest's wife is back and out doing some gardening. "Great sermon today," says the lay reader. "That's a surprise," said the wife, "because he only tried it twice, and he fell off both times!"

✶✶✶✶

A dull old maths teacher leaves a letter for his wife one Friday night:

> Dear Janet,
> As you know, I am 56, and by the time you read this letter I will be settled in at the Luxor Hotel, tucking into my beautiful, sexy, 21-year-old teaching assistant.

When the teacher arrives at the hotel he finds that a letter has been left for him:

> Dear John,
> As you know, I too am 56, and by the time you read this letter I will be settled in at the Excelsior Hotel, tucking into my handsome, virile, 21-year-old toyboy. You, being a maths teacher, will appreciate that 21 goes into 56 a lot more times than 56 goes into 21!

Mr Rennie was an old man and he lived in a nursing home. One day he walked into the nurses' quarters and told them his penis had died. None of them were shocked – this sort of thing happened all the time – and they just figured he was a bit bored and would get over it. A couple of days later, Mr Rennie bumped into one of the nurses walking down the corridor. His penis was hanging out of his trousers. The nurse said to him, "I thought your penis had died, Mr Rennie?" "It certainly did, young lady,' he replied, 'but today's the viewing!"

****

Four retired friends decide to go golfing. One of them pays the fees, while the other three go up to tee off. They are all bragging about their sons. The first man says, "Well, my son's in construction, and he's so successful that he gave one of his friends a brand-new house for free." The second man says, "Well, my son's a car salesman, and he's so successful that he gave one of his friends a Porsche for free." The third man says, "Well, my son's a stockbroker, and he's so successful that he gave one of his friends a share portfolio for free." At this point the fourth man arrives on the scene and they tell him, "We were just discussing how our sons were doing. Is yours successful?" The man says, "Well, my son is gay, and he's an erotic dancer in a gay bar." There is silence as the others look embarrassed for the man. "I'm not really thrilled about the dancing, but still," the man continues, "he does pretty well anyway. His last three boyfriends gave him a share portfolio, a Porsche and a brand-new house for nothing!"

****

A German is climbing in the Alps when he stops for a rest. He notices a bottle half-hidden in the pile of stones that he is sitting on. He uncorks it and WHAM! a genie pops out. "Thank you for releasing me, O Great One," the genie says. "I can grant you one wish – it can be anything you want." The man has a think, and eventually says, "I'm a big fan of schnapps and it's rather expensive. Could you arrange for me to piss schnapps?" "Your wish is my command, O Great One," says the genie, who waves his hand and then disappears. The man carries on with his walk and eventually gets home. That evening, after dinner, he goes to the toilet. As he is going, he thinks to himself, "I wonder if that genie was telling the truth...let's see, now that smells like schnapps, and it looks like schnapps, so..." And he pees a bit into a glass. He holds it up to the light and then tastes just a tiny bit. "Hurrah! It is schnapps, and good schnapps at that," he shouts, and drinks the entire glass. The man rushes out of the bathroom calling for his wife, "Helga, Helga, come quickly: it's a miracle!" Helga comes downstairs and he "pours" her a glass of schnapps. She is very apprehensive and it is not until he drinks some himself that she will try the liquid. She finds the taste fantastic as well, so the two of them get blasted on top-quality schnapps all night and have a great time. The next day after work the German tells Helga to take two glasses out of the cupboard because they will be having another party. She willingly agrees and the couple party the night away on the excellent schnapps that the man "produces". The next day after work the German tells Helga to take only one glass out of the cupboard because they will be having another party. "But, my love," she says, "why only the one glass?" The man fills his glass, lifts it to his wife and says, "Because tonight, my dear, you drink from the bottle!"

✳✳✳✳

Three men, John, Jack and Jim, are shipwrecked and washed up on the shores of Africa. They turn inland looking for food and safety but are captured by cannibals. The cannibal king tells them that normally they eat everything they find in the forest, but that he will give them a chance to live if they pass a small test. The test is in two parts: for the first part, all they have to do is gather ten pieces of the same type of fruit in the forest. "Easy enough," the men think, and they all run off quickly. First of all John comes back with his arms full and walks up to the king of the cannibals. "I have brought apples, O cannibal king," he says. The cannibal king then explains the second part of the trial... "You will have the fruit forcibly inserted into your arsehole without any pain, pleasure or sentiment to be shown on your face. Any sentiment or sound whatever will cause you to be skinned alive and eaten." So John is bent over and the second part of the trial begins. The first apple goes in easily, but the second one is bigger and John winces as it is forced. As he cries out, he is carried away, prepared for the pot and eaten. Shortly Jack comes back with his hands full and walks up to the king of the cannibals. "I have brought blackberries, O cannibal king," he says. The cannibal king explains the second part of the trial and Jack grins to himself as he bends over. The insertion begins. First one berry, then two, then three, then four, then five, then six, then seven, then eight. Jack keeps his cool throughout, but suddenly, on the ninth berry, he bursts out laughing and is taken away, prepared for the pot and eaten. The two men meet up in Heaven. John says to Jack, "What happened to you then? I saw that you picked berries and I'd have thought you would have got through that with no problem." Jack says, "Me, too, and I was nearly there when I saw Jim coming round the corner with an armful of watermelons!"

✳✳✳✳

Two cowboys are sat having a drink in a bar. One asks his friend if he's heard of the latest sexual position. Apparently it's called 'the rodeo'. The other says no and asks what you do. "Well," says the first cowboy, "first you mount your wife from the back, reach around her front and cup both breasts with your hands. Then you whisper softly in her ear, 'Oh baby, these are almost as nice as your sister's!' Then you see how long you can hang on for!"

✶✶✶✶

Nikos, a Greek man, was sitting in a bar talking to a young tourist. "So," he says, "you see that wall out there in that field?" He points to a huge stone wall separating two fields. "Can you see how well it's built? I spent a year of my life moving stones from down in the valley up to those pastures and carving them so they fitted. That's the strongest fence between here and Athens! And do they call me Nikos the wall-builder? No; they do not!" Then he continues, "So, you see the bar here? The one you are leaning on right now?" and he raps it with his knuckles. 'Can you see how well it's built? I spent a year of my life cutting and sanding and waxing this bar. This is the finest bar between here and Athens! And do they call me Nikos the bar-builder? No, they do not!" Then he continues, "So, you see the pier out there in the water?" He points to a long, solid pier that stretches out into the deep, deep water. "I spent a year of my life putting that pier together. I cut down the trees, I nailed the boards and I dug the holes for the poles. It almost killed me, and it is the finest pier between here and Athens! And do they call me Nikos the pier-builder? No, they do not!" Then he looks around and checks the bar before he continues, "So I fuck *one* lousy sheep...!"

✱✱✱✱

Jim and Nick are hanging out on the beach trying to pull. Nick has plenty of luck, but Jim's a bit short in the "front" so he says to Nick, "What's up, Nick? I'm just not having much luck with the ladies?" Nick replies, "It must be that you aren't appealing enough to the basic animal instincts. Try putting a nice big potato down your swimming trunks. The birds'll take one look and be all over you like a rash!" Now Jim knows that Nick pulls all over the place, so thinks he might as well give it a damn good go. The next day the two of them meet up again and Jim is in no better a mood. He says to Nick, "I tried it with that potato and you know, it did me no good at all. In fact, even more of the chicks are avoiding me than before. What's that all about?" Nick has a quick look and says, "Well, mate, I think it'd probably help a lot if you put the potato down the front!"

✱✱✱✱

Two explorers are walking through a rainforest when they are captured by a tribe of tiny, but highly aggressive, cannibals. Minutes later they find themselves tied up tight, sitting in a huge pot full of water and vegetables with an enormous fire burning underneath it. After a couple of minutes one of them starts to laugh. The other one is shocked and assumes the man has lost his mind. "What the heck is up with you?" he asks, "We're going to die in here and be eaten by a bunch of horrible cannibals. What on earth do you find funny about that?" The other replies, "I just peed in the pot!"

****

A businessman goes on a trip to Japan. As is traditional, he and his associates all go out with their Japanese equivalents and get totally drunk. Then they send the American upstairs with a prostitute. As he begins to have sex with her, she starts to moan, "Nai com chai, nai com chai." He has no idea what it means, but she doesn't look very happy, so the businessman stops and leaves. The next day, he is out playing golf with his associates when one of his Japanese hosts slices the ball horribly to one side and in frustration shouts, "Nai com chai!" The American businessman says to him, "What does that mean?" The Japanese businessman replies, "Wrong hole!"

****

One night a guy had a few too many at his local and decided to drive home very slowly, taking the "clever" route to avoid any policemen or other snoopers. As he did so, he passed a field full of pumpkins. Having been drinking, the man was feeling pretty horny so started to think about how pumpkins are soft and squishy on the inside, and how no one need ever know, and how it wouldn't really do any harm, would it? So he pulled over and picked out a nice soft pumpkin, cut the right-sized hole in the side and began to have a go. He really started getting carried away and before he knew it he was sweating away, oblivious to the world: so oblivious, he didn't even notice a police car turn up right behind him. The two policemen walk up behind him and one of them shouts, "Hey sir, sir, do you realize you're fucking a pumpkin?" The man jumps, realizes he's been rumbled and starts thinking. Quick as a flash, he says, "A pumpkin? Is it midnight already, officer?"

✱✱✱✱

Two mates are out for an evening in a bar. They happen to go to the toilet at the same time. As they are standing there, John notices that Thomas is pretty well-endowed and he can't help mentioning the fact. "Yeah," says Thomas. "But it wasn't always like that, you know. I was sick of only having a small one, so I had a transplant from a doctor in Harley Street. It was pretty expensive – £10,000 – but it was really worth it." A few months later, the two mates find themselves next to each other in a toilet again. John says to Thomas "I thought about what you said last time, and I decided to get myself a transplant, too. You got well ripped off, mate – mine only cost a grand!" Thomas leans across the urinals and has a quick look. "Not surprising," he says. "They've given you my old one!"

✱✱✱✱

Two men are changing after a sweaty game of squash. One notices that the other has a cork up his arse. He says, "Um, I couldn't help noticing, but how the hell did you get that cork up your arse?" The other man says, "Well, um, yes: it's a bit embarrassing, really. I was walking along a beach barefoot when I trip over this old bottle. I pick it up, take the cork out and whoosh! Out pops a huge red man with a turban on his head, floating in space in front of me. He says 'I am a genie. I grant you one wish. What will it be?' So I – rather foolishly, upon reflection – said, 'No shit!'"

****

A little old lady walks into a sex shop. She is having trouble walking and half hobbles and half hops over to the counter. She eventually makes it and holds on for dear life. She says the the boy behind the counter, "D-d-d-d-ooo yo-yo-you s-s-s-sell d-d-d-d-d-dildos-s-s-?" The boy says, "Yes, ma'am, we sell dildos. In fact we sell all sorts, in all shapes and sizes." The little old lady says, "D-d-d-d-d-o yo-yo-you h-h-h-h-have w-w-w-ww-wun th-th-th-th-that is sm-sm-sm-sm-small and b-b-b-b-black, s-s-s-s-s-ix i-i-i-i-i-inches l-l-l-l-ong b-b-b-b-b-but three i-i-i-i-i-i-inches th-th-th-th-thick?" The boy says, "Why, yes we do: that's one of the most popular models." "W-w-w-w-w-w-ell, c-c-c-c-c-c-can you t-t-t-t-t-t-tell m-m-m-me-e-e- how-w-w-w-w to t-t-t-t-t-t-turn-n-n-n-nn the fu-fu-fu-fucking thing-g-g-g-g-g- off-f-f-f-f-f-f-f-f-f-f?"

****

Two men and a woman were sitting in a bar discussing their lives. The first man says, "You know, I'm a YUPpie – that's Young, Urban Professional." The second man says, "Well, me and my missus, we're DINKs – that's Double Income, No Kids." Then the first man asks the woman, "So what are you?" She replies, "I'm a WIFE – that's Wash, Iron, Fuck, Et cetera!"

****

There's this really vain surfer type. He jogs and he lifts weights and he stretches and he tones. He's admiring himself in the mirror one day and he notices that all of him looks great apart from his willy – it is the only part of him that doesn't have a tan. So he tries instant tan from all sorts of places and tanning booths, but nothing works. Eventually he goes to see a doctor who tells him that because of the sensitive nature of the skin, he will only be able to tan his willy in proper sunlight. So the man goes to the beach. Sadly, there are no nudist beaches near where he lives, so he goes to a normal one and tries to get himself a tan without anyone noticing. He can't manage it, so he develops a plan: he digs a hole big enough to hide in and buries himself, apart from his willy, which he leaves sticking out, and his mouth. He puts on suntan lotion and falls asleep. A few minutes later, a couple of little old ladies walk past and one of them notices the willy in the sand. She prods it a couple of times with her walking stick and gets it to wake up a little bit. Then she sighs and says to her friend, "There's no justice, is there?" "What do you mean, dear?" her friend replies. The lady says, "Well, I've spent my life being curious about willies, enjoying them, asking for them, tasting them, praying for more of them, hoping they'll get bigger, and now here I am, 80 years old – they grow wild on the beach and I can't even squat down!"

****

An accountant is thrown in prison for fraud and is seriously disappointed to see that his cellmate is a huge body-builder type with no hair and covered in tattoos. His new cellmate says, "Don't worry, number-boy, I'm in here for white collar crime as well." The accountant says, "Phew, that's lucky, I'm in for insider dealing and tax evasion. What about you?" The cellmate replies, "I murdered three priests!"

****

Superman is flying through the skies of the city feeling horny and looking for opportunities to score. Suddenly he sees Wonder Woman sunbathing naked on the top of a building. "Aw, she won't mind; and besides, I'll be so quick she'll hardly notice!" he says to himself. He swiftly flies down, fucks her in quadruple-quick time and shoots off. Wonder Woman jumps up and says, "What the hell was that?" to which the Invisible Man replies, "I don't know, but my bum sure hurts!"

****

Three young female students all lived together in a flat and one night they all had dates at the same time. Around midnight they all got back and started comparing notes. The first girl says, "You know what? You can tell a good date when you come back home and your hair's all messed up." And the second girl says, "You know what? You can tell a good date when you come back home and your make-up's all smeared." The third girl says nothing, but just reaches under her skirt, removes her knickers and throws them against the wall. They stick there. "You know what? That's a good date," she says.

✳✳✳✳

A mounted policeman was on patrol one day when he comes across a little boy on a shiny new bicycle. The policeman leans down to the boy and says, "That's a nice shiny bike. Did Father Christmas bring it for you?" "He sure did," says the boy, all pleased with himself. Then the cop sits back up and writes the boy a £25 fine. "Next year, boy," he says, "ask Father Christmas to put a licence plate on it, too." The boy is really annoyed, so decides to get his own back. He looks up at the policeman and says, "That's a fine horse. Did Father Christmas bring it for you?" The policeman, thinking he will humour the boy, says, "He sure did," and is pretty pleased with himself. The boy then looks down underneath the horse and back up at the policeman before saying, "Next year, officer, perhaps you could ask Father Christmas to put the prick underneath the horse instead of on top!"

✳✳✳✳

Two village idiots go to a brothel and hammer on the door. "What the hell do you want?" shouts the madam."We've come for women," say the idiots. "How much money do you have on you?" shouts the madam again. The idiots scrabble through their pockets and see. "We've got a tenner!" they shout. "For that much you can go screw yourselves," laughs the madam. Just five minutes later, the idiots return and bang on the door again: "We've screwed ourselves: now we've come to give you the tenner!" they shout.

****

A couple had children who were very inquisitive, so were finding it hard to communicate about adult things like having sex. To avoid having to teach the children about the birds and the bees, they decide to use a code instead, using the word "typewriter" as a substitute for sex. A couple of days later the husband thinks it will be amusing to use the code for the first time, so he calls his five-year-old daughter over and says to her, "Go and tell your mother that Daddy would like her to come up and type a letter on the typewriter, please." The girl goes off and comes back a couple of minutes later. She says, "Mummy says that she can't type a letter for Daddy today because she's got a red ribbon stuck in the typewriter." A few days later the daughter comes up to the father and says, "Mummy told me to tell you that she can type that letter now." The father says, "Well, you go and tell Mummy not to worry because Daddy couldn't wait for the typewriter, so he decided to write the letter by hand!"

****

Once upon a time there was a sweet little girl who always wore pretty little dresses to school. However, at lunchtime every day she would sit on the bench by the tuckshop and cry. Nobody knew why, so one day one of her classmates, Tony, plucked up the courage to ask her why she always cried. She explained that she really loved chocolate but that she never had any money to buy some. So Tony says to her, "Tell you what: if you climb up that tree over there, I'll give you the money to buy some chocolate." "That's just great," the little girl says, and she runs off to climb the tree. As she does so, Tony and all the other boys in her class gather round and watch her climb. As she gets down, Tony gives her the money and thanks her. The next day the same thing happens and the sweet little girl climbs the tree again to get the chocolate. Again, all the boys watch her go up and down. This becomes a daily occurence at school and eventually the girl's mother asks her where she gets her chocolate money from. "It's easy, mum," the sweet little girl explains. "The boys in my class all give me money to climb the tree every day." "Oh, dear, don't do that: those nasty boys just want to see your underwear as you climb." "OK, mum," the girl says; but the next day at lunchtime there is an even bigger crowd by the tree as the sweet little girl climbs it. When she gets home that evening her mother asks her where she got her chocolate that day. "Oh, mum: I got it from climbing the tree," she explains simply, but the mother says, "Honey, I told you not to do that. Those boys just want to see your underwear!" So the sweet little girl says, "Don't worry, mum: I didn't wear any underwear today!"

✳✳✳✳

An Italian, a Frenchman and an Irishman are all chatting about their love-making prowess. The Italian begins by saying, "When I have feeneesh make-a love with my-a wife, I just stroke her-a buttocks and she-a float seex eenches above-a tha bed in total ecstasy." The Frenchman continues, "Zat's noseeng. When I av-a feeneeshed to make ze lurve wiz my wife, I leek ze solez of 'er feet and she float 12 eenches above ze bed in total ecstasy!" So the Irishman says, "Well, when I've screwed da woife, I git out da bed, wipe me dick on da curtins and she hits da fukkin' roof!"

****

A decent young man goes for dinner at his new girlfriend's house. He is very anxious and keen to impress his prospective in-laws. As the meal is served the family dog comes out of its basket, sits on the floor right beside the dinner table and proceeds to start licking its balls with a massively loud slurping sound. There is a shocked silence: nobody knows where to look or what to say. Driven to a state of wild nervousness, the man stutters, "Um, er, um…I er wish I could do that!" The girlfriend's family all look around in even greater shock and the mother says to him, "Well, if you gave him a biscuit I'm sure he'd let you!"

****

Three soldiers come back from active duty in Afghanistan. They are all due for retirement and are all summoned before their commanding officer. He tells them that in addition to their Army pension they will be paid a premium for services rendered in the Middle East and it will be calculated in the following way: each man will be paid $100 for a measurement from two points in their body, the two points to be stipulated by the men themselves. So the first soldier, a Sergeant, walks up to the front. "Where do you want the measurements to be taken from, Sergeant?" says the CO. "From the top of my shaved head to the tip of my toes, Sir!" A Lieutenant makes the measurement and tells the Commanding Officer it is 71 inches. "Seventy-one inches!" says the Commanding Officer. "That makes $7,100 for you." So the second soldier, a Corporal, walks up to the front. "Where do you want the measurements to be taken from, Corporal?" says the Commanding Officer. "From my left fingertip to my right fingertip, Sir!" says the Corporal. A Lieutenant makes the measurement and tells the CO it is 73 inches. "Seventy-three inches!" says the Commanding Officer, "that makes $7,300 for you." So the third soldier, a Private, walks up to the front. "Where do you want the measurements to be taken from, Private?" says the Commanding Officer. "From the top of my penis to the base of my balls, Sir!" says the Private. The commanding officer is a little surprised, but gets the lieutenant to make the measurement anyway. After a couple of seconds the Lieutenant says from down below, "Where on earth are your balls, Private?" and the private replies, "Back in Osama bBin Laden's bunker, Sir!"

✳✳✳✳

An ambassador from an African country was visiting Russia. The Russian ambassador to his country was entertaining him, and despite the obvious cultural differences, the two of them got on really well. The African gentleman was impressed by the hospitality that he was shown and on the final day of the visit the Russian offered to show him the traditional game of the country – Russian Roulette. The African man had not heard of this game, so the Russian explained the rules. "You pick up a revolver. You empty the cylinder. You replace one bullet. You spin the cylinder. You turn the gun to yourself and pull the trigger once." The African ambassador found this a bit scary, but coming from a proud warrior people he thought it would be exciting. The Russian man produced two revolvers and when both guns were loaded, both men turned them on themselves and pulled the triggers at the same time. There were two loud clicks and both breathed a huge sigh of relief. The African ambassador was very impressed with the game and thought about it all the way home. One year later, the Russian ambassador visited the Africa country to finalize a deal between the two countries. His hospitality was returned, much to his pleasure, and he and the African ambassador got on as well as before. On his last night, the African man said he would show him his country's traditional game. The Russian was impressed, and eager to see what the African had to offer him. The African ambassador led him to a plush room, deep in the state building. Standing before them were six beautiful women, all completely naked. The African said,

"These are the most beautiful women from each of the six tribes of the country. Any one of them will give you the best blowjob of your life – just choose one." The Russian was impressed, but he couldn't help feeling there was something missing from this game. He said to the African ambassador, "That's great and everything, but compared to the national game from my country there is something missing – where's the danger, the excitement, the chance?" The African ambassador, with a wide grin on his face, answers, "One of these women is a cannibal!"

✳✳✳✳

There were twin brothers by the name of Joey and John Jones. They had lived in the same fishing village all their lives. John was married and Joey had always been single. Joey owned a knackered old boat. One day, Joey's boat sank on exactly the same day that John's wife passed away. A couple of days later a kindly old lady met Joey in the queue for the Post Office and she thought he was John. She said to him, "So sorry for your trouble: you must be feeling awful and I'm not surprised." Joey, not at all worried about his crappy old boat, replied, "Well, I couldn't care less. She was a pile of crap right from the very beginning. Her bottom was all lumpy and she always stank of old fish. The first time I got in her she leaked faster than anything I'd ever seen before in my life. She had a crack and a huge hole in front that kept getting bigger and bigger every time that I used her. I could handle her fine, but when someone else was using her she leaked like a bastard and that's what finished her off, I reckon: three or four blokes from out of town came over looking for a good time. I told them that she was useless and much too creaky for all of them, but they really thought she looked all right. Anyway, all of them tried to get into her at the same time. It was just too much and she cracked right up the middle!" The little old lady fainted!

✱✱✱✱

On a sunny, hot afternoon a man is sitting on his porch drinking iced lemonade in a deckchair relaxing and watching as his wife grunts, groans and struggles with the lawnmower. The next-door neighbour can't believe her eyes and she storms over to the porch. "You should be ashamed of yourself, you caveman, letting your wife mow the lawn on a day like this. You ought to be hung!" "I am," says the man with a wry smile, "and that's exactly why my wife is mowing the lawn."

✱✱✱✱

One morning at breakfast, Chuck walks up behind his wife and pinches her arse. "You know, Daisy, if you firmed this up we'd be able to get rid of your girdle," he says. Now Daisy is most insulted by this, of course, but she decides to let it go – it's only breakfast time, after all. The next day, Chuck walks up behind his wife and pinches her breast. "You know, Daisy, if you firmed this up we'd be able to get rid of your bra," he says. Daisy can't bite her lip another time, so she turns around and grasps his cock firmly, saying, "You know, Chuck, if you firmed this up we'd be able to get rid of the postman, the gardener, the pool man and your brother!"

Blonde Ambition

Not for the Fair-haired

A blonde is walking down the street with a pig under her arm. She passes a man who, puzzled, asks "Where did you get that?" "I won her in a raffle!" the pig replies.

****

One day, a blonde went to see the doctor with a carrot in one ear, a cucumber in the other and two peas up her nose, complaining she wasn't feeling well. The doctor told her it was because she wasn't eating properly.

****

Three blondes witness a violent crime. Two days later, they are summoned by the police to identify a suspect. In order to check they are reliable witnesses, the inspector says he will show them a mug-shot for 30 seconds, then ask each one for a description. He shows the mug-shot to the first blonde for 30 seconds, then covers it and asks her if she thinks she would recognize the face. "Yes, easy," she replies. "The guy in the picture has only one eye." The inspector blinks in confusion, then says, "He's got only one eye because it's a profile shot!" Shaking his head, he repeats the procedure for the second blonde and again asks if she would recognize him. "Easy! He only has one ear," she answers. "Come on, what's the matter with you two? It's a profile shot! You're seeing this man from the side!" shouts the inspector. Expecting the worst, he repeats the procedure with the third blonde, then says, 'Would you recognize the suspect from this picture if you saw him in real life? And think before you give me a stupid answer." The third blonde looks hard at the photo, and remains silent for a minute, then says, "Yeah, it's easy: he's wearing contact lenses." This takes the inspector by surprise. He picks up the photo and looks really hard at it, but can't tell if the suspect wears contact lenses or not. With a suspicious look at the third blonde, he checks the full report on the suspect. Sure enough, when the mug-shot was taken, he was wearing contact lenses! Baffled, the inspector goes back to the third blonde and asks her, "How could you tell he was wearing contact lenses?" "Well," she says, "he can't wear regular glasses with only one eye and one ear, now, can he?"

****

Two blondes are waiting at the bus stop. A bus pulls up and the doors open. The first blonde steps in and asks the driver: "Will this bus take me to New Street?" "Sorry, it won't: you're at the wrong stop," the driver replies. The second blonde steps inside, throws her chest out, smiles devilishly and twitters: "Will it take ME?"

****

A blonde walks into a library and says to the librarian at the counter, "Can I have a burger and fries, please?" "This is a library," the librarian answers reprovingly. "Oh, I'm so sorry. *May* I have a burger and fries?" the blonde whispers.

****

A blonde is complaining to her friend about her boyfriend and men in general. "I've had enough with men. They're cheap, they cheat on you, they don't respect you… Next time I want sex, I'll use my trusty plastic companion instead." "Yeah, but what will you do when the batteries run out?" her friend asks. "I'll fake an orgasm as usual."

****

A guy approaches the window of the ticket office of a cinema carrying a chicken in his arms. "Hi: could I get two tickets, please? Oh – does my pet chicken have to pay full price?" "What do you mean, your pet chicken? Chickens aren't allowed into the cinema," the girl tells him. Outraged, he storms off, but after a few minutes, as he really wants to see this film, he decides to hide his chicken in his pants and try again. He returns to the booth and this time, to his delight, he is allowed to get a ticket. During the film, however, he can feel the chicken getting restless so he pulls his zip down and lets its head out for some fresh air. As it happens, he's sitting next to two blondes. One of them, turning to check what he's doing wiggling in his seat, turns to her friend and says: "Sally, the guy sitting next to me just unzipped his flies!" "It's OK; when you've seen one, you've seen them all," the other replies. "Yes, but this one is eating my popcorn!"

****

A blonde is looking at a bulletin board at her workplace and sees an ad which says, "Luxury Ocean Cruise Only 5." She copies the details, goes to the address and hands the ad and a fiver to the secretary. The secretary points to a burly guy sitting in a battered sofa, reading a newspaper. The guy stands up and knocks the blonde unconscious. When she wakes up, she's tied to a log and floating down the river. She starts to think maybe this wasn't such a good idea after all. Then she sees one of her colleagues (who is also blonde) floating right next to her. Sighing, she says, "So do you think they're going to serve us some food on this trip?" "They didn't last year," the other blonde replies.

****

A mother and her young blonde daughter have just finished shopping for food and all the groceries are scattered over the kitchen floor in plastic bags. While the mum busies herself putting things away, the daughter picks up a box of animal crackers and empties its contents on the table, making quite a mess. "What are you doing?" her mum yells. "Well, it says on the box, 'Do not eat if seal is broken.' I'm looking for the seal."

****

How do you know a blonde has been sending e-mail?
There's an envelope in the CD drive.

How do you know a blonde is having a bad day?
Her tampon's behind her ear and she can't find her cigarette.

How do you put a twinkle in a blonde's eye?
Shine a flashlight in her ear.

How do blondes' brain cells die?
Alone.

Did you hear about the new blonde paint?
It's not real bright, but it's cheap and it spreads easily.

How do you know that a blonde's been using a word processor?
There's Tipp-ex all over the screen.

What's a blonde's favourite nursery rhyme?
Humpme Dumpme.

What do blondes and doorknobs have in common?
Everyone gets a turn.

****

A blonde wanted to get her pet dog in a smooth-haired dog contest and decided to help her dog a little by going to the chemist for some hair-removal lotion. The assistant hands her a bottle of special shampoo and says: "Remember to keep your arms in the air for at least three minutes." "Er, it's not for my armpits," the blonde replies, blushing slightly, "it's for my Chihuahua." "In that case, don't ride a bike for three days," the assistant says.

****

A blonde is flying on a four-engined plane. Suddenly there's a loud bang, the pilot comes on the radio and says, "I'm sorry, but we seem to have lost an engine. We'll probably be delayed by 45 minutes." A few minutes later, there's another bang. Once again, the radio comes on: "I'm sorry, but we seem to have lost another engine. We'll probably be delayed by two hours." A little while later, the third engine shuts off. This time, the pilot tells the passengers that they will be delayed by around three hours. The blonde turns to the guy sitting beside her and says, "Man, if they lose the fourth engine, we'll be up here all day."

****

A blonde is taking a tour of a National Park and hears the guide say dinosaur fossils have been found in the area. "Wow!" she exclaims. "I'd never have thought dinosaurs would come so close to the motorway."

****

NASA sends a space shuttle up with two pigs and a blonde on board. While the shuttle is taking off, the NASA command centre calls the first pig and asks, "Pig One, do you know your mission?" The pig replies, "Oink oink. Get the shuttle into orbit and launch the trillion-dollar satellite. Oink oink." Then Mission Control asks the second pig, "Pig Two, do you know your mission?" The second pig replies, "Oink oink. Once Pig One has completed the trillion-dollar satellite launch, close hatch and land shuttle. Oink oink." Then NASA asks the blonde, "Blonde woman, do you know your mission?" The blonde woman replies, "Um... Oh yeah: I remember now. Feed the pigs – and *don't touch a goddamned thing!*"

****

A blonde walks down the street and sees a banana peel on the ground 100 metres ahead. "Here we go again," she sighs.

****

A blonde goes to the electrical appliance sale and finds a bargain. She stops a salesman and says: "I'd like to buy this TV, please." "Sorry: we don't sell to blondes," the salesman replies. She storms out of the shop and hurries home, where she dyes her hair. She comes back to the same shop and again tells the salesman: "I'd like to buy this TV, please." "Sorry: we don't sell to blondes," he replies again. "How did he recognize me?" she wonders. Mortified, she rushes back home again and goes for the complete disguise this time – haircut, new colour, new outfit, big sunglasses – then waits a full day before returning to the shop. "I'd like to buy this TV, please," she says to the same man. "Sorry: we don't sell to blondes," he replies. Frustrated, she exclaims, "But how do you know I'm a blonde?" "Because that's not a TV: it's a microwave," he replies.

****

"The guys down at the pub say the milkman has seduced every woman on our street except one," Bob told his blonde wife. She thought for a moment. "I'll bet it's that snooty Mrs. Jenkins."

****

A blonde went to the hospital emergency room with the tip of her left index finger blown off. "How did this happen?" the doctor asked. "Well you see, I was trying to commit suicide," the blonde replied. "By shooting your finger?" the doctor asked, baffled. "No, silly! First I put the gun to my chest and I thought, 'I just paid $6,000 for these boobs: no way I am blowing them off.' Then I put the gun in my mouth but I thought, 'I just paid $2,000 to get my teeth fixed: the teeth are staying!' So I put the gun in my ear and I thought, 'This is going to make a loud noise,' so I put my finger in my other ear before I pulled the trigger."

****

A blonde, a brunette and a redhead are running away from the cops when they stumble by chance upon an old barn to hide in. They find three big sacks on the floor of the barn and promptly jump in them. About a minute later, a police car comes to a screaming halt by the barn door and a policeman steps out. He enters the barn and spots the suspicious-looking sacks. He kicks the first one. "Meow," says the redhead. "It must be a cat," says the policeman, and he kicks the second sack. "Woof," says the brunette. "Must be a dog," mutters the policeman, and he kicks the third sack. "Potatoes," says the blonde.

****

A blonde finds her way to her doctor and tells him that she's really worried because every part of her body hurts. "Show me where," says the doctor, concerned. The blonde touches her own arm and screams, "Ouch!" Next she touches her leg, her nose, her elbow and every time she howls in pain. She looks at her doctor and says, "See? I told you: it hurts everywhere!" The doctor pokes her in the chest and says, "Don't worry; it's not serious. You've just got a broken index finger."

****

It is winter and a blonde decides to go ice-fishing. After having spent some time getting all the right tools, she drives toward the nearest frozen lake and starts cutting a circular hole in the ice. Then from the heavens a voice boomed, *"There are no fish under the ice."* Startled, the blonde moves a bit further down the ice, pours herself a mug of coffee from a thermos and starts cutting another hole in the ice. Out of nowhere, the voice booms, *"There are no fish under the ice."* This time the blonde is pretty scared, so she moves to the far end of the frozen lake. Just as she starts cutting another hole, the very loud voice says, *"There are no fish under the ice."* The awed, and very scared, blonde slowly raises her head and says, in a small, contrite voice: "Is that you, Lord?" The voice answers, "No. It is the manager of the ice rink!"

✱✱✱✱

A blonde orders a pizza. When it is done, the cook asks her: "Do you want me to cut it into six or 12 pieces?" "Six, please," she says, "I couldn't eat 12 pieces."

✱✱✱✱

A blonde and a brunette are out driving. As they've had a few beers, the brunette tells the blonde to look out for cops. They drive for a while, and then the blonde taps the brunette on the shoulder and says: "Hold on, there's a cop car behind us." "Shit!" says the brunette. "Are their lights on?" The blonde has to think for a moment, then says, "Er... Yes. No. Yes. No. Yes. No..."

✳✳✳✳

Two American tourists were travelling through Wales. As they approached Llangollen, they started arguing about the pronunciation of the town's name until they stopped for lunch. As they stood at the counter, one tourist asked the blonde employee, "Could you settle an argument for us? Would you please pronounce where we are very slowly?" The blonde leaned over and said, "Burrrrrr Gurrrrrr Kingggg."

✳✳✳✳

A blonde, a redhead and a brunette were looking at a dictionary for the hardest words they knew. The brunette's word was 'posthumous'. The redhead's word was 'deoxyribonucleic'. The blonde's word was 'dick'.

✳✳✳✳

A blonde, a brunette and a redhead are having a breaststroke swimming competition across the English Channel. The brunette finishes first, then the redhead second, but the blonde never finished. When the lifeboat found her, way behind, she said, "I don't want to be a telltale or anything, but the other two – you know? They used their arms."

✳✳✳✳

A blonde was having a great time at a party and was soon spotted by a guy who swiftly led her upstairs. He started to undress her, then, surprised, saw that she was wearing shower caps on her tits. "Hey, what's with the shower caps?" the guy asked her. "What shower caps?" she answered, "These are booby condoms!"

✳✳✳✳

A blonde, a brunette and a redhead go trekking one day and stumble upon a cave, in which there is an old magical mirror. The dusty book next to it says that this mirror will grant a wish only if you tell the truth – if you lie, you disappear in a puff of smoke. They find this pretty neat, so the brunette goes first. "I think I'm the smartest woman on earth." "Poof!" She disappears. The redhead goes up to try. "I think I'm the prettiest woman on earth." "Poof!" She disappears. The blonde goes up, decided to tell the truth and nothing but the truth. "I think…" "Poof!"

✳✳✳✳

A little boy is playing with his blonde friend when another, older boy comes in. "I found a condom on the veranda," he smirks. The blonde looks up and asks innocently: "What's a veranda?"

****

After watching a program about Egyptians on TV, a blonde decides to treat herself to a milk bath. She leaves a note to the milkman which reads, "30 litres of milk tomorrow, please." On finding the note in the morning, the milkman is a bit confused and knocks on the door. "You mean three litres, right?" "No, you read right, 30 litres, please," the blonde smiles back. "Er…OK. Pasteurized?" "No: just up to my tits."

****

A blonde, a brunette and a redhead are on a walk in the mountains when they find a bridge over a deep ridge. They are halfway across when a fairy appears out of nowhere. "Welcome to the fairy bridge," she says. "If you want to pass, you need to jump over and shout the name of an animal: then you will be transformed into this animal and land harmlessly." The brunette goes first and, as she jumps over the edge of the bridge, she shouts "Lion!" and, sure enough, whoosh! she gets transformed into a great lion which gently descends to the ground and disappears into the trees. When it is her turn, the redhead swings her legs over the edge of the bridge and shouts "Eagle!" and whoosh! she is transformed into a magnificent eagle which soars to the heavens. The blonde finds this pretty neat but, just as she jumps over the bridge, she realizes she hasn't thought about what animal she wanted to be. "Crap," she says.

****

A young blonde was on vacation in the depths of Louisiana. She had always wanted a pair of genuine alligator shoes and thought it was the perfect place to get some. She was disappointed, however, for the local shoe shops were still too expensive for her. Very frustrated, she decided to catch her own alligator so that she could get a pair of shoes at a reasonable price. Later in the day a man was driving home after a day of fly-fishing when he spotted the blonde standing waist-deep in the water, shotgun in hand. Just then, horrified, he saw a huge nine-foot alligator swimming quickly toward her. The blonde took aim, squeezed the trigger and killed the beast. She waded to the body and dragged it to the bank, where there were already half a dozen dead alligators lying in the mud. With an angry shout, the blonde flipped the alligator on its back, stared at it for a few seconds and howled out, "Damn it: this one isn't wearing any shoes either!"

****

A blonde was trying to put together a jigsaw puzzle. She got very frustrated, so she decided to ask her husband for help. "It's supposed to be a tiger!" she cried. "Honey," said her husband, "put the Frosties back in the box!"

****

A blonde and a brunette are sitting in a pub having a drink when the brunette's boyfriend comes in with a bunch of roses. The brunette receives the flowers with apparent pleasure, but makes a face as soon as her boyfriend is off to get a drink from the bar. "Crap: he's bought me flowers again," says the brunette. "What's the matter with you? You don't like flowers?" asks her friend. "Oh, I do," the brunette replies. "It's just that when he buys me flowers it means I'll have to spend the next two or three days with my legs wide open." The blonde asks, "You don't have a vase?"

****

A blonde has been asked on a date and is being treated to a seafood restaurant. On her way to her table, they pass an aquarium full of live lobsters. At the end of the meal, taking pity on the lobsters, she manages to get near the aquarium while her date is settling the bill and hides a couple of them in her bag. "Neat," she thinks triumphantly. "I'll ask Bill to stop by the woods and I'll free the poor creatures."

****

Two blondes take a stroll in the forest. Suddenly, one blonde stops and looks down. "Look at those deer tracks," she says to her friend. Her friend looks down and replies: "These aren't deer tracks: they're wolf tracks." "No way. They're deer tracks." "You're completely wrong. These are *wolf* tracks!" They kept on arguing for half an hour, at which point they got killed by a train.

****

A blonde walks into a clothing store. She looks around for a while and finally picks out a scarf and brings it to the counter to pay for it. As she seems very pleased with her purchase, the cashier is surprised to see her again a hour or so later, holding the scarf out for a refund. "But this colour goes so well with your hair," the shop assistant remarks. "Why do you want to return it?" "Because it's too tight!" the blonde replies.

****

A blonde, a brunette and a redhead have been stuck on a deserted island for a long, long time when one day a magic lamp is washed ashore. The redhead rubs it hard and out pops a genie. "Thank you for letting me out of this bottle," he says. "As a reward, I can give a wish to each of you." The redhead goes first: "I hate it here. It is too hot and boring. I want to go home!" "All right," replied the genie, and the redhead disappears in a puff of smoke. Then it's the brunette's turn. "I miss my family, my friends and relatives. I want to go home, too!" "No sweat," the genie says and off she goes. Then the blonde starts crying and says, "I'm lonely: I wish my two friends were back here with me!"

****

A butcher is introducing his blonde wife: "Hello, everyone," he says. "Meet Patti."

****

A nervous blonde goes to the dentist. To calm her down, the dentist decides to tell her a short story. He thinks for a while, while putting his latex gloves on, then he has it. "Do you know how they make these gloves?" he asks genially to his patient. "There's a factory in Wales where there's a big vat of latex. They employ people of all ages, with various hand sizes, to dip their hands in the vat. They walk for a while until the latex solidifies a bit; then they take the gloves off." This story seems to have done the trick, because the blonde is smiling, a dreamy expression on her face. "I wonder where they make condoms," she breathes.

****

A blonde is arrested at the airport check-in for having a bomb in her bag and is being grilled by the customs officer: "How come you have a bomb in your bag?" he barks. "It's just because I'm afraid of flying," the blonde wails. "You are afraid of flying, therefore you carry a bomb with you?" "Oh, I'm just afraid someone will bring a bomb on the plane." The customs officer shakes his head to try and clear his thoughts and asks again, in an incredulous tone: "If you're afraid of someone carrying a bomb with them on a plane, why do *you* carry one?" "It's simple," replies the blonde. "I figured the odds against two people carrying a bomb with them would be much higher, so the plane would be far safer."

****

Blondes know that coughing can have bad consequences. Especially coughing in the wardrobe.

****

There is no such thing as an impotent man – only incompetent blondes.

****

A blonde finds herself, inexplicably, in a university and meets a professor of psychology. Not wanting to appear as if she didn't belong here, she asks him: "Tell me, Professor, is it true there's a way to detect mental deficiency in people that appear completely normal?" "Oh, yes," the professor answers. "All you have to do is ask them a very simple question which anybody can answer, and then monitor their replies." "Really? Have you got an example?" the blonde asks, vaguely planning on fooling the professor next time she meets him. "Take this one: Captain Cook did three trips to the Pole and died during one of them. Which one was it?" The blonde laughs nervously and said: "Can you give me another example? I'm not very good at history."

****

A blonde walks up to the counter of the local library and complains to the librarian: "Here's your book back. It's the most boring book I have ever read. There's no plot whatsoever, and far too many characters." "Oh, thank you," the librarian replies. "You must be the person who borrowed our phone book."

****

A blonde has been in a taxi for some time when she realizes she doesn't have any money. "I'm sorry," she says to the driver, "you'll have to go back, I forgot my purse and it's already £10." The driver glances at her and says: "It's OK: I'll just stop in a dark alley and you can take off your bra." "I can't do that: you'd be cheating yourself," the blonde replies. "Cheating myself? How so?" "This bra only cost me a fiver."

****

A young man stops at an ice cream van and asks the blonde serving: "What flavours do you have?" "Vanilla, chocolate, strawberry..." then she sneezes violently and her throat makes a rasping noice. "Have you got laryngitis?" he enquires in a sympathetic voice. "No, only vanilla, chocolate and strawberry."

****

It is a beautiful day and a young blonde and her boyfriend are visiting the zoo. The blonde is dressed in a tight-fitting dress which shows quite a bit of shapely leg and boob – and there's plenty of it to show! They arrive in front of the gorillas' cage and it is obvious that her dress is impressing the male gorilla, as he starts jumping up and down staring at her. "It looks like he fancies you," the boyfriend says. He suggests she plays a game on the poor beast and she purses her lips, wiggles her bottom and plays along for a while. The gorilla is getting wild with excitement, pounding his chest and grunting, to the amusement of the blonde and her boyfriend. At this point, the said boyfriend suggests she "accidentally" drops one of the flimsy straps of her dress. The blonde does that and this sends the gorilla into such a sexual frenzy that he seizes the bars of the cage, pulls them apart, grabs the girl and drags her into the cage with him, squeezing the bars back into place after him and glaring at the boyfriend who says, a triumphant note in his voice: "Now, you tell *him* you have a headache!"

****

A young ventriloquist is touring the clubs and one night does a show in a pub in Shropshire. With his puppet on his knee, he's going through his usual dumb blonde routine when a blonde woman stands on her chair and starts shouting angrily: "I've heard enough of your stupid blonde jokes. What makes you think you can stereotype women that way? What does the colour of a person's hair have to do with her worth as a human being? It's guys like you who keep women like me from being respected at work and in the community and from reaching our full potential, because you and your kind continue to perpetuate discrimination against not only blondes, but women in general!" The ventriloquist, embarrassed, begins to apologize, but the blonde yells, "You stay out of this, buster! I'm talking to that little jerk on your knee!"

****

A blonde is sitting at the counter in a bar with a glass of vodka with an olive in it. She tries to pick the olive up with the toothpick but it always eludes her, skidding to the other end of the glass. This futile exercise has been going on for half an hour when the man next to her, exasperated, snatches the toothpick from her hand and adroitly skewers the olive in one stroke. "This is how you do it," he says to the blonde. "Big deal," the blonde mutters darkly. "I already had him so tired out, he couldn't get away."

****

Three blondes go to a funfair and buy a raffle ticket. As it is for charity, everyone wins a small prize. The first blonde wins a case of spaghetti sauce. The second wins a small Stilton cheese. The third wins a toilet brush. The following day, they meet at the first blonde's place and she says: "Wasn't that great? I love spaghetti!" "And I adore cheese," comments the second blonde, then asks the third: "How's the toilet brush?" "Not so good , I'm afraid," she answers. "In fact, I think I'll go back to paper."

****

How do you give a blonde a maths class?
Subtract her clothes, divide her legs and give her a square root.

Why couldn't the blonde add ten and seven on a pocket calculator?
She couldn't find the ten key.

What's the difference between a smart blonde and the Abominable
Snowman?
Maybe someday we'll find the Abominable Snowman.

What do you call a blonde with two brain cells?
Pregnant.

Why don't blondes take birth control pills?
Because they keep falling out.

What do blondes and shrimps have in common?
Their heads are full of shit, but the pink bits are nice.

What's the connection between a blonde and a halogen headlamp?
They both get screwed on the front of a Ford Escort.

What are a blonde's first words after two years of university?
"Would you like ketchupwith that?"

How do you give a blonde a brain transplant?
You blow in her ear.

How can you tell when a blonde rejects a new brain transplant?
She sneezes.

What does "TGIF" on blondes' T shirts stand for?
"Tits Go In Front."

How can you tell a blonde has been playing a game on the computer?
The joystick is wct.

What do you call a blonde who can't swim?
Shark bait!

What's the advantage of having a blonde as a girlfriend?
You get to park in handicapped zones.

To a blonde, what is long and hard?
Primary school.

What do a blonde and a car have in common?
They can both drive you crazy.

What did the blonde say when she saw a herd of elephants walking
across the plains with sunglasses on?
Nothing: she didn't recognize them.

How many blondes does it take to change a light bulb?
One hundred: one to hold the light bulb, the other 99 to rotate the
house.

What do a blonde and a taxi have in common?
Everyone's been in and out for a fiver.

What does a blonde use for protection during sex?
A bus shelter.

What do a blonde and a turtle have in common?
They're both screwed on their backs.

What does a blonde say after having multiple orgasms?
"Great work, team!"

What is it called when a blonde blows in another blonde's ear?
Data transfer.

How do you change a blonde's mind?
You buy her another beer.

What do you call a blonde with a runny nose?
Full.

What do a blonde and a beer bottle have in common?
They're both empty from the neck up.

Why do blonde mums only change their babies' nappies every month?
Because the instructions say, "Good for up to 20 pounds."

What do you say to a blonde with no arms and no legs?
Nice tits!

How do you play Space Invaders with a blonde?
You trap a fly in her head.

What did the little blonde girl say to her dad when she opened the box
of Cheerios?
"Look, daddy: doughnut seeds!"

What do you call five blondes at the bottom of a swimming pool?
Air pockets.

What do you call a blonde in a university?
A visitor.

Why did God create blondes?
Because sheep can't bring beer from the fridge.

Why don't blondes like to breast-feed their babies?
It hurts too much to boil their nipples.

What do you call a pimple on a blonde's bum?
A brain tumour.

✳✳✳✳

A blonde wanted to buy a personalized license plate for her new car but she couldn't afford it. So, instead, she decided to change her name to K34GML.

✳✳✳✳

A blonde was strolling down the avenue when she saw a student wearing a sandwich board saying "Free Big Mac". She went up to him and asked: "Why? What did he do?"

✳✳✳✳

A blonde, a brunette and a redhead go out sailing, but a storm damages their craft and they end up being blown onto a beautiful but uninhabited island. After a couple of days, they reach the conclusion that their absence has not been noticed. The redhead says, "Listen girls, we're trapped on this island; we have enough food for about two more days, but it can't be more than six or seven kilometres to the mainland and I'm sure I can swim there." With that she dives into the water. She is quite a strong swimmer and she thinks she is making good headway. Sadly, the wind is blowing off the mainland and she has actually gone less than halfway when she begins to get very tired. She tries to go on, but exhaustion takes over and she drowns. A day later, when nothing has been heard on the island, the brunette says, "Do you think our friend has forgotten us? I'm a very good swimmer and I'm sure I can make it to the mainland. As soon I get ashore I promise I'll get help for you." Off goes the brunette. She is a stronger swimmer, but she is also unlucky, because the wind is the in the wrong direction. She gets three-quarters of the way across before exhaustion gets the better of her and she too drowns. The blonde waits a couple of days for help to arrive, but of course, no one appears. Faced with the prospect of dying of starvation, alone on the island, or trying to swim for it, she decides to try to swim. Her luck is in because the wind has turned around and she quickly gets to within a half-kilometre of the shore. At this point she remembers that she left the fire burning on the island, so she turns back to put it out.

****

Animal Crackers

Beastly Jokes

A tiny zoo in Suffolk is given a very rare species of gorilla by an eccentric explorer. After a couple of weeks, the gorilla starts to go wild: it won't eat, can't sleep, becomes violent and causes all sorts of problems. The zoo owner calls the vet, determines that the gorilla is a female and, what's more, she's on heat. The only way to calm her down is to have someone mate with her. Sadly, there are no other gorillas of her species in captivity, so another solution will have to be found. It is then that the owner remembers Richard, the cage cleaner. Richard is a bit dumb, but he has a reputation for having sex with anything, so the owner decides to offer him a proposition: would he like to have sex with the gorilla for £500? Richard says he's interested, but that he'll need the night to think it over. The next day he says he'd be willing and that he'd accept the offer, but only if the owner meets three conditions. "First," he says, "I don't want to kiss her on the lips." The owner says that's fine. "Second," Richard says, "you must never, ever tell anyone about this." That's fine, the owner says again. "And third," says Richard, "I'm going to need another week to come up with the money."

****

A pig farmer is worried because none of his pigs is getting pregnant. His pigs are his livelihood, so he calls the vet and asks him what on earth he can do to make them procreate. The vet says that if the pigs really won't do the business he should try artificial insemination. The farmer doesn't have a clue what artificial insemination is, but he reckons it must mean he has to get the pigs pregnant by himself. So he loads them all into his truck, drives them to the woods and shags them all. The next day he calls the vet again and asks him how he will be able to tell if his pigs are pregnant. The vet tells him that the pigs will be lying down rolling in mud. The farmer looks out of the window and sees that all his pigs are really clean and all standing up in their field. So he herds them into his truck, drives them to the woods and shags them all again. The next morning the farmer gets up and looks at the pig field. All the pigs are still clean and all standing. So the farmer herds them yet again into his truck, drives them to the woods and shags them all. Early the next morning the farmer is exhausted so he asks his wife to have a look at the pigs to see if they are rolling in mud. His wife gets up, looks out at the pig field and says, "That's very odd: the pigs are all in your truck. Two of them are waving over here and one's tooting the horn!"

✱✱✱✱

Four dog owners were having a post-walk drink together on a Friday, and were all boasting about the merits of their dogs. The first man was an engineer. "Set-square! Set-square – do your thing!" he said to his dog. Set-square leapt up and ran over to the desk, opened a drawer, took out some paper, a pen and a set-square. He took it all over to the table and proceeded to draw a careful circle, triangle and some perfect parallel lines on the paper. There was a round of applause, but the second man – an accountant – insisted his dog could do better. "Slide-rule! Slide-rule – do your thing!" he said to his dog. Slide-rule trotted off to the kitchen and came back with a tin of biscuits. He opened them on the table, counted out 12 and then divided those into four piles of three. He pushed one pile towards each man and took the tin back to the kitchen. There was a round of applause, but the third man – a chemist – insisted his dog could do better. "Measuring-cup! Measuring-cup – do your thing!" he said to his dog. Measuring-cup ran into the kitchen and came back with three cans of beer and four glasses. He opened all the beers and poured them evenly into the glasses without spilling a drop. There was a round of applause and the fourth man – a civil servant – said his dog could do better. "Tea-break! Tea-break! Do your thing!" the man shouted loudly. After a lengthy pause, Tea-break leapt up, ate the biscuits, drank the beer, had a crap on the paper, groped up the other dogs, claimed he hurt himself while doing so, filed a complaint to the union for unsafe working conditions and went home sick!

****

A fly was hovering over a lake. A fish, swimming below the water, saw the fly and said to itself, "If that fly would just drop six more inches, I could get it." In the woods beside the lake, a bear was watching the fish and said to itself, "If that fly would just drop six more inches, the fish could get that fly and I could get that fish." Deeper in the woods, a hunter, sitting eating a sandwich, saw the bear and said to himself, "If that fly would just drop six more inches, that fish could get that fly, that bear could get that fish and I could get that bear." Just behind him a mouse was watching. The mouse said to itself, "If that fly would just drop six more inches, that fish could get that fly, that bear could get that fish, that hunter could get that bear and I could get that sandwich." Behind the mouse was a cat, watching intently. It said to itself, "If that fly would just drop six more inches, that fish could get that fly, that bear could get that fish, that hunter could get that bear, that mouse could get that sandwich and I could get that mouse!" Suddenly, the fly dropped six inches. The fish leaped up and snapped it up. The bear grabbed the fish, and the hunter jumped up and shot the bear. The mouse leaped for the sandwich and the cat jumped for the mouse, but was too excited, so shot past it and landed in the lake. The moral of the story? Every time a fly drops six inches, a pussy gets wet!

****

A man decided he wanted to become a hunter, so he set about getting himself all the equipment. Last on his list was a dog, so he went off to see the local dog breeder. The dog breeder took him out to the woods with his best dog so the man could see what a top hunting dog it was. The dog breeder snapped his fingers at the dog and shouted, "Go!" The dog ran off at top speed and they could hear much crashing in the undergrowth. The dog came running back, out of breath, and barked once. "What does that mean?" said the man. "One bark means that the dog saw one rabbit in the woods," said the dog breeder. The man thought this was cool, but that he'd better see it again in case it was a scam. Again, the dog merchant snapped his fingers and shouted, "Go!" The dog ran off at top speed and they could hear more crashing of undergrowth. The dog came running back, out of breath, and barked twice. "What does that mean?" said the man. "Two barks mean that the dog saw two rabbits in the woods," said the dog breeder. The man asked to see it one more time, and the dog breeder snapped his fingers at the dog and shouted, "Go!" The dog disappeared again, but this time he came back carrying a stick and began to hump the dog breeder's leg. "What the hell does that mean?" asked the man, astonished. "Well, that means he just saw more effing rabbits than you can shake a stick at!"

****

A jaguar was walking pugnaciously through the jungle, intimidating the other animals. He spotted a monkey and ran up to it, pinning it against the trunk of a tree. "Who is the fiercest animal in the jungle?" he roared. "You: you are," the monkey squeaked. Satisfied, the jaguar let him go and carried on, noticing with satisfaction that all the other animals were running away from him. He nonetheless managed to immobilize a bird and growled in a terrifying manner: "Who is the fiercest animal in the jungle?" 'You: you are," the bird stammered, and the jaguar magnanimously let him go. The jaguar then spotted a lion having a siesta and, giddy with self-importance, made the mistake of running up to him. "Who is the fiercest animal in the jungle?" he roared, eyes bulging. Hearing this, the lion stood up, picked up the jaguar by the tail, swung him around faster and faster and finally released him and sent him crashing heavily into a banana tree. "All right, all right," the jaguar said, standing up groggily and shaking his head to clear it. "Even if you don't know the answer, it's no reason to get pissed off."

****

A horse and a chicken are friends. They are playing around together one day when the horse tumbles into a pit and begins to sink. He begs the chicken to fetch the farmer to get him to pull him to safety. The chicken runs off but he cannot find the farmer. Ever resourceful, the chicken jumps into the farmer's Porsche (obviously a French farmer, full of EU subsidies) and roars off to the hole where the horse is rapidly sinking. He takes a tow-rope from the boot, ties it around the bumper and throws the other end to the horse. The horse manages to grip the rope in his teeth and the chicken pulls forward in the Porsche, thus pulling the horse from danger and saving his life. A couple of days later the horse and the chicken are playing the same game in the same place. This time, the chicken falls into the same hole and begins to sink. The chicken screams for help and the horse, even more resourceful than the chicken, straddles himself over the hole, positioning his penis over where the chicken is sinking. "Quick, chicken," he says. "Grab hold of this and pull yourself out!" The chicken follows his instructions and only a few seconds later, both animals are safely on solid ground. The moral of the story? If you're hung like a horse, you don't need a Porsche to pull the birds!

****

Hillary Clinton goes into a pet shop and sees the most beautiful parrot she has ever seen. "Does it talk?" she enquires of the shopkeeper. "He sure does, ma'am," the man replies. "Well, how come he only costs fifty bucks when all the other parrots are at least five hundred?" "Well, ma'am, that's a good question, and the answer is that he's got a bit of a fruity vocabulary on him. He used to live in a brothel and some of the things he says would even make a tart blush!" Hillary, used to foul language and deeds, says, "Not a problem for me. I'll take him right now." She gets home and places the parrot in its new cage in the front room. The parrot turns to her as soon as the cover goes off the cage, looks her square in the eye and says, "New house, new madam!" Hillary laughs and carries on with her day. Later on, Chelsea arrives with a friend and they go over to pet the new bird. The parrot turns to them, looks them square in the eye, and squawks, "New house, new whores." They run off, giggling. Later that night, Bill comes home after a hard day's work. He walks up to have a look at the new bird. The parrot turns to him, and with the briefest glance says, "Hey, Bill!"

✷✷✷✷

A plane crashes and five men are stranded on a desert island. They are all in their early 20s and very horny. After a month of survival John gets up and says, "I can't take it any more: I'm so horny I'm going to shag that female gorilla at the other end of the island." He grabs himself a bag and runs off. The other four guys follow him and they quickly catch the gorilla. Each of the guys grabs a limb and John pops the bag over its head, jumps on top of the animal and starts to screw it. The gorilla is pretty strong and doesn't put up with any nonsense, so pretty soon it gets an arm clear, and then another. It puts both of them around John's waist and holds on tight. Then it gets first one, then the other leg free as well. and it wraps both of them around John, too. The gorilla seems to be enjoying itself and John starts to shout, "Get it off! Get it off!" One of his mates says, "You must be joking: you're on top and she's wrapped around you tightly." John says, "Not the gorilla – I mean the bag: I want to kiss her!"

✳✳✳✳

A farmer has a prize cock which has sired hundreds of young. It used to take care of every single one of the farmer's 200 chickens. But one day the old cock dies and the farmer is forced to get himself a replacement. The farmer looks at all the ads in *Farmers' Weekly* and orders a mail-order rooster named Randy. A couple of days later the new cock arrives. It is a very impressive and fit-looking bird. Before the farmer lets the rooster loose to work on his chickens, he gives it a bit of a pep talk. "Now, look here, Randy," the farmer says, "I need you as a long-term investment. I don't need a new rooster for just the next couple of days: I need one for a very long time. So take it easy and pace yourself when you get in there, OK?" Randy nods and the farmer puts him into the coop. But no sooner have Randy's claws hit the ground than he is off at the first brace of hens. The farmer looks on amazed as he sees the rooster making his way through the entire flock, doing all of the hens first once and then twice! The rooster doesn't even pause for breath. When he's done, he looks around and sees a load of ducks out by the pond. He sprints over and does them too – twice each. The farmer, while obviously impressed, is worried that his superb new rooster won't even make it through the night if he's that horny already. The farmer's worst fears are confirmed the next morning when he leaves the house after breakfast: Randy is lying a hundred yards from the hen-coop with buzzards circling around him. The farmer, shaking his head, walks slowly up to the chicken and looks down at him. "What the hell did I tell you, Randy?" he begins, "I knew you wouldn't make it if you didn't pace yourself!" Randy opens one eye and looks up at the farmer, then up at the buzzards. "Sshhhh," he says. "They're getting closer!"

****

A koala bear escapes from the zoo, decides to get himself a night out on the town and chances upon a prostitute. He spends the entire night with her, but every time they have sex he stops to eat a sandwich. The prostitute is a little surprised but figures, "Hey, I'm having sex with a koala bear, so what the heck?" In the morning the bear gets up, has a shower and is starting to walk out of the door when the prostitute calls him back. "Aren't you forgetting something, honey?" she asks. The bear turns around, looks at her and shrugs his shoulders. She realizes he doesn't understand so she beckons him back and gets a dictionary. In it, she looks up the word "prostitute" and the definition is, "Someone who has sex and gets paid for it." The koala understands, but picks up the dictionary and flicks to the "koala" definition. It says simply, "Eats shoots and leaves."

****

Once upon a time, there was a beautiful, independent princess who was very self-assured. One day she was walking in the forest when she chanced upon a frog sitting on a rock in a stream. To her amazement, the frog begins to talk to her: "Fair princess, I am a handsome prince, trapped by a witch in the foul, slimy body of this poor frog. Won't you kiss me once to break the spell and we can live happily ever after in my castle with my mother and my father and my knights and you can bear my children and look after them and prepare my meals and clean my sheets and all will be well?" That night, as the beautiful, independent princess ate her frog's legs, she thought to herself and laughed out loud: "Not this time!"

****

At primary school one day, the teacher was reading the *Three Little Pigs* to her youngest class. When she got to the part about the pig building his house from straw she read, "And the little pig went to the farmer and said, 'Please mister farmer can I have some straw to build my house with?'" And then the teacher asked the whole class, "And what do you think the farmer said?" Little Johnny in the corner put up his hand and said, "I know, miss. He said, 'Blow me – a talking pig!'"

****

A Welshman is shipwrecked after a big storm and ends up on a desert island with only an Alsatian and a sheep for company. There is enough food for them all and there is plentiful fresh water, too. The weather is great and they all have a pretty good time. After a few months, the three of them get into the habit of walking up into the hills to watch the sun go down every night. One particularly balmy night, everything is just beautiful: the sea can be heard gently lapping in the distance, the cool breeze carries the sound of the crickets chirping and everyone is happy. The Welshman looks over at the sheep and the sheep looks back. They glance into each other's eyes and the Welshman starts to feel warm inside. The sheep continues to look at him, so he reaches out and puts his arm around the animal. As soon as he does this, the Alsatian begins to growl, and doesn't stop until the arm is removed. The three of them continue to watch the sunset, but there is no more funny business. After a few more weeks there is a huge storm and a beautiful woman is washed up on the beach. She is pretty ill and has to be tended night and day for weeks before she even has enough strength to talk. After a few months of tender, loving care the woman is perfectly well again and the four of them all get along fine. The Welshman, the sheep and the Alsatian introduce the woman to their nightly ritual of watching the sun go down, and one night they are all there and it is just magical. As before, they can hear the sea, smell the scented air and see the most beautiful sunset of their lives and as before, romance is most certainly in the air. The Welshman is getting his warm feeling inside so he turns to the beautiful, scantily-clad maiden at his side and just nuzzles his mouth up next to her ear. She tips her head to one side to hear what he has to say, as he whispers, "You wouldn't take the dog off for a walk, would you?"

****

An old man walks into a bar using a cane and carrying a crocodile. The barman says, "Sorry, mate, no animals allowed in here – especially dangerous ones like that." The man says, "Oh, go on: my croc can do a fantastic trick and it'll have people coming from miles around to see it. Let me show you." "Well, OK then," says the barman, "but if I think it's crap I'm going to chuck the pair of you out." So the old man says something to the croc, who gets up on his hind legs and opens his mouth. The man then drops his trousers and puts his pecker into the croc's mouth. The croc shuts its mouth tight around his pecker. The crowd in the bar all gasp out loud, but then the man picks up his cane and raps the croc's head with it three times – tap, tap, tap! The croc opens its mouth and the man's pecker is there – still attached – without even a scratch on it. Everyone in the bar starts clapping and cheering the old man. "Now," says the man looking around the bar, "Does anybody else think they're up to this fantastic trick? Would anyone else like a go?" There is silence and all the men look to the floor. Suddenly an old lady pipes up, "I'll have a try, but you only need to hit me on the head once!"

✱✱✱✱

A guy walks into his local with a giraffe and a monkey. All three of them get utterly blotto. The man and and the monkey manage to prop each other up and make it to the door, but the giraffe is too big for them to help and he collapses on the floor. As the man opens the door the barman shouts across the bar, "Oi, mate, you can't leave that lyin' there!" and the man shouts back, "That's no lion – it's a giraffe and I can't move him!"

✱✱✱✱

A local business was looking to employ someone to help in the office. The manager put a sign in the window saying: "Help wanted. Must be able to type, good with a computer and bilingual. We are an Equal Opportunities Employer." Soon afterwards a dog trotted up to the window, saw the sign and went inside. He looked at the receptionist and wagged his tail, then walked over to the sign, looked at it and barked sharply. Getting the idea, the receptionist fetched the office manager, who looked at the dog with surprise. However, the dog looked determined, so he led him into his office. Inside, the dog jumped up on a chair and stared at the manager. The manager said, in as friendly a tone as possible, "I can't hire you. The sign says you have to be able to type." The dog jumped down, went to the typewriter and proceeded to type out a perfect letter. He took out the page in his mouth and gave it to the manager, then jumped back onto the chair. The manager was stunned, but then told the dog, "The sign says you have to be good with a computer." The dog jumped down again and went to the computer. The dog proceeded to demonstrate his expertise with various programs. After a few minutes he produced a sample spreadsheet and database and presented them to the manager. By this time the manager was totally dumbfounded. He looked at the dog and said, "I realize that you are a very intelligent dog and have some interesting abilities. However, I still can't give you the job." The dog jumped down and went to a copy of the sign and put his paw on the part about being an Equal Opportunities Employer. The manager said, "Yes, I know, but the sign also says that you have to be bilingual." The dog looked at him straight in the face, and said: "Miaow."

****

A little old lady had two monkeys as pets for years. One day, one of them died of natural causes. Overcome with grief, the second monkey passed away two days later. Not knowing what to do with the remains, she finally decided to take them to the taxidermist and have them stuffed. After telling the owner of her wishes, he asked her, "Do you want them mounted?" "No. Holding hands will be fine," she said, blushing.

****

Two tall trees, a birch and a beech, are growing in the woods. A small tree begins to grow between them. One tree says to the other: "Is that a son of a beech or a son of a birch?" The other says he cannot tell. Just then a woodpecker lands in the sapling. The tall tree asks: "Woodpecker, you're a tree expert. Can you tell if that's a son of a beech or a son of a birch?" The woodpecker takes a taste of the small tree. He replies: "It is neither a son of a beech nor a son of a birch. That, my friends, is the best piece of ash I have ever put my pecker in."

****

Deep in the forest, a tortoise was slowly padding towards a tall tree. Ever so slowly she started climbing the tree. After a few days of this, she managed to climb high enough to reach the lowest branch, but it was apparently not high enough, as she carried on upwards. It took her a week to reach a suitable branch and then another three days to arrive at the end of the branch. Once there, she took a deep breath and hurled herself forward, instantly falling like a brick all the way down, finishing her trip with a thud in the dirt below. A couple of birds had been watching the whole process for a week and the male bird turned to his mate and chirped: "Dear, I know how much this will upset you, but we'll have to tell her she's adopted."

****

This guy had been dating this girl for some time when she invited him over to her parents' house for dinner to meet them. When they got there, the guy realized he was so tense that he was starting to get really bad gas. They sat down for dinner but he just couldn't hold it in any longer. A fart slipped out. The mother yelled "Spot!" The guy realized the family dog was under his chair, and was relieved that the dog had got the blame. A few minutes later he let another one go and the mother again yelled "Spot!" Again, the boyfriend was relieved that the dog had been told off, so he decided he might as well get it all out, and let this huge fart go. "Spot!" the mother yelled. "Get out from under there before he shits on you!"

****

A team of elephants had agreed to play a game of football against a team of ants. Things were going well for the ants – more agile and more nimble than the elephants – when the referee whistled loudly. Everybody from both teams gathered around the remains of an unfortunate ant, now completely squashed to bits on the pitch. "There you are," an ant complained bitterly. "You just can't trust the big people to play fair!" "I didn't want this to happen," the elephant said guiltily. "I just wanted to trip him over."

****

A frog goes into a London bank and approaches the teller. He can see from her nameplate that the teller's name is Patricia Whack. He says, "Ms Whack, I'd like to get a loan to buy a boat and go on a long vacation." Patti looks at the frog in disbelief and asks how much he wants to borrow. The frog says £30,000. The teller asks his name and the frog says that his name is Kermit Jagger and that it's OK, he knows the bank manager. Patti explains that £30,000 is a substantial amount of money and that he will need to secure the loan. She asks if he has anything he can use as collateral. The frog says, "Sure. I have this," and he produces a tiny pink porcelain elephant, about half an inch tall. It's bright pink and perfectly formed, but of no obvious visible value. Very confused, Patti explains that she'll have to consult with the manager and disappears into a back office. She finds the manager and reports: "There's a frog called Kermit Jagger out there who claims to know you, and he wants to borrow £30,000. He wants to use this as collateral," she says, holding up the tiny pink elephant. "I mean, what the heck is this?" The bank manager looks back at her and says: "It's a knick-knack, Patti Whack. Give the frog a loan. His old man's a Rolling Stone!"

****

An old man had a dog he just loved but this dog had the nasty habit of attacking anything that moved, including people. His friends told him if he had the dog "fixed", he would lose his aggression and quit this behaviour. Thinking it might be a good idea, the old man had his dog fixed. A few days later he was in his front room when the postman came up the steps. The dog jumped up, went right through the door and attacked the postman. The old man ran out, pulled his dog away and began apologizing. "I am so sorry," he said. "I don't know what to do or say. My friends told me he would quit attacking people if I had him fixed, but it didn't work. I just don't know what to do." The postman picked himself up and said, "You should have had his teeth pulled: I knew when he came through the door he wasn't going to screw me."

✷✷✷✷

It was Frank's first time at bear-hunting. After some time in the mountains, he spotted a small brown bear and shot it. Just then there was a tap on his shoulder. He turned around to see a big black bear. The bear said: "You've got two choices. I either maul you to death or we have sex." Frank decided to bend over. Even though he felt sore for two weeks, Frank soon recovered and vowed revenge. He headed out on another trip where he found the black bear and shot it. There was another tap on his shoulder. This time a huge grizzly bear stood right next to him. The grizzly said: "What a huge mistake, Frank. You've got two choices. Either I maul you to death or we have rough sex." Again, Frank thought it was better to comply. Although he survived, it took several months before Frank finally recovered. Outraged, he headed back to the mountains, managed to track down the grizzly and shot it. He felt sweet revenge, but then there was a tap on his shoulder. He turned round to find a giant polar bear standing there. The polar bear said: "Admit it, Frank. You don't come here for the hunting, do you?"

****

Two young nuns, freshly inducted into their order, were visiting the zoo when they stopped in front of the gorilla cage. Something about them made the gorilla mad with desire and, after beating his chest for a while, he ran to the bars of the cage, pulled them open, jumped on one of the nuns and ravished her before going back into his cage, contented. The nun picked herself up, brushed down her clothes and said to her friend: "Promise me never to talk about this – ever." To which the other sister agreed. Twenty-five years later, the two sisters found themselves together again and went to sit on a bench in a nearby park. "I know I promised never to talk about this incident," the nun said, "but there's a question I've always wanted to ask you…" "All right: ask your question, sister." "Did it hurt?" "Did it hurt?" the nun replied in a sad voice. "Oh, yes, it hurt. He never called… he never wrote… he never sent flowers…"

****

A ventriloquist is on a walking holiday in Wales and getting pretty bored. During one of his walks he stumbles across a farm and there, leaning on a gate, is a farmer, so the ventriloquist decides to have a bit of fun. "Hey, cool dog you have here, sir. Mind if I speak to him?" "My dog doesn't talk," the farmer says, surprised. "Hey, dog, how's it going?" the ventriloquist asks the dog. "Doin' alright." the dog says. The farmer stares at his dog in total disbelief, as he can't believe man's best friend can talk. "This is your owner, right?" the prankster asks the dog, pointing at the farmer. "Yep," says the dog. "How is he treating you?" "Real good. He walks me twice a day, feeds me great food and takes me to the lake once a week to play." The farmer is still shocked, starting to feel bad over rubbing his dog's nose into his own poop after last week's potty incident. "Mind if I talk to your horse?" the ventriloquist then asks. "Hey?" blurts the farmer. "My horse doesn't talk." The ventriloquist approaches the horse: "Hey, horse, how's it going?" "Cool," says the horse. "Is this your owner?" "Yep," says the horse. "How's he treating you?" "Pretty good, thanks for asking. He rides me regularly, brushes me down often and keeps me in the barn to protect me from the elements." By this time, the farmer is completely amazed and his eyes are bulging out of their sockets. The ventriloquist approaches the gate and says: "Mind if I talk to your sheep?" The farmer coughs loudly and says quickly: "Sheep lie!"

✳✳✳✳

Two whales, a male and a female, are swimming happily through the ocean. On seeing a boat, the male says to his friend: "Hey, I've got a great idea! Let's swim up under that boat and blow out really hard through our blowholes!" The female says, "Uh… I don't know…" "Come on, it'll be fun: just this once!" The female agrees and they swim up under the boat and blow out, capsizing the boat and sending the hapless sailors into the water. As they are swimming away, the male says, "Wow! That was fun, wasn't it? Hey! I've got another idea! Let's swim back there and eat all the sailors!" The female, exasperated, replies, "Look, I agreed to the blow job, but I'm not swallowing any seamen."

****

An ant and an elephant share a night of romance. Next morning the ant wakes up and the elephant is dead. "Damn," says the ant. "One night of passion and I spend the rest of my life digging a grave!"

****

A city man, completely ignorant of country life, was visiting Wales. He stopped at an educational farm, had a look around and went to chat with the farmer. "Nice pigs you've got there," he said. "How big are they?" The pig farmer puts one of the pig's tails in his mouth and bobbed his head up and down. "30 pounds," he said to the city guy. "What? I can't believe that's the way you weigh pigs! You're having me on!" "No, I'm not," the farmer said. He then called his son over and asked him to weigh the pig. The son put the pig's tail in his mouth, bobbed his head a couple of times and said the pig weighed 30 pounds. As the city guy still couldn't believe this was the way to weigh a pig, the farmer asked his son to go and get his mum so that she could weigh the pig, too. The boy left and came back alone a few minutes later, saying: "Mum can't come: she's busy weighing the postman."

✳✳✳✳

Mama Weevil gave birth to two identical twin weevils. They grew up together, but there came a time when they had to discover the world on their own, and tearfully they separated, each to go its own weevil way. One was very successful in Hollywood, got tons of girlfriends and money, while the other didn't have much luck in its life and ended up broke, alone and miserable. He was, therefore, known as the lesser of two weevils.

✳✳✳✳

A fisherman accidentally left his day's catch under the seat of a bus. The next evening's newspaper carried an ad: "If the person who left a bucket of fish on the number 47 bus would care to come to the garage, he can have the bus."

✳✳✳✳

A mother and baby camel were talking one day when the baby camel asked, "Mum, why have I got these huge three-toed feet?" "Well, son, when we trek across the desert your toes will help you to stay on top of the soft sand," the mother replied, "OK," said the son. A few minutes later, the son asked, "Mum, why have I got these great long eyelashes?" "They are there to keep the sand out of your eyes on the trips through the desert." "Thanks, Mum," replied the son, and went off to think on his own. After a short while, the son returned and asked, "Mum, why have I got these great big humps on my back?" The mother, now a little impatient with the boy, replied, "They're to help us store water for our long treks across the desert, so we can go without drinking for long periods." "That's great, Mum: so we have huge feet to stop us sinking, and long eyelashes to keep the sand from our eyes and these humps to store water. But Mum…" "Yes, son?" "Why the heck are we in London Zoo?"

****

Two vultures board an aeroplane, each carrying two dead raccoons. The stewardess looks at them and says, "I'm sorry, gentlemen, only one carrion per passenger."

****

A three-legged dog walks into a saloon in the Old West. He slides up to the bar and announces: "I'm looking for the man who shot my paw."

****

A wolf had been chasing a rabbit in the forest for an hour when they arrived near the Enchanted Oak, where the genie lived. They were making such a racket that they woke up the genie, who said (he was a bit of a hippy): "OK, OK: I see that there is no sleeping in peace in here until you two have resolved your differences. Therefore, I am going to grant you three wishes and you'll go on your way much happier." The wolf had the first go and he said: "I want all the wolves in this forest to be female." The genie sighed and said that it now was so. He turned to the rabbit and said: "What is your first wish, rabbit?" "I'd like a helmet," the rabbit says, a faint smile on his face. The genie finds it a bit odd, but a wish is a wish and the rabbit is fitted with a nice crash-helmet. "I want all the wolves in this country to be female," says the wolf for his second wish. The genie sighs again but complies and all the wolves in the country become female. "For my second wish, I want a motorcycle," the rabbit says. The genie says "OK" and grants the rabbit a nice, powerful motorbike which goes very well with the helmet. The rabbit's smile is getting bigger now. True to his character and showing remarkable consistency, the wolf says: "For my third wish, I want all the wolves in the whole *world* to be female!" Marvelling at the single-mindedness of the wolf's wishes, the genie complies and turns all the wolves in the world female. He then turns to the rabbit, who is grinning from ear to ear. "So what is your last wish, rabbit?" The rabbit straps the helmet on his head securely, climbs on the motorbike, revs up the engine and says: "I wish the wolf was gay!"

✳✳✳✳

Why do cows have bells?
Because their horns don't work.

✷✷✷✷

A labrador, a rottweiler and a chihuahua spot a nice-looking female poodle. They rush to meet her and the poodle, aware of her charms, pouts coquettishly and tells them: "I will go out with the one of you who can use the words 'liver' and 'cheese' in a proper sentence." The labrador goes first, racks his brains and blurts out: "I like liver and cheese." "What imagination!" giggles the poodle. The rottweiler growls and prances, then says lamely: "I hate liver and I hate cheese." "That's even worse than the labrador!" howls the poodle in glee. Then the chihuahua winks at her and says: "Liver alone. Cheese mine."

✷✷✷✷

A duck enters a grocery store and says to the man behind the counter: "Do you have any beer?" "I'm sorry, but this is a grocery store. We're not licensed to sell beer here." The duck leaves, but comes back the next day. "Do you have any beer?" he asks. "I told you yesterday! We don't sell beer here! This is a grocery store! If you come here again asking for beer, I'll nail your feet to the floor!" The duck leaves, but comes back the next day. "Do you have any nails?" The shop owner says: "No." The duck continues, "Do you have any any beer?"

✷✷✷✷

A burglar breaks into a house really late one night. He spies a nice new DVD player in the front room and starts to walk over to it when he hears the words, "Jesus is watching you." He jumps but stays in place and holds his breath. There is no more sound so the burglar takes another step forward. As he does so, he hears again, "Jesus is watching you!" He jumps again and looks around the room again. In one of the corners he sees what looks like a cage. He goes over to it and sees a parrot inside, looking at him. "Was that you talking about Jesus?" the man asks the parrot. "It sure was," says the parrot. The burglar relaxes and feels a whole lot better. "So, what's your name then parrot?" he asks the parrot. "Arbuthnot" says the parrot. The burglar laughs and says, "What a dumb name, who on earth named you that?" The parrot replies, "The same person who named the Dobermann Jesus!"

****

Two cows were standing in a field. One cow says to the other, "Moooooo." The other says, "I was just going to say that."

****

Why do gorillas have big nostrils?
Because they have big fingers.

****

What's yellow and smells like bananas?
Monkey vomit.

****

A man was walking on the sidewalk and noticed up ahead that little Johnny was wearing a red fireman's hat and sitting in a red wagon. It appeared that the wagon was being pulled slowly by a large labrador retriever. When he got closer to the lad, he noticed that Johnny had a rope tied around the dog's testicles, which probably accounted for why the dog was walking so gingerly. Smiling, he spoke to the little boy, "That's really a nice fire engine you have there, son, but I'll bet the dog would pull you faster if you tied that rope around his neck." "Yeah," little Johnny replied, "but then I wouldn't have a siren."

✶✶✶✶

A bloke was about to bring his new girlfriend home, so he warned his parrot not to make any offensive remarks; the parrot had a tendency to verbally abuse anyone who came into the house. The next night the guy walked in with his new girlfriend, and the parrot instantly began to insult her: "Who's a fat cow, then? Who's been hit by a truck, then?" The next day, the infuriated man decided to shove the parrot in the freezer to teach it a lesson. About two minutes later the parrot called out, "I'm sorry. I'm really sorry. I'm really, really sorry. I won't do it again!" The man let the parrot back out and said: "I hope you behave, otherwise it's back in the cooler!" For the next couple of months he didn't hear so much as a squeak out of the parrot. He couldn't believe how successful his freezer trick turned out to be. But finally one night the parrot got up enough courage to talk again. "Excuse me, please," the parrot said, very cautiously, "but what exactly did the chicken do?"

✶✶✶✶

Two mice walk into a bar for a few ales when a giraffe walks in. "Look at that. She's a beauty," says one mouse. "Well, why not try your luck?" his friend suggests. So the mouse goes over to the giraffe and starts talking to her, and within five minutes they're out the door and gone into the night. Next day, the second mouse is in the bar drinking away, when his friend staggers in. The mouse is absolutely stuffed, worn out, ruined – an ex-mouse. The mouse helps his pal up on to a stool, pours a drink down his throat and asks: "What the hell happened to you? I saw you leave with the giraffe: what happened after that? Was she all right?" The first mouse says: "Yeah, she was really something else. We went out to dinner, had a couple of glasses of wine and she invited me back to her place to spend the night. And oh, man! I've never had a night like it!" "But how come you look like you're so exhausted?" "Well," says the mouse, "between the kissing and the screwing, I must have run a thousand miles!"

✳✳✳✳

A farmer decides it's time to get a new cock to look after his hens. The old one is a bit of a ragbag and, despite doing a reasonable job, the farmer figures he hasn't got all that long to go, so he may as well replace him sooner rather than later. He buys a new cock and lets him out in the barnyard to mix it up with the hens and sort it out with the old rooster. Now, the old rooster is pretty wise, and not the sort to take anything lying down, so he thinks to himself, "I'll have the last laugh here: I'm not ready to become lunch and dinner quite yet." So he walks up to the new cock and says, "So you think you're good enough to take over, then, do you? Well, I'll tell you what: instead of fighting and all that stuff, if you can beat me in a simple running race – just ten times around that old hen-house – I'll just leave quietly and not cause any fuss at all. I'll leave all the hens to you." "Old man, you've got yourself a deal," says the young rooster, puffing himself up and checking himself out in a mirror. "I'll even tell you what," continues the youngster with growing confidence, "you can have a half-lap head start – I know I'm going to win, after all!" So the race starts with the old rooster a good half-lap in front of the younger one. The old one has still got some strength left so he keeps a good pace for the first lap – he's not lost any distance. By the end of the second lap he is flagging just a little and by the end of the third the young rooster is noticeably gaining on him. By the time the fourth lap is over the old cock's lead has slipped seriously and at the end of the fifth the younger rooster can reach out and touch the older one. Still they run. At this point the farmer hears some noise from the chicken run. He walks out of the house, does a double-take, runs back in again and comes out with his shotgun. He stands and looks at the two roosters running for all they are worth around the hen-house, takes aim and BANG! blows the young rooster away. As he turns and walks away he mutters to himself, "Unbelievable: that's the third gay rooster I've bought in as many weeks!"

****

One day a lion was walking around the jungle, sad, lonely and bored stiff, when he spotted a monkey high up in a tree. He yelled up to the monkey to come down and play, but the monkey was too scared. So the lion asked the monkey what he could do to make him feel comfortable enough to come down. The monkey said, "If you tie yourself up, I'll come down." The lion tied himself up, but as the monkey came down he started shaking. The lion said: "Hey, monkey, you don't have to be scared! I'm not going to eat you; I'm tied up real tight." "I know," said the monkey. "That's not why I'm shaking." "Why are you shaking, then?" "It's the excitement," explains the monkey. "I've never fucked a lion before."

****

Did you know sharks will only attack you if you're wet?

****

A man was out walking his pit bull and decided to stop in the local tavern for a quick beer. Some time later, a second man entered the establishment and asked: "Who owns the pit bull outside?" The first man answers: "I do. Why?" The second man says: "Well, my pet chihuahua's out there killing it." "What rubbish! I don't believe it!" the first man says. "Suit yourself, but he's choking to death on it."

****

A penguin is on holiday in Arizona. He's driving around the desert when he sees the oil light on his car light up. He quickly stops at the next garage, just up the road. He asks the mechanic if he can take a look at the car and the mechanic says he can but he'll have to do a couple of other things first, so could the penguin leave the car and come back soon? "Sure," says the penguin and he goes off to find an ice cream parlour thinking that, as a penguin in Arizona, a bowl of ice cream will cool him down nicely. Having no hands, it's not easy to eat ice cream if you're a penguin, so he ends up covered in ice cream and has to hurry back to the garage to see what's up with his car. He asks the mechanic what's up with it and the mechanic replies, "It looks like you've blown a seal." The penguin, shocked, says, "No, no: it's just ice cream, I promise!"

****

Why did the turkey cross the road twice?
To prove he wasn't chicken.

****

A non-too-bright zebra escaped from a zoo and ended up in a field full of cows. He walked up to one and said: "Hi there! What do you do around here then?" "I eat grass all day and get milked morning and night," replied the cow. "Oh," the zebra said. He walked idly about and met another cow. "Hi there! Say, what do you do around here then?" he asked again. "I eat grass all day and get milked morning and night," replied the cow. The zebra nodded, pleased by the quietness and the sense of purpose of the cows' lives, then walked over to a bull. "Hello," he said. "What do you do around here?" The bull looked him up and down and said: "Get those pyjamas off and I'll show you."

****

Forgive Me Father

Jokes for the Faithful

A man is rushed to his nearest hospital in New York, Our Holy Mother of BeJesus, after a heart attack. The surgeon performs heart surgery and the man survives, no problem. Afterwards, the man is lying in his bed and one of the nuns is comforting him. "Don't worry sir, you'll be just fine, it's all over now," says the nun. "But we would like to know, sir, if you don't mind the asking, as to how you intend to pay your bill for the operation and the care. Would you be covered by an insurance policy?" "Well, actually sister, I don't think I am," the man replies. "Oh dear," continues the nun, "maybe you've got a load of money lying around and you'd like to pay by cash?" "Er, no, I don't think so sister," the man replies. "I'm not really a man of much material wealth." "Well," says the nun, "perhaps you've some close family who could help out?" "Well, not really, sister," the man replies, "I've just the one sister in County Kerry in the old country, but she's a spinster nun." The nun replies, "Nuns are not spinsters, sir, nuns are married to God." "In that case," says the man, "perhaps you could get my brother-in-law to foot the bill!"

✳✳✳✳

Two nuns walk into an off-licence and pick up the biggest bottle of whisky that they can find. When they get to the cashdesk the salesman says, "I'm not sure that I can sell booze to you ladies, now, can I? I didn't think you were supposed to drink that stuff." "Don't be worrying yourself about that, now, will you?" replies one of the sisters, "it's not for lowly nuns like us, 'tis for the Holy Mother

Superior – she has constipation!" "Oh well, sister," says the salesman, "I'm so sorry, in that case, have the bottle on the house and wish her my best." The nuns thank him and leave quietly. A couple of hours later the salesman shuts up the shop and leaves. As he is walking to the bus stop he hears laughing and sees the two nuns sitting on a park bench laughing their heads off, rolling around and drinking all the whisky he gave them. He is disgusted and runs over to them. "You lied to me, sisters!" he begins, "you told me that whisky was for the Holy Mother Superior's constipation." "And so it is," replies one of the nuns, "and so it is – when the Holy Mother Superior sees us in this state she's sure to shit herself!"

****

Brother William is on his way back from teaching children at a local school. It is late at night and the Abbey's car that he is travelling in breaks down. He knows that he hasn't run out of petrol because he's just filled up, so he opens up the bonnet and starts to have a look at the engine. A few minutes later a car pulls up next to him and the window is wound down. A red-faced man pops his head out and says, "Hello, old chap, what's the matter with you, then?" "Piston broke, I think," says the monk, to which the man in the car replies, "Me too, but what's up with the motor?"

****

A man is walking along a remote beach on the south coast of England. After about 20 minutes he hears a deep, booming voice say, "DIG!" He looks up, down, left and right, but he cannot see where the voice could possibly have come from, so he carries on. "I SAID DIG!" says the same deep, booming voice. The man figures that the sensible thing to do under these circumstances is to do as he's told, so he starts digging in the sand at the point where he first heard the voice. After about ten minutes he digs up a little metal box, about one foot square. On the front of it is an old rusted padlock. He hears a deep, booming voice say, "OPEN!" so he pulls and pushes and tweaks and bends until the padlock breaks. Inside, the box is full of gold coins. The deep, booming voice says, "TO THE CASINO!" so the man packs up the box, puts it in his car and drives to the nearest casino. He's had a right result so far, he reckons, so he may as well carry on. He changes the coins for a big stack of chips and starts to wander round the casino when the deep, booming voice says, "ROULETTE!", so he goes to the roulette table. There are a few people playing, but he has no problem getting in on the game. Just then, the deep, booming voice says, "TWENTY-SEVEN" so he puts a couple of chips on that number. "ALL OF IT," the deep, booming voice says so the man loads all the rest of the chips on to number 27. The croupier spins the wheel and rolls the ball. The crowd gathered around the table is silent as the ball spins. And spins. And spins. Eventually, it stops on… number 26. And the deep, booming voice says, "SHIT!"

****

A priest is shopping in the local town when he returns to his car and discovers he has been given a parking ticket. The traffic warden is still writing out the ticket when he arrives. The priest asks, "Oh, you couldn't waive the ticket could you now son?" But the traffic warden replies, "Oh, Father, I'm so sorry, but I've begun to write it and I'm not allowed to stop halfway through. If you'd just been a minute quicker…" "Oh well," says the priest, "I'm terrible with parking, I never remember what the time is or where I've parked, to be sure." "That's very decent of you, Father," says the traffic warden, "quite often when this happens us traffic wardens get given a whole load of abuse." "Oh my goodness, that's awful," says the priest, "after all you're only doing your job aren't you? Now, there's a tea party at the abbey this Sunday, would you like to come over?" "Well, Father, that's very nice of you to ask, I'd love to. And thanks again for being so understanding," says the traffic warden. "And perhaps you'd like to bring your father and your mother, too," says the priest, "I could marry the pair of them while I'm at it!"

✳✳✳✳

A man joins an order of silent monks. He doesn't say a word for ten years. After that time, there is a meal held in his honour and the head monk says to him, "Brother Peter, you have been with us for ten years now, you are permitted to break your vow of silence and to say whatever you'd like to say." Brother Peter says, "I'd quite like to have some more food in the evenings please, I've been getting hungry lately." Another ten years pass and another meal is held in Brother Peter's honour. The head monk makes another speech: "Brother Peter, you have been with us for another ten years now, you are permitted to break your vow of silence and to say whatever you'd like to say." Brother Peter says, "I'd quite like to have some more wine in the evenings, please, I've been getting thirsty lately." Another ten years pass and another meal is held in Brother Peter's honour. The head monk makes his customary speech: "Brother Peter, you have been with us for another ten years now, you are permitted to break your vow of silence and to say whatever you'd like to say." Brother Peter says, "Father, I think I'm going to leave the order, I don't really think I'm cut out for this life," to which the Father replies, "I'm not surprised, Brother Peter you've done nothing but complain since you got here.'

✳✳✳✳

Two nuns are shipped in from Ireland to the United States of America. As they are walking from the docks to the convent, they walk past a hot dog stand. "Well, would you look, at that sister. I did not know that they ate dogs in this country. How weird," said one nun to the other. Her companion replied, "Yes sister, but now that we are to live here, should we not do as the Americans do? I think that we should at least try to eat some dog should we not?" Both of the nuns go over to the vendor and they buy a hot dog each. The vendor hands them each a foil-wrapped dog. The nuns walk off, unwrapping their food. The first nun stares at hers, and then leans over her friend's shoulder before asking, "Um, so, er, sister, which part of the dog did you get then?"

✳✳✳✳

A man is confused about sex and the Sabbath day. He just cannot work out whether having sex on the Sabbath is a sin or not because he doesn't know whether it is work or play. He goes to see his local priest and asks him what his opinion is on this question. The priest gets his Bible down and flicks through it, reading a passage here and a passage there. Eventually he tells the man, "Well my son, after consulting the Good Book I have decided that sex is closest to work and that therefore you should not practise it on the Sabbath." The man thanks the priest but, as that wasn't really the answer he was looking for, he decides to go and see the local minister, who is married and may see things a bit more his way. He asks the minister the question and, to his disappointment, the minister gives him the same answer as the priest, "No sex on the Sabbath." The man decides to go and see another type of holy man – the local Rabbi. The Rabbi is asked the question and he ponders it over. Eventually he says, "Well my son, I have come to the conclusion that sex is definitely play so therefore you can have sex on the Sabbath." The man says, "That's great Rabbi, but how do you come to that conclusion when so many others disagree?" The Rabbi thinks a little and then says quietly, "If sex were work, my wife would get the maid to do it!"

✳✳✳✳

Three rabbis were playing golf one day. Another fellow, who had no golfing partner, asked if he could join in to make up a foursome. The rabbis were more than willing and they all had a jolly good round of golf. At the end of the game the man had lost miserably, and his score was a good 30 shots higher than all the rabbis. He found this confusing, because he's quite a keen weekend golfer, and the rabbis were men of the cloth. So he asks, "How come you guys are all such good golfers?" One of the rabbis replies, "Well son, when you lead a good, religious and pure life as part of a temple, your rewards are many. Being good at golf is just one of our rewards." So the man goes home and has a think, and decides, what the hey, I don't have much going on in my life anyway, I may as well go for it and try to improve my golf. So he finds a temple near where he lives, he joins it and attends classes three times a week. One year later the four of them all play golf again, but it is the same story: the man loses miserably again. "So what's that all about?" he asks the rabbis again. "I joined a temple, I go three times a week and I lead a good, pure life." One of the rabbis replies, "Which temple did you join?" and the man says, "Shalom Shalom on 4th Avenue." The rabbi says, "Oh no! That one's for tennis!"

****

A Sloaney Londoner is getting old so she decides to make her will and to include her final requests. She is talking to her priest and she tells him that when she has been cremated she would like to have her remains scattered in Harvey Nicks, dear. "But why's that?" asks the priest. The woman replies, "I want to be sure that my daughters will visit me at least once a week!"

****

There are two priests who ride bicycles to their parish church every week. One day one of the priests shows up to 'work' without his bicycle. The other priest says to him, "Where has your bike gone Father Michael?" to which Father Michael replies, "I'm not really sure, but I think it's been stolen!" The other priest tells him to read out the Ten Commandments at the next sermon he gives, and by the time he gets to "Thou Shalt Not Steal", someone will own up to stealing the bicycle from him. The next time the two priests see each other they are both on bicycles again. The other priest asks Father Michael, "So you made the thief own up, then, did you father?" Father Michael says, "Well, not really. I took your advice, sure enough, and I was reading out the Ten Commandments. I got to 'Thou Shalt Not Commit Adultery', when I all of a sudden remembered where I'd left my bike!"

****

A drunk staggers into church and manages to make his way into one of the confessionals. He sits there in silence. The priest coughs once to get the man's attention, but the man just ignores him and sits there. The priest can see that the man isn't asleep so he coughs again, only this time louder. The man still ignores him. The priest then knocks on the divider in a last attempt to get the man to speak. This seems to have the desired effect, and the man shouts to the priest, "It's no use knocking, there's no paper in this bloody one either!"

****

A woman goes to see her priest because she has a problem with the couple of female parrots that she owns – they just will not behave themselves. All they can say is, "Hello, we are prostitutes. Do you wanna have a good time?" The father agrees that that's a terrible situation, but he realizes very quickly that he, himself can provide a simple solution. He asks the woman to bring her two parrots over to his house, because he too has two parrots – his are male – and he has bought them up to read the Bible and to pray and all that sort of "good" stuff. He figures that his good parrots will be a very good influence on her "bad" parrots and that all will live happily together eventually. The next day, the woman brings her two female parrots over to the priest's house. She sees the priest's two parrots in their cage. They are praying, burning incense and fiddling with their rosary beads, all in a very devout manner. The woman puts her parrots down next to the priest's parrots and hers pipe up, "Hello, we are prostitutes. Do you wanna have a good time?" Upon hearing this, one of the priest's parrots turns to the other one and says, "Put the Good Book away my man, our prayers have been answered!'

****

A man goes to confession. In the booth he says, "Forgive me, Father, for I have sinned. I... almost... had an affair with a woman." "Almost? What do you mean 'almost'?" says the priest, not really understanding what the man is going on about. "Well, Father," the man continues, "we got undressed and rubbed against one another, but then we both thought better of it and so we stopped." "Very good," says the priest, "but rubbing up against it is just the same as putting it in. You must not go near that woman again. You must say five Hail Marys and you must put 50 in the donation box by the door." The man thanks the priest and walks to the door of the church. He stops by the donation box, pauses and then starts to leave. The priest runs up to him and says, "Oi, I saw that – you didn't put anything in the donation box did you?" "Well no, I didn't Father," the man says, "I rubbed up against it, and as you say, that's the same as putting it in!"

****

A priest and a nun were travelling through the desert on a camel. It was a very long, hot journey and the camel became ill and died, leaving the two of them stranded in the middle of the hot desert. After a couple of days, the pair of them are resigned to their fate and discuss all sorts of things, including sex. The priest is talking about how he's never had sex with a woman, so he pulls out his knob and says to the nun, "This is my life-giving tool." The nun, ever hopeful, says, "Oh, really? So why don't you stick it in the camel and give us a chance of getting the hell out of here?"

****

Ex-President Bill Clinton dies and goes to Hell. Satan, who's been waiting for him at the gate, greets him warmly. Now it turns out that Hell is a bit full at the moment, so Bill will be replacing some lucky person, who will get to go up to "the other place" instead. The good news for Bill is that he gets to choose who he can replace. Satan tells Bill to follow him as he leads him to three doorways. Satan opens the first door and Bill sees a man chained to the wall, smashing big rocks into smaller ones with a big hammer. At the sight of this, Bill goes pale and says, "Oh, no, I couldn't handle that: no way." Satan opens the second door and Bill sees a man up to his neck in mud, just able to breathe and keep his head above water. At the sight of this, Bill goes even paler, and says, "Oh, no, I couldn't handle that, no way." Satan opens the third door and Bill sees a man tied to a pole, totally naked. Kneeling in front of him is Monica Lewinsky, giving him a blowjob. At the sight of this, Bill gets a bit of colour back in his cheeks. "Well, I think I could handle this," he says. "Great choice," says the Devil. "Monica – you can go now."

✳✳✳✳

An Amish boy and his father decided to visit a shopping mall. They were amazed by everything they saw, but especially by two shiny, silver walls that moved magically forward and backwards together by themselves. The young boy said to his father, "Daddy, what is this for? What miracle is this?" and the father replied that he did not know. As the two watched, an 80-year-old lady walked in and the doors closed. Lights above the doors flashed upwards and then down again, before the doors opened again, silently, and a beautiful 25-year-old woman walked out. The father and son looked at each other before the father said to the boy, "Go and get your mother!"

✱✱✱✱

A little boy is sitting with his mother at a service when the sermon is about to start. He turns to her and says, "Mummy, I don't feel well. I think I am going to be sick." The mother is rather embarrassed, but it appears the rest of the congregation hadn't heard him. "You can't be sick here," she tells him. "I tell you what, go out now, before the sermon starts, and if you have to be sick, then at least you won't disrupt the priest or the service." The boy disappears and when the sermon ends, he makes his way back and sits down next to his mother. "Well, were you sick?" she asks felicitously. "Yes, Mummy, I was and I feel much better now." "Good, I am pleased you were so quiet. But, tell me, where were you sick?" she asks, thinking about the mess she would have to clear up. "I knew exactly where to go," he said proudly. "There was a big box at the back of the church with 'For the sick' written on it."

✱✱✱✱

Boys & Girls

19

Jokes About the
Birds and the Bees

Little Johnny's dad picks him up after school because Johnny has been trying out for a part in the school play. Johnny is all excited and his dad says, "So, son, it looks like you got a part – that's great!" Johnny says, "Yes, dad, I did: I get to play the part of a man who's been married for a quarter of a century." "That's great, son," says his father, "and if you keep trying harder and harder, one day you'll get a speaking part!"

✳✳✳✳

Jake moves to Australia after working all his life in the City. He buys a farm in the remotest part of the Outback he can find. His post arrives once a week, his groceries once a month and he can call the Flying Doctor on his radio if he has an emergency. One night, after six months of this, Jake is finishing his dinner when he hears a knock on the door. He walks up, opens it and sees a huge outbacker standing in front of him. "G'day, mate," says the outbacker. "I'm your nearest neighbour, Bruce Sheldon, from 20 miles east. I'm having a party Saturday night and I thought you might like to come along, mate." "That'd be great," says Jake. "I haven't really spoken to anyone for six months. Thanks a lot." Bruce is about to turn away, but instead says, "I think I'd better warn you, though: there'll be some serious drinking going on." "Not a problem," says Jake, "I like a couple of pints myself." Bruce is about to turn away again, but instead says, "Better warn you, though, there'll probably be some fighting, too." "Not a problem," says Jake, "I know how to keep out of trouble." Bruce is about to turn away again, but instead says, "Better warn you though, there'll probably be some pretty wild sex, too." "Not a problem," says Jake, "I've been alone for six months, remember. Now, what time should I show up?" Bruce turns once more and says, "Whenever you like, mate: there's only going to be me and you there anyway!'

✳✳✳✳

A man and woman have been married for what seems like for ever. They have eight grown-up children and countless grandchildren. On their 60th wedding anniversary they have a very candid conversation. The wife says to her husband, "Honey, since we are so old now and we've been together for so long, I'm going to be totally honest with you. Is there anything you'd like to know about me and our relationship over the past six decades that you'd like to ask me about? If there is, I promise that I will answer you with total honesty." The husband pauses for a while, and then says, "Dear, this isn't easy for me to say, but there is actually something that has been eating away at me for quite a few years now. It's just that of all our kids, there's one who looks decidedly different from the others. You know the one I mean, I'm sure, and I'm sure it's nothing but, as I say, I've wondered about this for years and I would like to know if he had a different father from the rest of the kids." The wife looks down at her feet and sighs loudly. "Well, dear, I'm sorry to say it, but you're right. I cannot tell a lie: that child did indeed have a different father from all the others." The husband looks miserable, but he's still curious. "And who would that be?" he asks. "Well, dear…" begins the wife slowly, "…you."

****

At the National Improvised Poetry Competition, there were two finalists. One was an Oxford graduate, the other a dustbin man from Suffolk. As a tiebreak they had two minutes to make up a poem containing the word 'Timbuktu'. The Oxford graduate read his poem first:

> We came across the desert,
> Miles across the sand,
> Both on camels, me and you,
> On our search for Timbuktu.

The audience cheered and thought the bumpkin would have no chance against so eloquent an effort. However, the dustbin man won hands-down with his effort:

> Me and Tim a-huntin' went
> Met three birds in a field in Kent
> They were three and us but two
> So I bucked one and Timbuktu!

****

A young mother teaches her son to go to the bathroom by numbers. She teaches him the following lesson: "1. Unzip your flies. 2. Gently lift out your family jewels. 3. Pull back the foreskin. 4. Let nature take its course. 5. Slide the foreskin forward. 6. Replace the family jewels. 7. Zip back up." The mother would often check that he was following instructions by listening outside the door of the bathroom. She would hear, "One, two, three, four, five, six, seven. All done!" However, one day she was walking past the bathroom and was disturbed to hear, "Three–five, three–five, three–five, three–five…"

****

A farmer is having trouble with his prize stud bull, which has a herd of 300 cows to sort out. It won't do what is required of it, so the farmer takes it to the vet. Without even examining the animal, the vet hands the farmer a small bottle of pills and says, "Grind one of these into its feed, stand back and watch it go!" Two weeks later, the farmer returns to the vet and says, "Veterinary, that was truly incredible. I did what you said and as soon as he'd eaten the feed he leaped over the fence and screwed all 300 cows in less than an hour!" The vet says, "So what's the problem then – why are you back?" The farmer says, "Well, I was wondering: it's a bit personal, but I've got a hot date with a 21-year-old tonight and I could really do with one of those tablets. I'm not really the man I used to be, after all." "Well, I can't really let you have a whole one," says the vet, "but I guess a quarter of a pill wouldn't do much harm!" So he gives a quarter-pill to the farmer, who goes off to prepare for his date. A few days later, the farmer is back at the vet's again. "What is it this time?" asks the vet. "Well, the pill worked fine – 40 times that one night," says the farmer. "So what's up, then?" asks the vet. "Well, now I need something for my wrist," says the farmer. "She never showed up!"

****

It was the night before Christmas and a rather lonely lady, who hadn't got laid in a very long time, was waiting for Father Christmas to come down the chimney at her house. When he did, she removed her shirt and said, "Oh, Santa, please stay a while." Santa said, "Ho ho ho, lady: I'd love to, but I've got toys to deliver to children around the world." So she dropped her skirt and says, "Oh Santa, please stay a while." Santa says, "Ho ho ho, lady, I'd love to, but I've got toys to deliver to children around the world." So she stripped naked and said, "Oh, Santa, please stay a while." So Santa said, "Well, I'm never going to get up the chimney with my dick in this state, so I guess I'd better stay a while!"

✳✳✳✳

A guy walks into a gun shop. "I'd like to buy a laser sight for a rifle, please." The salesman fetches one and encourages him to try it out. The man is looking around the neighbourhood when he sees, through a window, a man and a woman on the job. "Whoa! Check this out!" he says to the salesman, who has a look for himself. His eyes nearly jump out of his head as he sees that it is his wife with another man. No decent shot himself, he makes the guy the following offer: "If you can shoot him in the dick and her in the head I'll give you the laser sight and the rifle of your choice." "Sure thing," says the guy, and he takes aim and looses off a shot. "What luck – two for one: job done," he says.

✳✳✳✳

A man is out shopping one Saturday when he finds a new brand of condom. He is impressed by the brand: "Olympic Condoms – for winners." When he gets home he shows his wife, who asks him, "What's so special about Olympic, then?" "That's the cool thing," he says. "They come in three colours: gold, silver and bronze." "And which colour will you be wearing tonight?" the wife questions. "Well, gold, of course, darling," the man replies. Quick as a flash, the wife quips, "Why don't you try silver? It'd be nice if you came second for a change!"

****

A mother walked into the bathroom one day and was shocked to find her son scrubbing away furiously at his cock using a toothbrush and toothpaste. "Oh, my God: what on earth's going on?" she said. "Don't try and stop me, Mum," the boy said. "I'm doing this three times a day because if you think I'm going to end up with a cavity that looks as bad as my sister's you've got another think coming!"

****

One morning the farmer's son got up early to go and play on the farm, but his mother told him he would have to do chores because now he was old enough to be helping out. The boy didn't like the thought of this much, but didn't have a lot of choice. He started in the barn, where he milked the cow. When he'd finished he booted the cow up the arse. Then he went to feed the pig. When he'd finished, he booted the pig up the arse. The he went to feed the chickens. When he'd finished, he booted the chickens up the arse. Now his chores were done, he went back to the house for breakfast. His mother gave him a bowl of dry cornflakes. "What about milk and my fried breakfast?" asked the boy. "Well, you don't get any milk because you kicked the cow up the arse," said his mother. "And you don't get any bacon because you kicked the pig up the arse," she continued, "and you don't get any eggs because you kicked the chickens up the arse." At that moment, the farmer walks in as the cat walks past the door. In a bad mood, the farmer launches a kick at the cat and gets it up the arse. The boy is silent for a while, then looks at his mother and says, "Do you want to give him the bad news or shall I?"

****

A robber escapes from prison and breaks into a house occupied by a young couple. He ties them up and leaves them alone in the bedroom for a while. As soon as they are alone, the husband turns to his young wife, skimpily dressed in her black nightie, and says, "Now listen, dear. This man probably hasn't had sex with a woman for years. If he wants to have sex, just go along with it and pretend that you're enjoying it. It will probably mean the difference between living and dying for us." "I'm so glad you feel that way, my darling," said the wife, "because he just told me he loves your smooth skin and firm arse!"

****

A drunken bum is sitting on a bar stool when a really high-class bird sits down next to him. He immediately turns around and says to her, "Hey, darlin'. How's about you and me getting together for a bit of how's your father? I've got a couple of Euro and you look like you could do with a little cash!" The woman looks at him coldly before replying, "What makes you think I charge by the inch?'

✱✱✱✱

Janine had been married to Tim for 75 years. When he passed on she just couldn't envisage life without him, so she decided to end it all by herself. Remembering that Tim had an old army pistol and some live ammunition, Janine did some research. She found out on the Internet that a shot to the heart would be the best way to get it over with quickly. She read a page that said her heart would be a couple of inches below the left breast. She said her last rites, turned off the gas, cancelled the milk and pulled the trigger. Later that night Janine was admitted to the local hospital with a bullet wound to the left thigh.

✱✱✱✱

A young secondary school teacher is informed that, due to cutbacks, she will have to give her class their sex education lessons herself. Not wanting to have to explain much or draw pictures, she decides to use a mathematical approach and gets some flashcards for the following day's lessons. At the start of the lesson she holds up the first card, a picture of a breast, and says to the class, "Does anyone know what this is?" Susan puts up her hand and says, "I know; I know. It's a breast, and my Mummy has two of them." "That's very good, Susan," says the teacher and holds up the next card. It's of a penis. "Does anyone know what this is?" she asks. Tim puts his hand up and says, "I know; I know. It's a penis, and my Daddy has two of them." "Well, that's very good, Tim: it is a penis, but your Daddy can't have two of them." Tim replies, "He does, miss. He's got a little one he pees with and a great big one he brushes Mummy's teeth with!"

****

Christopher invites his nosy mother over for dinner. She's been encouraging him to find a wife for years, and when she arrives she notices that the live-in housekeeper is a very attractive woman who gets on very well with her son. She can't help wondering if maybe there's something going on – they get on so well – but her son denies everything: "Mother, I assure you that my relationship with my housekeeper is strictly professional." A few days later, the housekeeper tells Christopher that ever since his mother came over for dinner she has been unable to find the silver tray that the brandy is always served on. A curious affair indeed, thinks Christopher: I wonder what my mother is up to now. So he writes his mother a letter:

> Dear Mother,
> Regarding my silver tray. I'm obviously not saying that you did take it, and I'm not saying that you did not take it, but the fact remains that I have been unable to find it since you came over for dinner.
> Love, Christopher.

A couple of days later, Christopher receives a reply:

Dear Christopher,
Regarding your housekeeper. I'm obviously not saying that
you do sleep with her, and I'm not saying that you do not
sleep with her, but the fact remains that if she was sleeping in
her own bed she would have found the silver tray by now!
Love, Mother.

✳✳✳✳

A man and woman are sitting next to each other in the first-class
compartment of an aeroplane. Suddenly the man sneezes, but instead
of wiping his nose, he pulls out his penis and wipes the tip with a
handkerchief. The woman cannot believe it and thinks she must be
imagining things. A couple of minutes go by and the man sneezes
again. It's the same story – he pulls his penis out and wipes it with a
handkerchief. The woman is absolutely astonished and stares at the
man, who doesn't seem to notice. Five minutes later the man sneezes
again. He goes through the same process and this time the woman can
bear it no longer. She turns to him and says, as calmly as she possibly
can, "That's three times you have sneezed, and three times you have
wiped your penis on a handkerchief. It's absolutely disgusting! What
kind of sick, twisted individual are you?" The man replies,
"Goodness. I'm so sorry that I offended you, but I suffer from a very
rare condition which means every time I sneeze I have an orgasm."
The woman feels slightly guilty and replies, "Oh, I'm sorry: I should

have realized. You poor thing. What on earth do you take for it?" The man turns around, looks her square in the face and says, "Pepper."

****

A young wife was frustrated by the lack of spice in her and her husband's sex life, so she decided to see what she could do about it. Straight after work she went shopping and bought herself a pair of crotchless panties in a sex shop. She ran home and put on her new panties, along with a particularly short skirt. When her husband came home from work she fixed him a drink and sat across from him as he drank it. "Now you've had some of that, sugar…" she cooed as she slowly spread her legs, "… perhaps you'd like some of this?" "God, no!" screamed the husband. "Look what it's done to your underwear!"

****

One Sunday, a man is working in the garden as his wife gets up and bathes. He is clearing leaves and soon realizes that he cannot find his rake, the essential tool for the job. He can see his wife in their bedroom window, so he shouts up, "Where's my rake?" The wife doesn't understand him and mouths, "What?" Again the man shouts, "Where's my rake?" The wife still doesn't understand, so shrugs her shoulders to signify a lack of comprehension. The man, tiring of shouting, points to his eye, then his knee, and then makes a raking motion with both hands. The wife is still clueless, so shrugs again, to say, "What?" The man repeats the gestures, and mouths "eye, knee, the rake" as he does so. The wife understands finally, and signals her reply. She points to her eye, her left breast, her arse and finally her crotch. The man's eyes nearly pop out and it is obvious he hasn't got a clue what she is going on about. Giving up, he walks into the house and runs upstairs. "What the hell was that all about?" he says. The wife replies, "Eye, left tit, behind, the bush!"

****

Why are Monica Lewinsky's cheeks so puffed up?
She's withholding evidence.

What did Bill Clinton say to Monica Lewinsky?
"I didn't, say "Wreck my election",' I said …".

****

One day in a jewellery shop a man is in the process of buying a really expensive necklace with a lovely silver locket on it. The jeweller asks him, "Would you like her name engraved on it?" The man has a think and then replies, "No: just put, 'To my one and only love.' That way, if we split up and she throws it back in anger, I'll be able to recycle!'

****

A man gets himself an Audi TT with a share bonus windfall at work and takes Friday night to drive it around the M25. As he gets more used to the car, he starts to go faster and faster. Eventually he winds up at over 100 miles per hour. Just as the needle goes over the hundred, he sees flashing lights in his rearview mirror and he pulls over. The policeman walks up to his window, leans in and says, "Look here, mate, I've had a rough day, I'm nearly off, so if you can give me an excuse I've never heard before I'll let you off the ticket, the fine and the driving ban." The man can't believe his potential luck and excitedly says, "Well officer, my wife ran away with a policeman last week and I was driving so quickly away from you 'cos I thought you were trying to give her back!" "You take it easy sir, and have a good weekend," said the policeman as he turned to go back to his car.

✱✱✱✱

An old guy begins to feel his age, and at 50 decides to treat himself to a facelift. When it's done, he feels really good – years younger. On his way back from the surgery he stops off at a newsagent to get the paper. He chats to the shopkeeper, and eventually says, "I hope you don't mind me asking, but how old do you reckon I am?" "No problem," says the shopkeeper, "about 35?" "It's my 50th birthday!" says the man, overjoyed. Next, he goes to get some fish and chips. He chats to the assistant and eventually says, "I hope you don't mind me asking, but how old do you reckon I am?" "No problem," says the chipper, "about 32?" "It's my 50th birthday!" says the man, overjoyed again. The man decides to get a taxi home, and stands in the queue to get one. Behind him is an old lady and they get talking. The man says to her, "I hope you don't mind me asking, but how old do you reckon I am?" "No problem," says the old lady, "but I'm 85 and my eyesight's not so good. If I put my hand down your trousers and play with your balls for a couple of minutes I'll be able to tell exactly how old you are." This came as a bit of a shock to the man, but he figured what the hell, and let the old lady put her hand down his trousers. After a couple of minutes the old lady says, "It's your 50th birthday." The man is amazed. "That's incredible," he says. "How on earth did you know that?" The old lady replies, "I was standing behind you in the fish and chip shop!'

****

There once was a beautiful young woman who wanted to use her good looks to get rich quick. So she started to hang around older men in the hope of netting one for herself to marry and to shag them to death on their wedding night. She pretty quickly found herself a rich 80-year-old who looked frail, and their romance went quickly and effectively. Three months later it was their wedding day. All went well and in the evening they found themselves in a five-star hotel in Paris. They both retired to their separate bathrooms and she emerged first, seductively dressed as she slipped between the satin sheets of the huge bed they were to share. The man's bathroom door opens and he walked out sporting a condom over a 12-inch erection. He was carrying a pair of earplugs and some nose plugs, too. The woman's heart sank and she began to suspect something was up. Tentatively, she asked, "Er… what are those for, dear?" The old man replies, "These take care of the two things I can't stand the most: the sound of women screaming and the smell of burning rubber!'

****

A masked man runs through the door of a sperm bank. He is brandishing a shotgun. He leaps over the counter and points the gun at the receptionist. "Open the safe!" he barks at her. "What?" she says. "There's no money here: we're a sperm bank, not a money bank." "Just do it!" the guy continues. "Just open the goddamned safe and don't talk back. Don't make me hurt you, lady." So the lady leads him out back and opens the safe. It is just a big refrigerator full of sperm samples. "Now take a sample out," the guy snaps. The woman obliges. "Now, drink it," the guy says. "But it's sperm," the woman says. "Don't make me mad – just do it!" shouts the man. Fearing the worst, the woman pops the cap off the bottle and drinks the sperm. She chokes a couple of times but drains the bottle. "Another one," says the guy. She takes another bottle from the racks and drinks it. At that moment the man drops his gun and pulls off his mask. The woman cannot believe her eyes – the man who just had a gun at her head is her husband! "You see," he shouts at her, "it wasn't that bloody difficult, was it?"

****

A top executive lawyer decides that he needs some holiday and to improve his golf, so combines the two with a week's-worth of golf at his local course. On the first round of the first day, he is playing behind a woman whom the lawyer notices is very attractive – and not bad at golf, either. He makes the effort and catches up with her quite quickly. He suggests to her that they play together and she agrees. They begin to play and it soon turns out that they are very evenly matched. Eventually the woman wins with the last stroke on the last hole. They have got on really well, so the man offers his congratulations and offers the woman a lift home. As they are driving, the woman tells the man how much fun she's had, and that she is surprised at how well they got on and how close the competition was. They stop at her place, and she says, "I'd like to show you just how much I appreciated the game and your company," she says, and proceeds to give the lawyer a blowjob. The next morning the lawyer sees the woman teeing off at the first and again suggests a partnership. She agrees, and they play another round of close, competitive golf. The man is pretty disappointed that he didn't manage to win the previous day's game so he really puts everything into it, but it is to no avail. The lady wins once more, again by just one stroke. Again, he gives her a lift home and she gives him a blowjob. This pattern carries on all week, with the woman winning the golf every day. The man is pretty sick about this, but he's getting to spend a lot of time with a beautiful woman who performs sexual favours for him, too, so he's not really complaining. On the Friday night as he is driving her home, he announces that in honour of spending such a great time with her, he's booked them a table for a candlelit dinner at the most exclusive restaurant in town, and then a penthouse appartment at the best hotel. Upon hearing this, the woman bursts into tears, sobbing, "I can't; I can't." The lawyer asks her what on earth is wrong. She sobs out that she just can't go with him, not because she doesn't want to, but because she isn't really a woman – she is, in fact, a transvestite. The guy is gobsmacked and says nothing. "I'm so sorry," she cries. "You total bastard!" he screams suddenly, all red in the face, "You bloody cheat. You've been playing off women's tees all week!"

****

There was a farmer with three daughters. One Saturday night they each had a date. One by one the dates arrived and the farmer answered the door each time. The first fellow knocked on the door. The farmer answered and the fellow said, "Hello, Mr Farmer. My name is Joe, I'm here to take your daughter Flo out to eat some dough." "That's just fine," said the farmer, and off went Joe with the eldest daughter. The second fellow knocked on the door. The farmer answered and the fellow said, "Hello, Mr Farmer. My name is Freddy, I'm here to take your daughter Betty out to eat spaghetti." "That's just fine," said the farmer and off went Freddy with the middle daughter. The third fellow knocked on the door. The farmer answered and the fellow said, "Hello, Mr Farmer. My name is Chuck – " "Get the hell out of my house," yelled the farmer.

****

A man is drinking in his local watering-hole in New York when he spots a bit of top totty hanging out with a really cheap, loser type. He's amazed that a dullard like that can pull such top crumpet, so he goes up to the bartender and asks him about it. He discovers that the woman is a prostitute, so he keeps an eye on her and, sure enough, a while later, she leaves on the man's arm and comes back later with someone else. The next night the man is in the same bar and in comes the prostitute. He still thinks she looks magnificent, so he goes up to her and asks her what her rates are. She is totally unfazed, and says, "Well, my rates start at $100 for a handjob and go up from there." "A hundred dollars," the guy interrupts, "for a handjob? You must be joking!" "Listen, buddy," says the woman, pointing out of the window at a huge Mercedes outside, "I bought that car for cash with the money I made from giving handjobs! Trust me: it'll be worth it." The man is certainly impressed, and thinks for a few seconds before deciding to get himself a handjob from the woman. They leave together and the man gets what he thinks is probably the finest sexual experience that he's ever had with anyone. The next night he is back in the bar, eagerly awaiting the woman. When she shows up, he walks straight up to her, saying, "Last night really was incredible." "Of course it was: I told you, didn't I?" the prostitute replies, "but just you wait until you try one of my blowjobs." The man is tempted, but he asks, "and how much would that be?" The woman replies, "$1,000." "One thousand dollars?" the guy almost shouts, before the woman says, "Listen, buddy: I bought myself a ten-storey downtown condominium for cash with the money I made from giving blowjobs. Trust me: it'll be worth it." The man is impressed again and, based on the evidence of the previous evening, decides to get himself a blowjob from the woman. They leave together and the man gets what he knows is far and away the greatest single experience of his life – he nearly faints! The next night he is back in the bar, waiting again. He is so excited he can hardly sit in a chair. When the prostitute does eventually show up, he runs up to her and says, "You're the best: you're the best: just tell me what it'll cost for some pussy!" The woman grabs his hand and pulls him outside the bar into the street. Away in the distance he can see Manhattan. She says, "You see that island?" To which the guy replies, "Come on – you can't be serious!" The prostitute nods her head and says, "Yup: if I had a pussy, I'd own Manhattan!"

✳✳✳✳

An Italian, a Frenchman and a Texan were talking about making love to their partners. The Italian began, "Last-a night, I make the love to my-a wife three times. She have three times joy. She was hin ecstasy this-a morning." The Frenchman continued, "I made lurve to mah wife seeks times last night. Zis morning she make me ze omelette and she say to me zat she could never lurve anozzer man een er life!" The Texan doesn't say a word, so the Frenchman said to him, "And ow many times did you make ze love wis your wife last night?" "Just the once," the Texan replied. "Only once!" snorted the Italian, "and what did your poor wife-a say to you this morning?" "Don't stop," drawled the Texan.

✳✳✳✳

A man had a beautiful but very demanding wife. She always wanted the latest fashion clothes and beautiful jewellery, but he didn't really make enough money to get her all that she wanted. One day she comes home showing off a brand-new diamond necklace. "Wow," he says to her, "where did you get that?" "Oh, I won it at bingo, darling," she says, rather unconvincingly. The next day the wife comes home wearing a brand-new mink coat. "Wow," he says to her, "where did you get that?" "Oh, I won it at bingo, darling – I've had a lucky week, you know." The next day the wife comes home in a brand-new Porsche. "Wow," he says, "where did you get that?" "Oh, stop asking me all those awkward questions, please. Leave me alone and do something useful. Go upstairs and run me a bath, there's a dear." The wife comes upstairs and into the bathroom. There's only a tiny amount of water in the bottom of the bath. The wife says, "What's up with the depth of that bath? That's not even going to reach my pussy!" And the husband replies, "Didn't want to get your bingo card wet, dear!'

✳✳✳✳

A man dies while having sex but his erection stays hard. At the funeral parlour they discuss the situation with his wife and she gives them permission to cut it off in order to get the lid on the coffin. The wife keeps the penis, and later that night steals back and shoves it up the dead man's rear end. The next day, at the funeral, she peers over the coffin and, noticing a tear in the dead man's eye, whispers, "I told you it hurt, you heartless bastard!"

✳✳✳✳

An old soak is looking for a whorehouse and stumbles into a chiropodist's office. He walks up to the front desk and is directed to one of the inspection rooms. Without looking up, the receptionist waves him over to the inspection table and without looking up says, "Stick it through the curtain." Thinking, "How cool is this?', the drunk pulls his plonker out and sticks it through the middle of the curtain. "That's not a foot!" screams the doctor on the other side. "Well, lah-di-dah," says the drunk, "I didn't know there was a minimum!'

****

A woman is tidying up around the house one day when she hears a strange humming noise coming from her daughter's bedroom. The mother knocks on the door but just opens it immediately. She walks in and finds her daughter lying naked on the bed, pleasuring herself with a vibrator. The mother is a little shocked, but retains her composure and says, "What on earth are you doing that for, dear?" The daughter replies, "Well, mother, I am nearly 40 years old and I live at home with my parents. I never date guys, so I figure this is the nearest thing I'll get to a husband!" That night her father can't sleep, so he wanders downstairs and hears a strange humming noise coming from the front room. He walks in and finds his daughter lying naked on the sofa, pleasuring herself with a vibrator. The father is a little shocked, but retains his composure and says, "What on earth are you doing that for, dear?" The daughter replies, "Well, father, I am nearly 40 years old and I live at home with my parents. I never date guys, so I figure this is the nearest thing I'll get to a husband!" The next day the mother is once more tidying up around the house when she hears that same humming noise coming from the front room. She walks in and, to her surprise, she sees her husband watching TV with the vibrator just placed on the sofa beside him. "What the hell are you doing?" she says to her husband, shocked. He replies, "Just watching the game with the son-in-law."

****

A well-to-do woman visits her doctor, saying, "Doc, my problem is a bit embarrassing and I'm going to have to show you rather than explain it." "That's fine," says the doc, used to such things, "just show me where the problem is." The woman lifts up her skirt and opens her legs. There, right at the top of each thigh, on the inside of each leg, are large, green circles. "Do you know what it is doc? It's been troubling me for weeks now and I've no idea what the cause could be." The doctor drops to his knees and spends some time examining the area that has turned green. After a while he says, "I've never seen anything like it, unless..." "Yes, doctor?" says the woman expectantly. "Unless – let me think – have you been seeing someone who wears large earrings lately?" The woman is somewhat surprised but says, "Well, yes, doc; I have, as a matter of fact. But why do you ask?" "Well, perhaps you should tell them that their earrings aren't real gold!"

****

After his first day at school, Timmy comes home full of questions for his parents. Unfortunately, some of them are not really what his parents hoped he'd be learning at school. So Timmy goes up to his mother and says, "Mummy, what's a pussy? Everyone says that word in the playground and I don't know what it means." Timmy's mother picks up an illustrated dictionary and flicks to the page with a cat on it. She shows him the picture. Then Timmy says, "Mummy, what's a bitch? Everyone says that word in the playground and I don't know what it means." Timmy's mother picks up the dictionary and flicks to the page with a dog on it, and shows Timmy the female. Timmy is still curious so he goes to find his father. He says, "Daddy, what's a pussy? Everyone says that word in the playground and I'm still not sure what it means." Timmy's dad figures it is time to teach the boy a thing or two, so he picks up a jazzmag, draws a circle around the pussy that's on the page and shows the picture to the boy. "That's a pussy," he says. Then Timmy says, "Daddy, what's a bitch? Everyone says that word in the playground and I'm still not sure what it means." Timmy's father replies, "Everything outside the circle!"

✳✳✳✳

In the distant future, a couple of humans land on a distant planet in their spaceship. They are greeted by a couple of natives of the planet, who look remarkably human and who speak the same language. They talk for hours, comparing everything on Earth and on the alien planet. Things are a lot closer than they would have all imagined and the aliens have computers, cars, television, guns and all the other things we have that make life great. Eventually the couples get on to social interaction and, in particuar, how they have sex on their respective planets. It turns out that the aliens have sex pretty much the same way that Earth people do, so the two men suggest that, in order to see the differences, the couples should swap partners and see how things are

done on the other planets. The women both agree to this and they all
retire for the night. The Earth woman is in the bedroom with the alien
man and they both undress. She is a little worried because the alien's
member is tiny: a couple of centimetres long and only about a
centimetre thick, even when it's hard. "This isn't going to be easy,"
she says. "What's up?" says the alien, "the size bother you? Not a
problem." And he slaps himself on the forehead. As he does so, his
member grows longer. He continues to slap and with each hit he gets
bigger until he is very impressive-looking. "That's pretty good," says
the Earth woman, "but it could do with being a bit thicker." "Not a
problem," says the alien again and he begins pulling his ears. With
each pull, his member increases in thickness until it is even more
impressive. "Amazing!" exclaims the Earth woman, and they shag
wildly all night. The next day she meets her husband at breakfast.
"How was it for you?" he asks her. "Well, I must admit, they've got
some pretty exciting stuff over us," she replies, "but how was it for
you?" "Well, I must admit I was a bit disappointed," he says, "I just
got a headache. She kept slapping my forehead and pulling my ears
all night!'

****

A little boy comes home early from school one day and catches his
parents having sex. In fact, the wife is giving the husband a blowjob.
The boy asks, "Mummy and Daddy, what are you doing?" so the
parents reply, "Making fish-sticks," because they figure he's only
young and he's never going to know what they're up to, and what
does he care anyway? A couple of nights later the boy walks in on

them again and as they turn around he says, "Are you making fish-sticks again?" Both parents say "Yes". So the boy says, "Well. Mummy, you've got some tartare sauce stuck on your lip!"

****

A little old lady lives in a nursing home. She's losing her marbles and one day she walks up to one of the male patients and lifts up her skirt. She points down and says, "Super pussy," then drops her skirt and walks away. She walks up to another male patient and lifts up her skirt. She points down and says, "Super pussy," then drops her skirt and walks away. Then she walks up to a third male patient and lifts up her skirt. She points down and says "Super pussy" once more. The man looks up at her and says, "I think I'll take the soup, thanks!"

****

A couple have been married for years and years. On their 60th anniversary they decide to go on a second honeymoon. "Let's go to all the same places that we did just after our wedding," the wife says. "Sure," says the husband. "And let's do all the same things that we did just after our wedding," the wife says. "Sure," says the husband. "And we'll make love just like we did after our wedding," the wife says. "Sure," says the husband, "only this time it's me who gets to sit on the side of the bed crying, 'It's too big, it's too big!'"

****

A young newly-wed couple decide to have a romantic weekend away in the mountains in the winter: candlelit dinners, roaring fires and peace and quiet. They arrive in their winter cabin and the husband goes out to chop wood as the wife prepares their lunch. After a while he returns, saying, "Wow! It sure is cold. My hands are freezing." "Well', his wife tells him, "pop them between my thighs, baby: it's pretty hot down there, and sure to warm them up." He does so. After lunch he realizes they are low on wood again, so the husband goes out to chop some more. After a while he returns, saying, "Wow! It sure is cold. My hands are freezing." "Well," his wife tells him, "pop them between my thighs, baby: it's pretty hot down there, and sure to warm them up." He does so again. Later in the evening the husband goes out to chop wood again. After a while he returns, saying, "Wow! It sure is cold. My hands are freezing." But this time the wife says, "For goodness' sake! Don't you ever get cold ears?"

✳✳✳✳

A woman and a man are involved in a really nasty car accident. Both their cars are totally demolished, but neither of them are hurt. After they crawl out of their cars, the woman says, "So you're a man – that's interesting. I'm a woman. Wow, just look at our cars! There's nothing left, but we're unhurt. This must be a sign from God that we should meet, get acquainted and live together in peace for the rest of our days." The man feels great at having such good luck, so says, "Oh, yes; I agree with you completely! This must be a sign from the Lord!" The woman continues, "And look at this – another miracle. My car is demolished, but this bottle of wine didn't break. Surely God wants us to drink this wine and celebrate our good fortune." She hands the bottle to the man, who nods his head in agreement, opens the bottle and drinks half of it before handing it back to the woman. The woman takes the bottle and immediately puts the cap back on. The man asks, "Aren't you having any?" The woman replies, "No. I think I'll just wait for the police!" The moral of this story: Women are clever. Don't mess with them.

****

It is Christmas, and a little boy is taken to the local Santa's Grotto to meet the big man himself. Santa picks the boy up, places him on his knee and begins to ask him about what he wants for Christmas. The boy says he doesn't really know what he'd like for Christmas, so Santa makes some suggestions, spelling the words out as he does so, and prodding the boy's nose, so the boy can surely understand. Santa asks him if he'd like a B-I-K-E or a T-R-A-I-N and so on, but the little boy doesn't seem to want any of the "normal" Christmas stuff. So Santa eventually says, "Come on, kid: what do you want for Christmas?" The little boy replies, "I want some P-U-S-S-Y and I know you've got some because I can smell it on your finger!"

****

One day, a sweet little girl goes home to find that her dog has died. He is lying on the lawn on his back with his poor little legs sticking straight up in the air. She quickly runs to her father and asks him why her dog is lying down with his poor little legs in the air. "Well," her father explains, "that's because Jesus will be coming down to help poor doggy up to Heaven, and if his legs are up in the air like that it'll be a whole lot easier for him to go." The very next day when the father comes home, the sweet little girl runs up to him in a dreadful state. "Daddy! Daddy! Mummy almost died today – I'm sure of it!" "Oh, my!" says the father. "How do you know – is she OK?" "Yes, Daddy," the girl says, "she's OK now, but earlier on Mummy's legs were up in the air and she was shouting 'Oh Jesus, I'm coming, I'm coming; and if the postman hadn't been there to hold her down I think she'd be in Heaven now!"

****

A hippy, long-haired youth was on a hitch-hiking holiday through the southern states. In Georgia he got a ride from a really nasty-looking trucker in a check shirt and dungarees. After 30 miles of scorched earth, the youth said to the trucker, "Well, aren't you going to ask me?" "Ask you what?" drawls the trucker. "If I'm a boy or a girl," answers the youth. "Don't matter none to me," says the trucker, "I'm going to shag you anyhow!"

****

A little boy starts to notice the loud, heavy bouncing noises of his parents having sex at night. Curious, he asks his mother what the noises are. She doesn't really want to go into it, so just explains that she bounces on top of his father to help him to stay thin and to make his stomach smaller. "I don't think it's going to work," says the boy. "Why ever not?" asks the mother. "Because every morning after you go to work, Elsie from next door comes over and blows Daddy back up again!'

****

A barman is delighted when a really top bird walks up and calls him over. She's a real stunner and he's feeling lucky already. "I wonder," she begins in a low, sexy voice, "could I speak to the manager, please?" "I'm afraid he's busy right now," the barman says, not wanting to share this one with anybody or to lose the chance of such a top bird. "Perhaps I can help you instead?" he continues. "I'm not really sure," she says cautiously, stroking him gently on the shoulder. "It's quite a personal issue and I'm not sure you're in charge of the situation." "Oh, I'm in charge; I'm in charge," the barman blurts out. "I'm sure I can take care of your problem." "Well," says the woman, as she touches his face gently and begins to stroke his cheek, "it's like this…" and she slides her fingers into his open mouth, sending him into a fit of joy and excitement, "…can you tell the manager…" "Yes! Yes!" the barman is thinking, "… can you tell the manager there's no toilet paper left in the ladies'?"

****

Two men are walking home from work one hot, sweaty Friday in London. The first man says, "First thing I'm going to do when I get home is rip my wife's knickers off!" "Steady on, mate," says the second. "You've got the whole weekend: why are you in such a hurry?" The first man replies, "They've been chafing my groin all day!"

✱✱✱✱

A couple of OAPs – a man and a woman – are sitting outside their old folks' home talking of the old days. All of a sudden an ice cream van pulls up at the gate with the tune playing. The woman says, "I'd love an ice cream, you know," to which the man replies, "Would you like me to get you one?" "Don't bother," the old dear says, "by the time you get to the van you'll never remember what I wanted anyway." "Don't be silly," says the man, "I won't forget. Now, come on: what do you want?" "Well, OK, then," says the woman, "I'll have a double-scoop of strawberry with chocolate sauce, nuts and a flake on top." "A double-scoop of strawberry with chocolate sauce, nuts and a flake on top coming right up," says the man and off he goes. Five minutes later he comes back carrying four hot dogs and two large Cokes. "Oh, my God," says the woman, "I knew I shouldn't have trusted you – where's the gravy?"

✱✱✱✱

A man is talking in his favourite bar with his favourite friends on a Sunday night. He says, "So, check this out – last night when I was down here with you lot, a bloody burglar broke into my house." "Well out of order," says his mate. "Did he get anything?" says another. "Yup," says the man, "a smack in the face, a kick up the arse, a plank in the nuts and a dinner-plate over his head – the missus thought it was me coming home pissed again!'

****

A guy breaks down while driving through Wales. Luckily, a farmer stops and offers him a lift to the nearest town, only about 20 miles away. They set off, and after a few minutes they pass by a field full of sheep. All of a sudden the farmer slams on the brakes and leaps out of the van. He hops over the fence, grabs a sheep, sticks its head in the fence and begins to hump it from behind. The guy jumps out and walks up to the fence. "What the hell are you doing?" he asks the farmer. "What the hell does it look like? Why: do you want some?" moans the farmer. "Sure do," says the guy, "but not if you're going to do that with my head."

****

A funeral service is being held for a woman who has recently died. Right at the end of the service the bearers pick up the coffin and begin to carry it to where it will enter the cremation chamber. As they turn a corner in the chapel the coffin hits the wall and there is a loud, audible "OUCH!" from inside it. They drop the casket to the floor and it turns out that, wonder of all wonders, the woman is actually alive. The woman lives for two more years and then dies – presumably for real this time. Everyone goes through the same ceremony, but this time, as the bearers round the corner, the woman's husband shouts out, "Careful, you lot: watch out for the wall!"

****

A man was on a blind date. He had spent the whole evening with this woman he just couldn't stand: she was everything he didn't like in a woman, so he was really bored to death. Luckily he had prepared for just this eventuality and had asked one of his mates to call the restaurant he was eating at, just in case he needed a getaway plan. So when the call came, he rushed over to the phone and feigned surprise and shock. When he returned to the table, his date looked up and asked, "Is everything all right?" He replied, "Not really. I'm afraid I'm going to have to go: my grandfather just died." "Thank God for that," the woman said. "If yours hadn't, mine would have had to!"

****

Jolly Good Sport

20

Jokes with
Balls

After a two-year study, the National Association for Sports and Activities announced the following results on the USA's recreational preferences:

1. The sport of choice for unemployed or imprisoned people is basketball.
2. The sport of choice for maintenance-level employees is bowling.
3. The sport of choice for blue-collar workers is football.
4. The sport of choice for supervisors is baseball.
5. The sport of choice for middle management is tennis.
6. The sport of choice for corporate officers is golf.

Conclusion: The higher you rise in the corporate structure, the smaller your balls!

****

Tiger Woods was having a quiet holiday far away from the sport paparazzi, driving around North Wales in his Volvo. One evening, noticing that he is almost out of petrol, he stopped at a station to fill up. An old man came out from behind an antiquated counter and approached the car. "Fill her up," Tiger Woods said, getting out of the car to stretch his legs. As he did so, a tee fell from his pocket and landed at the feet of the old timer. The petrol attendant picked it up, turned it around in his hands, obviously puzzled, for a full minute. Then, defeated, not able to figure out what it was, he turned to Tiger Woods and asked: "Say, what is this, young man?" "Oh, this is called a tee," the champion golfer answered. Seeing the lack of comprehension in the old timer's eyes, he elaborated: "It's to rest my balls on when I am taking long drives." The man looked him up, then at his car and said admiringly: "They really think of everything at Volvo."

****

Albert Einstein arrives at a party and introduces himself to the first person he sees and asks, "What is your IQ?" to which the man answers: "241." "That is wonderful!" cries Albert in delight. "We shall talk about the Grand Unification Theory and the mystery of the missing mass." The next person Albert introduces himself to is a woman and he asks her: "What is your IQ?" To which the lady answers, "144." "That is great!" responds Albert, very pleased with this party indeed. "We can discuss politics and current affairs. We will have much to discuss!" Albert goes to another person and asks, "What is your IQ?" to which the man answers, "51." Albert responds, "Spurs are doing well this season aren't they?"

****

Two friends are playing golf together, when the first woman swings a mighty shot…that goes up, and up, and down, smack amid a male foursome playing on the next hole. The women watch in horror as the ball actually hits one of the guys, apparently in a most delicate place. They are powerless as they witness the man yelping in pain, both his hands on his crotch and collapsing in a foetal position on the grass. The woman, guilty of the disastrous swing, rushes to meet the foursome and says to the guy in agony on the grass: "Listen, I can help. I am a physiotherapist. I can ease your pain, trust me." "I am alright," the bloke says between clenched teeth. "Come on, I can really help." The man agrees and manages to stand up. The physiotherapist then gently unzips his trousers and reaches inside to massage him. "Now?…Are you feeling better now?" "Yeah," the man admits, "that's great, but my thumb still hurts like hell!"

✳✳✳✳

A man has been on a desert island for five years. One day, while he was knee deep in the the sea spearing a fish, he notices a strange movement in the water. A few minutes later, a few feet away from him, a gorgeous woman in a tight wet suit stands up. Dumbfounded, he simply watches her approaching, dripping with water, teeth flashing, hips swaying. "How long has it been since you last had a cigarette?" she asked in a throaty voice. "Man, it's been ages," the guy answers in a shaky voice. The woman diver opens the zip of her breast pocket and fishes out a packet of cigaretes and a lighter. She places a cigarette in his mouth and lights it. She lets the guy take a drag and then asks: "How long has it been since you last had a nice Scotch?" "A long, long time," the guy replies, holding his breath. The woman pulls down the front zip of her wet suit, just enough to reach down and bring out a bottle of bourbon. She places her hands around the neck and gently twists the cap open. She takes a swig, licks the liquid on her lips and passes the bottle to the guy and then asks, her finger toying suggestively with her front zip, "Tell me, how long has it been since you last played around?" "Oh my God," breathes the guy. "Don't tell me you have golf clubs in there, too…"

****

A beautiful young woman is trying out skiing. By the fourth day, she feels confident enough to take the lift with her husband to the top of a gentle slope. While on the lift, stress takes its toll and the desire to visit the bathroom builds up, until it becomes unbearable. Unfortunately, on top of the slope, there is nothing as far as powder rooms go, so the husband, seeing that she desperately needs to go, suggests that she just uses the nearby thicket to do her business: her all-white suit would provide adequate camouflage. The woman weighs her options and realizes that this is the only solution she has if she doesn't want to pee in her suit, so off she goes. The woman is quite a novice at skiing, however, and doesn't really know the position to leave her skis in and, slowly, inexorably, starts sliding down the slope. Gathering speed, she somehow manages to stay on her skis, her bottom bare and her undies wrapped around her ankles. "And this is what happened, doctor," a young man, laying on a hospital bed said to the surgeon. "I was on the lift when I saw this gorgeous woman sliding backwards, half naked and her pants around her ankles. I bent over to get a better view and I fell off the seat and broke my leg." "I see," the surgeon said. "But tell me, how did you break your arm?"

****

Two guys are trying to get in a quick 18 holes, but there are two terrible lady golfers in front of them hitting the ball everywhere but where it's supposed to go. The first guy says, "Why don't you go over and ask if we can play through?" The second guy gets about halfway there, stops and comes back. The first guy says, "What's wrong?" His friend says: "One of these two women is my wife and the other one is my mistress. There is no way I could be seen with both of them! You'll have to go." The first guy laughs: "Yes, I can see that could be a problem! You're right, I'll go over." He gets about halfway there and comes back. The second guy says, "What's wrong?" "Small world," the first guy says with an apologetic grin.

✳✳✳✳

A primary school teacher explains to her class that she is a Manchester United fan. She asks the little ones to raise their hands if they are Manchester United fans, too. Not knowing what a Manchester United fan is, but wanting to be liked by their teacher, their hands fly into the air. There is, however, one exception. A little boy named Johnny has not gone along with the crowd. The teacher asks him why he has decided to be different. "Because I'm not a Manchester United fan," he retorts. "Then," asks the teacher, "What are you?" "I'm a proud Arsenal fan!" boasts the little boy. The teacher is a little perturbed now, her face slightly red. She asks Johnny why he is a Gunners fan. "Well, my Dad and Mom are Arsenal fans, so I'm a Arsenal fan, too," he responds. The teacher is now angry. "That's no reason," she says loudly. "What if your Mom was a moron, and your dad was an idiot. What would you be then?" Johnny smiles and says, "Then I'd be a Manchester United fan."

✸✸✸✸

A London mortician has a new apprentice who is learning the art of embalming. One day, after a particularly eventful post-match session at Highbury, the cadaver of a Manchester United fan ends up lying on the table of the embalming room. The mortician notes to his apprentice that he is to start the procedure while he finishes filling in a report. The apprentice nods, gathers the tools of his trade and begins examining the body. He rolls it over and, to his amazement, finds a cork in its rectum. Mystified, he pulls it out and immediately hears the 'Glory Glory Man United' song come out of the guy's arse. Startled, he shoves the cork back into the cadaver's butt and runs up the stairs to find the mortician: "Sir, you've got to come down and help me, you won't believe what I saw!" Slightly annoyed by the naivety of his assistant, the mortician follows him downstairs. "There, look at the cork in the arse of that body, I couldn't imagine what it was doing there so I pulled it out. You do it." The mortician is a bit surprised to see the cork, too, so he walks to the table and removes it as instructed. The 'Glory Glory Man United' song starts playing again out of the dead guy's arse. Sighing, he replaces the cork in its appointed position, turns to his assistant and says: "What's so surprising about that? I've heard thousands of arseholes sing that song."

✸✸✸✸

Moses and Jesus were part of a threesome playing golf one day. Moses stepped up to the tee and hit a long drive. The ball landed on the fairway, but rolled directly towards a water hazard. Quickly Moses raised his club, the water parted and the ball rolled to the other side, safe and sound. Next, Jesus strolled up to the tee and hit a nice long drive directly towards the same water hazard. It landed right in the centre of the pond and kind of hovered over the water. Jesus casually walked out on the pond and chipped the ball right up onto the green. The third guy got up and sort of randomly whacked the ball. It headed out over the fence and into oncoming traffic on a nearby street. It bounced off a truck and hit a tree. From there, it bounced onto the roof of a shack close by and rolled down into the gutter, down the drainpipe, out onto the fairway and straight towards the pond. On the way to the pond, the ball hit a little stone and bounced out over the water and onto a lily pad, where it rested quietly. Suddenly, a very large bullfrog jumped up on a lily pad and snatched the ball into his mouth. Just then, an eagle swooped down and grabbed the frog and flew away. As they passed over the green, the frog squealed with fright and dropped the ball, which bounced right into the hole for a beautiful hole in one. Moses turned to Jesus and said: "I hate playing with your Dad."

****

Three convicts were on their way to prison. Each had been allowed to take one item with them to help them occupy their time while behind bars. On the bus, one turned to another and said, "So, what did you bring?" The second convict pulled out a box of water paints. "I am going to learn painting. I will produce masterpieces and get filthy rich," he says. Then he asked the first fellow: "What did you bring?" The first convict pulled out a deck of cards and grinned and said: "I brought cards. I can play poker, solitaire and gin, and any number of games. I'll get filthy rich in jail." They both turned to the last convict, quietly sitting by himself, grinning insanely. "Why are you so smug?" the others asked. "What did you bring?" The guy pulled out a box of tampons and said: "I brought these." The other two were – understandably – puzzled. "What can you do with those?" The guy winked and said, pointing to the box: "Well according to this, I can go horse riding, swimming, roller-skating…"

✳✳✳✳

A 75-year-old golfer comes back home after a game. "How was your golf game, dear?" asked his wife. "Well, I was hitting the ball pretty well, but my eyesight's gotten so bad I couldn't see where it went," the man said, sounding dejected. "You are 75 years old, Jack," said his wife gently. "I'll tell you what: why don't you take my brother Scott along?" "But he's 85 and doesn't even play golf anymore," protested Jack. "Yes, but he's got perfect eyesight. He could watch your ball for you," Tracy pointed out. The next day Jack teed off with Scott looking on. Jack swung, and the ball disappeared down the middle of the fairway. "Do you see it?" asked Jack. "Yup," Scott answered. "Well, where is it?" yelled Jack, peering off into the distance. "I forgot."

✳✳✳✳

A woman had been driving 16 hours straight when she decided she'd had enough: she was still at least six hours away from her destination, it was almost seven o'clock in the morning and she had dozed off and nearly crashed into a telegraph pole. She decided to pull on to a side road and rest for a bit before carrying on. She turned off the car and closed her eyes... drifting off to sleep, precious sleep... All of a sudden an old man in a bright blue jogging suit knocked on her window, scaring her half to death. "Sorry to wake you," he huffed, jogging in place. "But can you tell me what time it is?" The woman glanced at her watch. "7:15," she said through the glass. "Thank you," the jogger said, and left. "Just my luck," the woman muttered angrily. "I'm parked on someone's jogging route." She considered driving off and parking somewhere else, but she was too tired, so she settled back into the seat, trying to re-capture the beautiful dream she was having... Suddenly another jogger knocked on her window. "Hi, do you have the time?" he said. The woman sighed and looked at her watch. "7:19," she said. "Thanks," the jogger said, then trotted off. She looked down the road and saw more joggers coming her way. Irritated, she retrieved a pen from the glove box and scrawled "I DO NOT KNOW THE TIME" on the back of a magazine. She jammed the hastily-constructed sign in the window with her shoulder and settled back to sleep. A jogger knocked on the window just as she started dozing off. The woman pointed at the sign and shouted, "Can't you read?" "Sure I can, ma'am. I just wanted to let you know: it's 7:27."

****

A guy is having a quiet breakfast when he is suddenly interrupted by his wife, who starts yelling at him: "I found this piece of paper in your pocket! Who is Marylou?" "Oh, that's nothing dear," the bloke says. "It's a horse. I bet on this horse last week you see." His wife smiles contritely, realizes she's made a fool of herself and lets it go at that. The bloke goes to work and when he comes back home, he finds his wife on the porch, her face like a thundercloud, having made a mess of his stereo and his collection of CDs on the front lawn. "What is the matter, honey?" he asks. "You got a call from the horse."

****

The Game Warden, fresh out of school, spots a man walking on the bank of the lake carrying two fish in a bucket. "Can I see your fishing licence, sir," he asks. "I did not catch these fish," the fisherman says. "They are my pets. Everyday I come down to the water and whistle and these fish jump out and I take them around to see the sights only to return them at the end of the day." "I do not believe it... You know it is illegal to fish without a licence." "If you don't believe me, then watch," the guy says as he throws the fish back into the water. "Now whistle to your fish and show me that they will come out of the water," the warden says in an ironic tone, to which the man replies: "Fish? What fish?"

****